Praise for
GREEN LIGHT, GO!

"Like a pioneering start-up company, the US Army's SFAB epitomizes the spirit of innovation, resilience, and adaptability by introducing a new service to the marketplace and revolutionizing the way the Army assists and trains partner nations."

—Chris Curry, CEO of Peak+

"Dave Rowland's story of how our Army's NCOs and officers encapsulate the American entrepreneurial spirit is inspiring and encouraging. *Green Light Go!* captures the essence of what it means to have grit and be a pioneer while contributing to our national security."

—Honorable Steve Watkins, Former US Congressman, Cofounder of TDY Rentals

"Partnerships are the lifeblood of our national security. *Green Light Go!* tells the remarkable story of how Army NCOs and officers applied business and start-up best practices to create lasting partnerships and relationships in the most strategically consequential area of the world—the Indo-Pacific region. This book is as applicable to business leaders as it is to national security practitioners. A remarkable and consequential accomplishment!"

—General Joseph Votel, USA (Ret.), Former Commander of US Special Operations Command and US Central Command, Former President/CEO of Business Executives for National Security

"*Green Light Go!* is an amazing story of a 'start-up journey' with valuable lessons for leaders, whether they are from the business world or the military. Taking an idea and making it into reality is at the heart of this book. Learn how this group of innovators launched and delivered a new, effective, and unique product in the market."

—Greg Harkins, President of CWTSato Travel

"*Green Light Go!* is an engaging read, detailing the struggles and successes of setting up a new unit for a new mission. The story highlights the ingenuity, creativity, and grit that exemplify both the best of the US Army and America's entrepreneurs since our founding as a nation."

—Jack Kemp, CEO of Phase Three Brands, Army Veteran

"Dave Rowland's *Green Light Go!* is an authentic story of leadership lessons dealing with colossal challenges, disappointing failures, and ultimate strategic successes. A must-read for those recruiting talent, navigating bureaucracy, or running distributed operations. A reminder that America remains a place for innovation and creativity."

—Craig Mullaney, *New York Times* Bestselling Author of *The Unforgiving Minute*, Rhodes Scholar

"Having the honor to help stand up, man, train, and equip one of the most consequential units of our time was the highlight of my professional life. The men and women of the 5th SFAB will always live in my heart as the absolute best of our conventional force. America can rest assured that the Vanguard BDE will always be forward and always be relevant!"

—Rob Craven, Former Command Sergeant Major of 5th SFAB and the United States Corps of Cadets at West Point

"Col. David Rowland's modern-day story of an Army start-up echoes inspirations from many successful contemporary business start-ups. *Green Light Go!* chronicles this little-known story of the Brown Berets in their infancy and their critical role in developing partnerships in the Indo-Pacific region. Just like building an incomparable team in sports or business, *Green Light Go!* tells how bringing talented people together to achieve an important mission requires engaged leadership and ingenuity."

—Richard LaMotte, Award-Winning Author of *Follow His Lead*, *Pure Sea Glass*, and *The Lure of Sea Glass*

"*Green Light, Go!* by Col. David B. Rowland offers an incredible insight into the formation of a decentralized, highly mobile unit somewhat unconstrained by the red tape and 'hurry up and wait' that is so embedded in bureaucratic structures and the military. Building the Brown Berets from scratch in the midst of the Covid restrictions, complicated by working internationally, was a massive undertaking in and of itself. This book also provides much-needed insight to many established models of business into the value of always looking to improve and to think outside the box."

—A. Monique Taylor, JD, Historian, Author of *Suicide Jockeys: The Making of the WWII Combat Glider Pilot*

Green Light Go!
by Col. David B. Rowland

© 2023 Col. David B. Rowland

ISBN 979-8-88824-153-0

All rights reserved. No part of this publication may be reproduced, stored in a retrieval system, or transmitted in any form or by any means electronic, mechanical, photocopy, recording, or any other except for brief quotations in printed reviews, without the prior written permission of the author.

Published by

köehlerbooks™

3705 Shore Drive
Virginia Beach, VA 23455
800-435-4811

GREEN LIGHT, GO!

THE STORY OF AN ARMY START UP

COL. DAVID B. ROWLAND

VIRGINIA BEACH
CAPE CHARLES

TABLE OF CONTENTS

FOREWORD | 1

PROLOGUE | 5

INTRODUCTION | 7

    Why Did We Exist? | 7

    Our Role in US Army History | 12

    What an SFAB Formation Looks Like | 15

PART I: BUILD STAGE | 23

CHAPTER 1: It Started with a Phone Call | 25

    Building Something New | 27

CHAPTER 2: Breaking Ground and Eating Dirt:
                 Finding and Hiring the Right Team | 31

    Recruiting: Convincing Others to Join the SFAB | 32

    Arrival at JBLM, the Real Beginning | 36

    The Meeting of the Minds: Cofounders Coming Together | 39

CHAPTER 3: Building a Team of Experts | 45

    Assessment and Selection: Getting the Right People | 45

    The Beginning of a Series of Firsts | 49

    Guns and Shooting | 53

    Mission Pivot | 57

CHAPTER 4: Seed Stage: Test Runs and Trials (Beta Mode) | 67

    What Makes us Ready to Launch | 69

    Testing Ourselves: Beta Testing | 75

    Managing COVID Risk | 78

    Test Team | 81

    The Battalion's Minimum Viable Product | 86

PART II: THE TRAINING CYCLE | 107

CHAPTER 5: Prelaunch (Growth Stage) | 109

   Brigade Training | 110

   Generating Business and Demand: The Start of Double Work | 125

   The Pitch: Becoming a Salesman | 135

   Our First Loss: A Plankholder Departs | 148

CHAPTER 6: The Final Test: The Brigade's Big Exercise | 151

   Step 1: Pretraining | 158

   The Crucible | 167

   Into the Breach | 177

   By, With, Through . . . and Sometimes For | 190

   The Hardest Places | 200

PART III: INTO THE INDO-PACIFIC | 215

CHAPTER 7: Green Light! | 217

   Getting out the Door: Self-Motivation | 219

   Air Force Tale of Woes: Persistence | 222

   The Subcontinent: Innovation | 226

   Where to Park the Headquarters:
   Singapore Attempt – Long Term Focus | 231

   The Paradise Mission: Branding | 236

   The Hermit Kingdom: Patience | 241

   The Philippines, Pearl of the Orient: Adaptability | 251

   The Land of Tigers and National Heritage Sites:
   Structured Experimentation | 260

Back to the Original Early Adopters: Self-Motivation | 273

The One That Got Away—Stuck in Paradise:
Comfortable with Failure | 280

Our Last Frontier, the Land of the Rising Sun: Tenacity | 287

Mongolia: The Far Reaches of America | 292

The Battalion Headquarters | 302

CHAPTER 8: Exit Phase, Transitions | 312

Back to Washington | 312

Final Farewell | 315

CHAPTER 9: The Entrepreneurial Bureaucracy | 318

GLOSSARY OF TERMS | 332

LIST OF IMPORTANT FIGURES | 338

1/5 SFAB TIMELINE | 348

END NOTES | 352

ACKNOWLEDGMENTS | 357

FOREWORD

Working with Allies and partners is in my blood. It all started with my time as a Special Forces officer, and it continued as the brigade commander of 2nd Brigade, 10th Mountain Division. While in command of 2/10, I spent a lot of time alongside my Iraqi counterpart, but there was a better way for the Army to perform our "advise and assist" missions. As an Army and as a Nation, we have always fought with our partners and allies, going back as far as the Revolutionary War. And in recent generations, we fought with partners and allies through groups like the Korean Military Advisory Group (KMAG) and the Military Assistance Command Vietnam (MACV). We did it in Afghanistan and Iraq with Military Transition Teams (MiTTs) and Security Force Advisory and Assistance Teams (SFAAT). However, all these teams were ad hoc organizations. We know that relationships are built over time, with trust developed through shared experiences and shared sacrifices—temporary and dynamics programs did not provide enough to keep the relationship strong.

Working with our partners and allies is, and always will be, essential for the security of the United States. We face challenges from China and Russia as they attempt to build their military might, spread their influence, and expand their span of control. Moreover, North Korea remains a destabilizing regime in the North Pacific, Iran threatens its neighbors with growing weapons programs and with proxy forces, and Violent Extremist Organizations still threaten our interests at home and abroad.

The US Army must prepare to face multiple challenges. To be a stabilizing force in the world, the Army must remain focused on Readiness and Modernization. Readiness with the equipment we currently have and modernizing to face the threats and challenges of the future. To do both we needed a professional organization that aligns with our partners and allies while our brigade combat teams both train and use the latest weapons and technology. Creating and building the Security Force Assistance Brigades (SFABs) played a critical role in allowing our Army to build readiness, modernize, and develop interoperability with our partners and allies simultaneously.

It's critical to select the right people when building a new organization. That's why I chose Scott Jackson to command 1st SFAB and complete the SFAB's first combat rotation to Afghanistan. Scott and his team faced challenges and learned a lot of lessons along the way, but on all accounts, they accomplished their mission. While 1st SFAB was still in Afghanistan, I briefly met Dave Rowland in Iraq. He was already deeply involved in his own advise and assist mission as the squadron commander for the 1st Squadron, 3rd Cavalry Regiment and was working closely with his Iraqi counterparts in Baghdad to eradicate ISIS. I was happy to see the close relationship he had developed with the Iraqis and what they accomplished together.

Following his time in Iraq, Dave volunteered for SFAB service. Just like all his fellow Brown Berets, Dave is an expert with the proven skills and experience to lead our SFAB formations. He was part of transforming something temporary and provisional into something deliberate and professional. I truly appreciate him and all the other SFAB commanders and command sergeant majors (CSM) who accepted the challenge to do something new. It takes a unique individual to accomplish what they built. Dave led by example by being the first person in his new battalion to attend the Army's Survival, Evasion, Resistance, and Escape level C (SERE-C) school, the course in which students experience the physical hardships of capture. And he did it as a forty-three-year-old.

Dave's mission with the 5th SFAB was unique from that of all the other SFABs. Instead of rotating to Iraq or Afghanistan first, the 5th SFAB would head directly into the Indo-Pacific to work with our partners and allies in the expansive region. Dave and his team built, trained, and deployed eighteen SFAB teams to eleven Indo-Pacific countries in less than a year and a half. Green Light, Go!: The Story of an Army Startup, tells the detailed account of executing my vision of the SFAB mission and building relationships side by side with conventional foreign armies. Once given the green light to move out into the Indo-Pacific, they forged ahead.

Strengthening our alliances and partnerships is an enduring priority for our Army. In the Indo-Pacific, the 5th SFAB fostered relationships with conventional partner and ally units that our Special Forces couldn't achieve. Dave's book talks about the struggle of the Brown Beret NCOs and officers as they helped change our framework to engage our partners and Allies. He and the 1/5 SFAB team were professional problem solvers and demonstrated the grit and "can-do" attitude of our Army's finest people.

Their team helped set the conditions for larger USARPAC exercises for our brigade combat teams as the brigades improved their readiness and focus on modernization. Their Brown Berets are symbols of working on the ground with their counterparts, training and fighting side by side, and doing it all in the dirt. They were on the ground with their counterparts whether on the steppes of Mongolia, the hills of Korea, or the jungles of the Philippines and Indonesia.

Dave's work building, training, and deploying 1/5 SFAB is one example of how our Army works to improve our interoperability. Each year our forces train alongside other nations in fifty-eight multinational and joint exercises involving over 110,000 partner nation soldiers. I am proud he took the time and opportunity to tell the Brown Beret story. While his story is unique in that 1/5 SFAB was focused on the Indo-Pacific, it also describes some of the commonalities and challenges the 1st, 2nd, 3rd, and 4th SFABs faced as they recruited, built, and trained their formations, then shifted to their assigned region of the world. The book also highlights the capabilities that the SFABs bring to our Combatant Commanders and why they must remain a vital organization in our Army.

Our Army is about people and Green Light, Go! highlights the entrepreneurial ingenuity of our great officers and NCOs that stand in our ranks. There are leadership lessons, and stories of persistence, failure, and accomplishment. You will join the Brown Berets on their path through the trials and tribulations of attempting something new, learning, adapting, and overcoming challenges. It's a story worth telling. I hope you enjoy it.

>General Mark A. Milley
>United States Army (Retired)
>Former Chairman of the Joint Chiefs of Staff
>and former Chief of Staff of the Army

PROLOGUE

The two-hump creatures ambled awkwardly across the road in front of us, causing our four-vehicle convoy to come to a complete stop. This allowed us the opportunity to get out, stretch our legs, and take some pictures. We had been driving along this pitted two-lane road for four or five hours at this point, so this was a welcome diversion, even if unplanned. As we gazed about, we noticed that there was a thick layer of dust wafting up and settling atop the barren land around us making things look dull and dingy.

The animals were a herd of two-hump camels that my ten-year-old daughter Abi would later properly instruct me on their official name, Bactrian. She had learned about them in school earlier that year and knew the ungainly animal's precise label. She was extremely excited to know I would see them face-to-face. As I took the pictures, I thought that a year ago, if someone had told me I'd be traveling south into the Gobi Desert in southern Mongolia to link up with one of the battalion's advisor teams partnering with a Mongolian Army unit, I would have laughed in their face. We had not one, but five teams of Brown Berets in Mongolia, not including my battalion headquarters. During the battalion's deployment, our unit, which hadn't even existed two years before seeing the Bactrians lumber across the empty road, would have people in a total of eleven countries spread throughout the entire Indo-Pacific region. An insurmountable task that many would say could never happen.[1]

In light of the many bureaucratic obstacles, the officers and noncommissioned officers displayed the characteristics normally associated with those of an entrepreneur building a start-up—curiosity, structured experimentation, adaptability, decisiveness, team building, risk tolerance, comfortability with failure, banding, patience, persistence, tenacity, self-motivation, innovation, and a long-term focus.

These officers and noncommissioned officers recruited people into an unknown and untested organization while simultaneously acquiring facilities and equipment to start training and preparing for its nationally important mission in the Indo-Pacific. The COVID pandemic propelled them into a full mission rehearsal in Thailand as part of its seed stage's test runs and trails. They morphed into a cohesive unit and eventually embarked on their crucible training event in the swamps of Louisiana, where the Army tested new training concepts. Meanwhile, these "Brown Berets" became their own unit salesmen to convince a sometimes-apathetic Army bureaucracy, hesitant US Embassy personnel, and skeptical foreign army partners and allies that the unit was a valuable teammate for international military-to-military relations.

This story is about how this unique group of people took General Mark Milley's (then US Army Chief of Staff) vision of building a conventional Army unit to work with America's partners and allies and transformed it into something tangible, adaptable, and eventually sought after by other national militaries and US Embassy teams across the Indo-Pacific. It is the story of the ups and downs of doing something new, trying and failing, and building a brand, all within the framework of the large Army bureaucracy—an organization not normally known for cutting through red tape, streamlining processes and procedures, or having a flexible mindset. This group of noncommissioned officers and commissioned officers alike—underdogs really—prevailed and turned their story into that of an Army start-up.

INTRODUCTION

Why Did We Exist?

Back in 2016 when Gen. Mark Milley was the Chief of Staff of the US Army, he knew the Army needed to change.[2] The Army had been focusing on the wars in Afghanistan and Iraq, and it needed to modernize for future conflicts while simultaneously revitalizing its partnerships around the world. He needed to determine how to accomplish both of those tasks with limited resources in terms of people and money. The result was the establishment of the Security Force Assistance Brigade (SFAB). The creation of the SFAB marked "the first instance of a permanent organization dedicated solely to foreign advisory operations."[3] The SFAB was a creative way to solve these two concurrent problems—it was a completely new unit.

When entrepreneurs start a business, they try to solve some type of problem. As an inventor, Thomas Edison tried to solve all sorts of issues as the United States went full steam into the Gilded Age and saw a surge in industry and technology. One of his most famous inventions, the light bulb, is a great example. He was trying to figure out how to safely light homes and businesses using electricity. Constructing what we know as the carbon-filament incandescent light bulb took creativity and perseverance not only from Thomas Edison but from his whole team as they developed over three thousand different prototypes before arriving at his 1880 patent.[4] Edison and his team continued to innovate and eventually developed a safe and effective way to harness electricity. Most importantly, Edison created a systemized approach to inventing while at the same time focusing on items that could sell and were marketable.[5] He laid the foundation and culture within his business that could continue to innovate and create without his direct supervision. The result years later was an American company called General Electric (GE) that went on to produce a wide variety of products, from washing machines to giant electric turbines used to power cities. GE, starting with inventions like the light bulb, was the fortunate product of Edison trying to solve problems and innovate.

Similarly, Gen. Mark Milley, while serving as the Army chief of staff, identified a requirement for a conventional Army unit to work with conventional foreign partner forces around the world to develop relationships and interoperability. Working with allies and partners has always been an essential element of America's National Security Strategy.[6] Fostering close relationships with allies and partners keeps the United States safe and helps maintain maximum flexibility to respond to threats. As a nation and as an army, the United States has always worked with partners and allies. One could argue that this began with requesting the help of the French during the American War for Independence, clearly seen again during both World Wars and even in contemporary times during the War on Terrorism.

While US Army units were rotating through Iraq and Afghanistan, Gen. Milley realized we were not strengthening conventional foreign partnerships or building committed teams with a shared vision in regions around the world in our partner's home country. Normally Army brigade combat teams, the Army's basic fighting formation, are aligned with various training exercises with foreign allies and partners on a regular basis. Instead of being sent to exercises that had been ongoing for years, units were trained, validated, sent to Iraq or Afghanistan, and then returned to repeat the cycle. I experienced this cycle when stationed with the 173rd Airborne Brigade in Italy. During the forty-eight months I was stationed there, I spent twenty-six in Afghanistan, and during the time I was home, our unit trained for the next rotation. We rarely trained with any of our NATO allies.

In the Indo-Pacific, "departures of the 25th Infantry Division to support the wars in Iraq and Afghanistan left large holes in the number of sizable ground forces immediately available to respond to needs" throughout the region.[7] This decreased our influence, relationships, and interoperability with the many nations scattered across the Indian and Pacific oceans.

The Army's, and Gen. Milley's, quandary was to figure out how to strengthen relationships and build trust with our foreign partners while at the same time allowing our large combat formations, brigade combat teams (BCTs), to rearm, modernize, and train for large-scale combat operations after years focusing on fighting counterinsurgencies in Iraq and Afghanistan. Gen. Milley was limited by the budget, time available, and the size of the Army—it could not grow. Unfortunately, the answer wasn't, and couldn't be, using Army Special Forces formations. He had to bridge the gap between partnering with foreign armies, which the Special Forces originally started doing (watch John Wayne's film *The Green Berets*) during its inception, and what happened during the War on Terrorism. During the Global War on Terror, Special Forces were in high demand in Iraq and Afghanistan and no longer had the time to partner with conventional foreign units.[8] In other cases, many countries were establishing or revitalizing their own counterterrorism or special operations forces. This subtle shift left our highly trained Special Forces working with foreign special operations or special police forces and not self-sustaining conventional army units, which was less than ideal, but required, nonetheless. The US Army needed a conventional force that could partner with foreign armies designed for large-scale operations.[9] Could the Army find a way forward that allowed them to build committed teams of smaller highly trained units to renew their relationships with those foreign armies and create value for their stakeholders?

The model used by the Army was not working. In many cases,

the Army just needed the experienced leaders—officers and senior NCOs—found in a brigade combat team to work with Afghan and Iraqi army units, but not the majority of the soldiers. The brigade combat team (BCT) is the basic deployable unit of maneuver in the US Army, typically consisting of two to three combat arms battalions, a reconnaissance and surveillance squadron, an artillery battalion, an engineer battalion with organic intelligence and signal companies, and a sustainment battalion. The brigade is commanded by a colonel (O-6). Sizes vary between 4,400–4,700 personnel and can surge even higher if other specialized Army units get attached to the BCT. There are three types of brigade combat teams: infantry, Stryker, and armored. The team is designed to perform a variety of functions across a full range of military operations, including offensive, defensive, counterinsurgency, and stability operations. The challenge with BCTs is that they must train for those specific missions and cannot perform all of them at every point in time proficiently.

Because that traditional structure wasn't producing the desired results in Iraq and Afghanistan, the Army broke up its BCTs into parts and deployed them piecemeal. For instance, in 2016, the 101st Airborne Division sent its 2nd Brigade Combat Team's 1,300 leaders to Iraq to support Operation Inherent Resolve.[10] They went to train, advise, and assist their Iraqi counterparts. A light infantry BCT typically has about 4,000 soldiers, but the unit left almost 2,700 soldiers back at Fort Campbell without most of their leadership. The cost of sending only part of the unit to Iraq came on the "backside," or post-deployment timeframe. While the unit was in Iraq, its combat capability actually decreased because the soldiers back at Fort Campbell were not doing all the training necessary to maintain full combat readiness nor were the soldiers in Iraq always training on key and essential combat tasks. This may sound counterintuitive for many, but in reality, fighting a counterinsurgency is very different from fighting a near-peer adversary with tanks, helicopters, and fighter aircraft. Meanwhile, the soldiers back at Fort Campbell, with no leadership, were unable to complete platoon- and company-level live-fire exercises, tactical command post exercises, or other collective training exercises needed to be ready to fight that peer adversary. This gap in mission training and leadership between brigades during these deployments created a need for them to retrain upon return to the United States. The retraining cost the Army time—from nine to twelve months—and money. Therefore, 2nd Brigade, 101st Airborne was not combat ready to fight a peer adversary for the nine months the leaders were in Iraq plus the year required to go through the training cycle—a total of eighteen months not ready for a near-peer threat.

I experienced splitting a unit when I deployed only half of my infantry squadron (battalion) to Iraq in 2018–2019. The designation of this mission did not require US infantry platoons to patrol Baghdad. Therefore, I deployed my infantry troops (companies) to pull security at designated bases in both Iraq and Syria. My squadron headquarters partnered with the Baghdad Operations Center to provide liaison and support functions to our Iraqi counterparts. We worked with our Iraqi partners every day. This left over three hundred infantry and other soldiers at Fort Hood (today known as Fort Cavazos) without a mission but also unavailable for deployment since the majority of the leadership was absent. When we returned from Iraq, we began our multi-month process to prepare for fighting future peer adversaries.

This tactic wasted time and broke apart formations; neither was good for the soldiers or their leaders. Gen. Milley said, "I need to get those units back and get their readiness up to speed."[11] As such, the Army and Gen. Milley decided they would build something new. What was their vision of that new fighting force, and what was their focus?

Gen. Milley was an advocate of keeping the combat formations focused on fighting peer adversaries (combat readiness) but also believed the Army needed a formation of experienced officers and NCOs that could efficiently and effectively train with our foreign allies to enable them to become capable of conducting major combat operations as they arise, commonly known as interoperability training. Specifically, this required an adaptation to a shared-value team-building approach that took into account the changing landscape of war and threats around the globe using an innovative mindset. One solution was the formation built around small, low-cost, twelve-person teams composed of talented and experienced noncommissioned officers (NCOs) from various military specialties and an officer. These small teams were easier to move and provided a higher rate of return on their initial investment. They were filled with experienced noncommissioned officers and officers that had served in other Army units and could leverage their knowledge with foreign units. Neither were currently present in the Army. Therefore, change the Army must.

Our Role in US Army History

The United States Army has a history of creating new units to fight its nation's wars.[12] The Army created numerous infantry regiments to fight in the American Civil War, then sent cavalry regiments out West to secure trails and wagon trains as the young nation expanded westward. However, most of the time, the Army repurposes and redesigns existing formations to meet the requirements of the new realities of combat. The near-constant drive came with each new requirement to understand, evaluate, and re-evaluate organizational designs and effectiveness.[13] The innovation of young Americans was tested when American tanks needed to figure out how to breach the hedgerows that prevented them from maneuvering in Normandy's countryside following the famous D-Day invasion of France in 1944. The modern era continued to see the United States Army create new units and ways to fight when it paired helicopter technology with the fighting American infantrymen of the 1/7 Air Cavalry, most famous for their Battle of the Ia Drang in 1965.[14] Thanks to the industrious forward-thinking of then Lt. Col. Hal Moore, infantry soldiers from the 1st Squadron, 7th Cavalry were moved faster around the battlefield with the assistance of the UH-1 Iroquois "Huey" helicopter. This maneuver set the stage for the future movement of troops across wide battle zones.

The creativity, innovation, and entrepreneurial mindset that Lt. Col. Moore exhibited allowed our Army to try something new, using the helicopter with tactics that are still relevant today. The innovation by 1/7 Cav. was an adaptation of an existing unit to try something new. Doing something new at any point in the Army's history, especially building a new unit with a new type of capability, requires an extraordinary type of people. The geographic combatant commands required small, highly skilled formations to partner with foreign military forces from the Army while the Army simultaneously needed to preserve brigade combat teams for modernization efforts and combat-readiness training. Therefore, to meet both competing exigencies, Gen. Milley created Security Force Assistance Brigades (SFABs). For our part at Joint Base Lewis-McChord, Washington, a group of officers and NCOs had the unique opportunity to be part of Gen. Milley and the Army's solution to this unique problem.

The 5th SFAB's development was part of the US Army's overall radical transformation to meet the changing character of warfare in the twenty-first century and confront new threats. We, members of the 1st Battalion, 5th SFAB, were a small part of this transformation. According to Gen. James McConville, the chief of staff of the Army, the last time the US Army had faced such a significant transition was during the aftermath of the Vietnam

War in the 1970s.[15] It was during the 1970s that the US Army developed its AirLand Battle doctrine. This doctrine and forward-thinking built the modern-day Ranger regiment and created the Big Five system—the M1 Abrams tank, AH-64 Apache helicopter, UH-60 Blackhawk helicopter, Bradley Fighting Vehicle, and the MIM-104 Patriot air-defense system—to face off against the Soviets during the Cold War. The Army achieved lasting force-structure transformations during the post-war period by adding new organizational constructs like the US Army's elite 75th Ranger regiment. New personnel frameworks required modernized equipment and procedures designed to counter, deter, and—if necessary—win a war toe-to-toe with the USSR. Just like the transition of the Army during the 1970s, the modern force was changing to adapt to the new environment, part of which meant building SFABs.

Transitional change is difficult to enact because it means that an organization—in this case, the US Army—has taken advantage of opportunities to restructure, consolidate, or merge. Doing so means that they must adopt new procedures, policies, and processes in order to transform. Transitional changes usually have definite beginning and ending dates. Personnel dynamics can be complicated when people are asked to adapt to a new environment. Change also means meeting the demands of the customer base that may or may not always understand what they want or need. We later learned we had multiple sets of clients in the Indo-Pacific region that included the US Army Pacific (USARPAC) Headquarters, US Embassy teams, and foreign military partners.[16] Members of 1st Battalion, 5th SFAB (1/5 SFAB) learned how to be innovative and adaptable while performing unique missions within unfamiliar governmental frameworks not often employed in traditional military units.

During our inception period, we quickly realized that the entrepreneurial skills required for success during a transformation and establishing a new unit are alive in the Army. The possibility to build something new from the ground up led to creative approaches in essential areas like training, problem identification, and organizational communication of potential solutions. The process of creating the newest SFAB revealed parallels between skills required for success in both the business world and the military. For instance, transformation requires a shift in cultural mindset, as well as changes in cultural behavior. Oftentimes, change can be met with resistance. Resistance to change can be curtailed by including all stakeholders in that change. That said, we would need to attract people who were curious about trying something different or outside of their traditional professional career timelines and those who might also be seeking a new opportunity. They would need to be comfortable with experimentation within the context of a large bureaucracy and develop divergent competencies such as negotiation skills, cultural awareness, and empathy. These individuals needed to be able to adapt to changing circumstances and challenges while at the same time understanding what level of risk they could accept, given their rank and experience. As in all Army organizations, members had to be good teammates, possess a "never give up" attitude, be okay with failure and be willing to learn from mistakes. Once given the green light to accomplish a mission, they had to be capable of doing it without additional guidance. Most importantly, they had to be innovative since the Army had never permanently organized conventional Army units to do the type of mission we were taking on.

What an SFAB Formation Looks Like

The creation of the SFAB was different from any other conventional formation in existence. Gen. Milley designed the SFAB specifically to work with conventional foreign partners in large-scale operations at echelon. The SFAB was his, and the Army's, solution to developing relationships with foreign militaries while allowing other Army formations to prepare for future conflicts. The extraordinary mission required a unique design.

The foundation of the SFAB is the twelve-person maneuver advisor team, or MAT, led by a captain who has already served as a company commander and a sergeant first class that has previously served as an infantry platoon sergeant in a combat arms formation, usually an infantry battalion.[17] Then there are two infantry staff sergeants, generally in charge of two sections. The first section consists of an intelligence sergeant, military police staff sergeant, fires (field artillery) sergeant, and an explosive hazards sergeant, a position usually filled by a combat engineer.[18] The second section consists of a medical sergeant, logistics sergeant (usually a supply specialist), communications sergeant, and maintenance sergeant (usually a mechanic). Each SFAB infantry battalion consists of nine MATs and is designed to work with battalion-level equivalent foreign armies. An SFAB infantry battalion is infantry in name only; eight of the twelve people on the MAT are non-infantry, unlike an infantry platoon in which all thirty-six personnel assigned are trained infantrymen. One significant advantage to the SFAB MAT is the density of experience across a wide variety of specialties in such a small formation. The small but impactful size makes the MAT easy to move yet at the same time remain extremely capable of working with foreign partner battalion-size or equivalent organizations.

The infantry company advising team, or CAT, is similarly designed but with more experience and rank and serves as a company headquarters for three subordinate MATs. The commander is a senior major who has already served as a battalion or brigade operations officer or executive officer. The company first sergeant already successfully served as a first sergeant in another infantry organization. The CAT also has a captain who has graduated from the Maneuver Captains Career Course but has

INTRODUCTION | 17

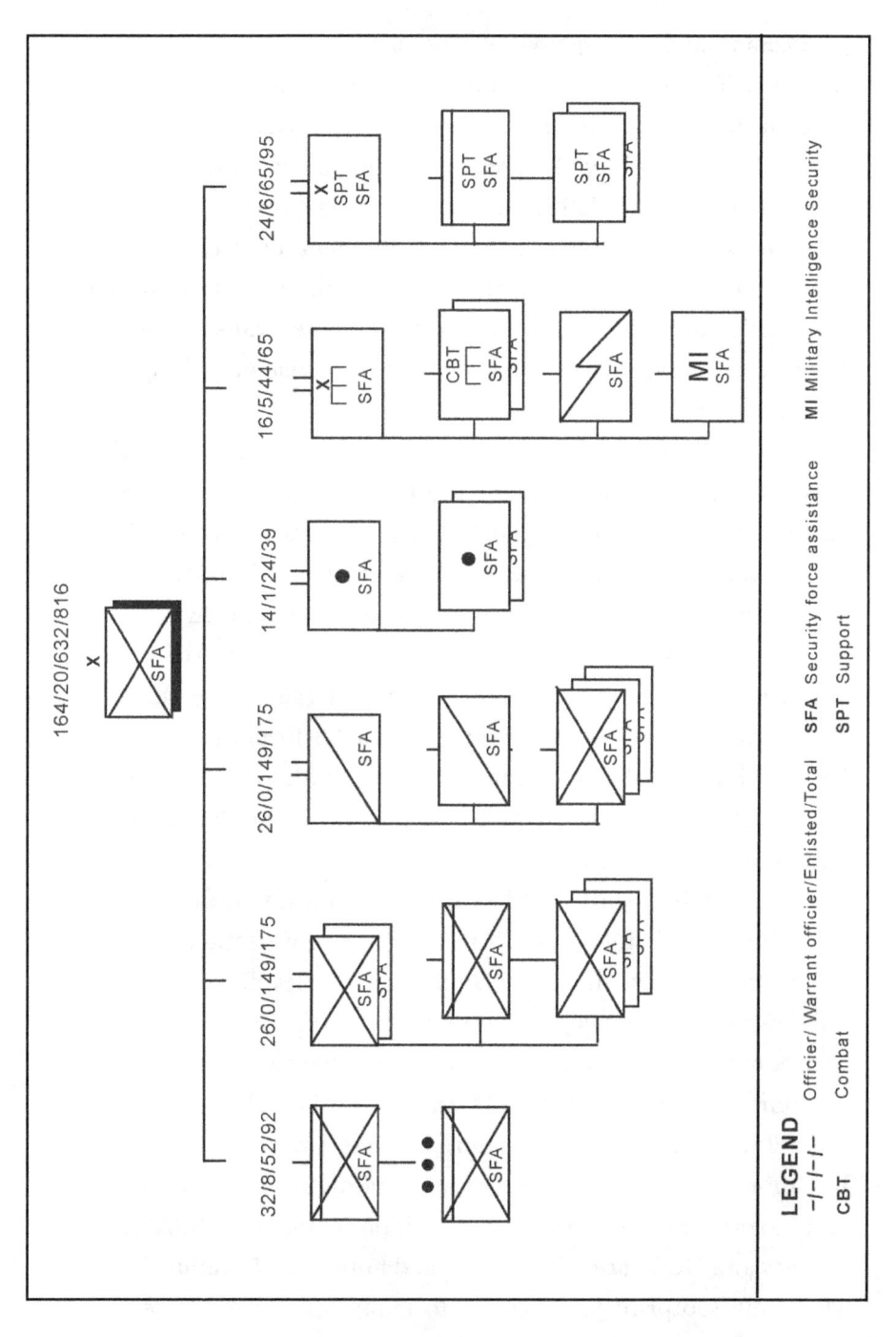

Security Force Assistance Brigade organizational chart.[21]

yet to command a company. They are usually referred to as junior captains. The CAT's senior operations sergeant is a sergeant first class mortarman and a sergeant first class fire support sergeant, i.e., artillery. The rest of the team are staff sergeants: medical, signal, mechanic, intelligence, logistics, infantry, and an expert ordnance disposal (EOD) technician, usually filled by a combat engineer. Each sergeant first class and staff sergeant has previously successfully served at their assigned rank in another Army assignment. All these people have expertise in their specific specialization.

The CAT must serve two functions. First, it is designed to conduct partnered activities at the brigade level with a foreign partner force: advise, support, liaise, or assess (ASLA). The second function is to perform command responsibilities similar to what's found in other companies throughout the Army, such as administrative and logistics functions, standards and discipline enforcement, and training management for the rest of the unit. The SFAB company level is where the SFAB formation starts to have dual responsibilities for mission command, termed command and control, and ASLA. There are three CATs in an SFAB infantry battalion.

The battalion staff, just like the companies, is lean and built to do both mission command and work with a partner force, in the battalion's case at the division or higher level. The staff has only twenty-seven people assigned, including the commander and command sergeant major. For example, while the typical personnel S1 staffing section in an infantry battalion is eight to ten soldiers, the SFAB battalion only has two. Since the SFAB battalion must still perform various administrative requirements and extra duties prescribed in regulations and law, SFAB staff officers and NCOs are usually assigned multiple additional duties. The small footprint is appealing to many foreign militaries and US Embassies, which helps reduce the US military signature when necessary. However, to achieve outsized results, the personnel must be experienced, capable, and independent thinkers.

In a full SFAB, there are two infantry battalions, a cavalry squadron, a fires battalion, an engineer battalion, and a support battalion. The cavalry squadron is organized identically to the infantry battalion, except that the cavalry squadron is filled with cavalry scouts (19Ds and 19As) in similar positions filled by infantry NCOs and officers (11Bs and 11As) in the infantry battalions. The fires, engineers, and support battalions typically attach their specific specialty teams to infantry battalions and the cavalry squadron when deployed. In the case of 1/5 SFAB, the brigade would attach artillery, engineer, and logistics teams to the battalion as part of our inaugural deployment into the Indo-Pacific.

Some may say that what the Army built in the SFAB was another version of the Special Forces A-Team, which is also a twelve-person team.[19] That model was under consideration when designing the SFAB's MATs and other advisor teams. The new SFAB teams are instead filled with conventional Army NCOs from various specialties with previous experiences in conventional Army units.[20] By contrast, when soldiers join the Special Forces, they go through about two years of training and permanently become a Special Forces soldier. In the SFAB, when a mechanic joins, they get selected, wear the Brown Beret, and serve in the SFAB as a mechanic. When their tour is complete, they return to the rest of the Army as a mechanic. This is notable because the Army retains this particular NCO in their designated military occupational specialty with the training, certifications, and experience needed in other Army formations. The mechanic NCO also has the option to return to the SFAB after gaining experience at their next rank in conventional units, thus creating a cycle of experiences between SFABs and the rest of the Army. Conventional Army NCOs are well-suited to work with conventional foreign counterparts, especially in areas like large-scale maneuver, artillery, and logistics operations. Many of the problems SFAB NCOs encounter with their partner forces are comparable to the ones in the US Army. Thus, the SFAB has the right type and mix of specialties inside the MATs and CATs to work properly with foreign conventional forces. This blend of skill sets in such a small organization does not exist anywhere else in the US Army.

The human capital cost for building an SFAB is significant, even though the eventual long-term benefit outweighs this cost. The density of experienced officers and NCOs necessary to staff an SFAB means that these talented soldiers are unavailable for other essential Army assignments like recruiting, drill sergeant, or observer/controller-trainer (O/C-T) at a combat training center (CTC). The Army bureaucracy pushed back on the idea of diverting many of these seasoned soldiers for SFAB service. The Army had to start asking some tough questions like "Where do we place our talent?" in the short and medium terms. This question remained one of the most formidable ones to answer when Gen. Milley still needed to prepare units for peer-competition combat. One additional difference between all those assignments and the SFAB is that you must volunteer for the SFAB and pass the selection process. This meant the Army bureaucracy could not simply assign officers and NCOs to positions in the SFAB, as it had for almost all other billets. In the case of SFAB service, the SFAB had to identify qualified personnel, recruit them, convince them to volunteer, then conduct additional screening. Recruiting talented professionals to join the SFAB was essential when building a new organization that was capable of partnering with foreign armies.

Ultimately, under Gen. Milley's leadership, the Army identified a need to solve a particular problem and created a unit structure to solve it. But what other SFAB leaders and I were to learn later is that just because the Army built a specific type of unit structure didn't mean the entirety of the Army or Department of Defense enterprise knew how to use it or that others needed it as well. The members of 1st Battalion, 5th SFAB were about to find out that not only did we have to build a unit from scratch, but we also had to get out and "sell" our product to the rest of the Army, military leaders responsible for the Indo-Pacific, the State Department, and of course our foreign partner forces.

Our challenge was just like the one you would find in the account of any start-up company. We had a great idea and needed to realize it. So, we devised a solid plan, and now we needed to secure funding and support from all stakeholders. We were a bit like entrepreneurs. We surrounded ourselves with the right personnel and established a program, policies, and protocols to market and sell the SFAB idea and product to the powers that be—the USARPAC, US Embassy teams, and foreign partners. This was challenging because of the good old-fashioned governmental bureaucracy. Could we prevail?

This book is the story of how the Brown Berets—as we referred to ourselves due to our distinctive headgear—recruited, built, tested, and deployed 1st Battalion, 5th SFAB for its inaugural deployment to the Indo-Pacific Command (INDOPACOM) Area of Responsibility, which stretches from India in the west to Samoa in the east, then Mongolia in the north down to New Zealand in the south. We were determined to do something that had never been done before.

PART I

BUILD STAGE

CHAPTER 1

It Started with a Phone Call

LIKE ALL GOOD STORIES, they begin with a problem that requires solving or a question that needs to be answered. My personal part of the 1/5 SFAB story started with my own problem—really a simple question. What should I do following two years of infantry squadron (battalion) command? For many, the command of a battalion is the pinnacle of a twenty-year Army career. Being selected to lead and serve with America's sons and daughters is a privilege few get to experience. Things seem to have gone well for me in command of the 1st Squadron, 3d Cavalry Regiment at Fort Hood. Though I hadn't received my first evaluation (which, as a commander, is the piece of paper that would determine my future service in the Army), I hadn't gotten into trouble, and I had a great boss, Colonel Jon Byrom. He was an exceptional commander and Army officer.

My dilemma was deciding what to do after squadron command following a nine-month deployment to Iraq supporting Operation Inherent Resolve. I knew I would redeploy from Iraq, have a few months in Texas, then need to move on to the next assignment. I had heard of the 1st SFAB forming at Fort Benning (today known as Fort Moore) from one of my previous battalion commanders, Colonel James Dooghan (who would later command 4th SFAB at Fort Carson). His rockstar battalion commander was a West Point classmate of mine, Lieutenant Colonel Brian Ducote, who was pulled early out of battalion command to form this unique unit called 1st SFAB.

When I had last seen Brian in 2015, he and I were both serving as aides-de-camps for three-star generals while our bosses had a short meeting in Kuwait. Then, during the Army's Pre-Command Course (PCC) for battalion and brigade commanders, many of my fellow PCC classmates and I appropriated all the great command products Brian had put together. Sitting in my squadron headquarters at Fort Hood, I decided to write Brian and ask him about the SFAB experience—it seemed like something interesting I might like to do.

Brian was then serving in the first SFAB deployment to Afghanistan that April of 2018 and graciously fielded my phone call. He described the ups and downs of building the unit and his experiences thus far in Afghanistan. It wasn't all rosy, but it did sound like a challenge. Many factors contribute to a mission's success. One such critical component is having the right people in the right positions. Throughout the conversation, he kept coming back to the people. He was excited to work with such talented and mission-focused NCOs and officers.

I kept thinking about that phone call as my squadron headquarters settled into a routine in Baghdad with our partner Iraqi unit four months previous. I routinely advised, supported, and liaised with the Baghdad Operation Center and multiple two- and three-star Iraqi general officers. We shared information and intelligence, surveillance, and reconnaissance platforms as we attacked the elements of ISIS in Baghdad and the surrounding area. It was challenging, sometimes frustrating, but also very rewarding. I kept thinking to myself that I was practically already doing an SFAB mission, and I enjoyed it. So, after discussing the SFAB idea with Col. Byrom and my wife, Amy, I decided to volunteer and applied for the opportunity to command again. There were other, less palatable options out there for former battalion commanders—most were staff jobs, which did not have the same appeal as the SFAB. The SFAB was another opportunity to command again. My favorite part of command was working with the people, training, mentoring, and most importantly, learning from them. I also unabashedly love to travel to foreign countries and learn about the people, history, and culture. The SFAB seemed to potentially combine both of those elements I particularly enjoyed, command and travel. Finally, it was a unique opportunity to try something groundbreaking and be on the cusp of a renewed way of working with foreign military partners. The SFAB sounded like a unique challenge.

In October 2018, I found out I would command 1st Battalion, 5th SFAB following my assignment with the 3rd Cavalry Regiment. So now I would join something I didn't fully understand, build it from scratch, train it, and deploy it. At this juncture I had more questions than answers.

Building Something New

The Army can be quite adaptable and innovative when attempting to determine how best to fight a conflict. However, it rarely builds new units from scratch. Usually, the Army takes an existing unit with people, a chain of command, equipment, and most importantly, a supply room and repurposes it for a new mission, such as the case for Lt. Col. Hal Moore and the 1/7 Cavalry in the battle of Ia Drang. Then it transforms the equipment and people, almost like a *pivot* in the business world. Transforming an existing Army unit is nearly identical to how Patagonia began by exclusively selling climbing gear but then did a one-eighty and morphed into an outdoor clothing business.

My unit, the 3rd Cavalry Regiment (Stryker), had undergone a similar transformation in recent history. The unit was previously called the 3d Armored Cavalry Regiment, equipped with tanks, Bradley Fighting Vehicles, and helicopters and had fought in Desert Storm and Operation Iraqi Freedom as that type of formation. In

2009 it converted to a Stryker formation with the eight-wheeled vehicles, complementary support, and engineer equipment and divested itself of the tracked vehicles and helicopters. The Army pivoted the 3d Cavalry Regiment from one way of fighting an organization to another. The organization still had the heraldry, culture, and many of the same people; however, it was a different type of unit with a new mission.

Back in the 1970s and 1980s during the Cold War, the US Army had built other now-notable units like the 75th Ranger Regiment, 160th Special Operations Aviation Regiment, and other special operations units to meet the needs of the defense environment during that era. Units like those had to find people, equipment, and patrons that kept the unit's development moving, like the well know General Creighton Abrams. They also built strong quality reputations over the years and went through their own learning curves as they decided on how to staff, equip, and train for their specific missions.

However, unlike those transformations, I, and other leaders in 5th SFAB, were tasked with building something unlike other existing conventional Army formations from scratch. In the present day between Army chiefs of staff General Milley and General McConville, the Army decided that it would transform and change to meet a new operating environment with units like the Multi-Domain Task Forces (MDTFs), Army Cyber Command, and Security Force Assistance Brigades (SFABs), which I now found myself a part of. However, in the case for the Joint Base Lewis-McChord (JBLM)-based 1st MDTF, USARPAC first did test runs then formed the MDTF out of the 17th Field Artillery Brigade.[22] In the case for Army Cyber Command, the Army formed it out of NETCOM/9th Signal Command and portions of the 1st Information Operations Command (Land).[23] 5th SFAB was different in that it was not built out of any existing unit or formation. The question remained: would our experiment succeed without having an existing unit to start from?

The Army has also failed in building units before. Some units were not effective, did not endure, or were only transitory. Some older, now deactivated, units had similar functions and missions to the SFAB. During the height of the Afghan and Iraq wars in the first decade of the 2000s and into the 2010s, they had names like Security Force Advisory and Assistance Team (SFAAT), Military Transition Team (MiTT), or Embedded Training Team (ETT). Their effectiveness was controversial. Many of the challenges the MiTTs, ETTs, and SFAATs had included the selection of the right personnel, the ad hoc nature of creating the teams, predeployment training shortfalls, and unity of command.[24] However, even when they did perform well they did not receive the recognition they deserved.[25] Most importantly, SFAAT, MiTT, and ETT assignments for officers and NCOs were not looked at favorably by the Army and meant they were not always rewarded with promotions and choice subsequent assignments.[26] For career-oriented officers and NCOs this led to a negative view of advisor units that filtered into the Human Resources Command and the general psyche of the conventional Army. This unfavorable history had a significant impact on the SFAB's ability to recruit talented officers and senior NCOs to volunteer for its ranks. In many ways early volunteers were taking a considerable career risk by joining the SFAB. It was an unproven step in the Army corporate ladder.

Recruiting talented people was a significant hurdle. Fortunately, much like an angel investor for a fledgling start-up, the SFAB had Gen. Milley as a patron. After serving as the chief of staff of the Army, he provided strong support to the SFAB enterprise as the chairman of the Joint Chiefs of Staff. Unconfirmed Army rumors and hearsay indicated that he and a few other four-star Army generals pointedly asked for top talent from various conventional Army units when 1st and 2nd SFABs first started. Additionally, some, but not all, Army officers and NCOs had favorable experiences with 1st, 2nd, and 3rd SFABs during their deployments to Afghanistan and Iraq. The 1st, 2nd, and 3rd SFABs created the mostly, but not decisively, favorable SFAB brand.

Now it was 5th SFAB's turn to build a unit from scratch. I had volunteered, that was the easy part. Now I was tasked with constructing a battalion with little more than a simple piece of paper with the names of other battalion commanders on it—my peers. I knew that my future boss, Colonel Curt Taylor, was coordinating with various Army agencies and units at JBLM, Washington to secure facilities and some bare bones equipment to work with, but I had no idea what to expect. I also knew that Lieutenant Colonel Marty Wohlgemuth, the future fires battalion commander, was already at JBLM, but he was still in command of his battalion in 17th Fires Brigade. From my I perspective still at Fort Hood, Texas, 1st Battalion, 5th SFAB could still be described by the pronoun "I" as opposed to a "we." So when I walked into what would eventually become the brigade headquarters for the first time, which consisted of some random desks and chairs, I was shocked to hear I wasn't the first person assigned to 1st Battalion. That honor belonged to First Sergeant Travis Keen. In fact, he was the first person officially assigned to 5th SFAB, which makes him the original plankowner for 5th SFAB. *Plankowner* is a borrowed Navy term that refers to the first member of the crew to serve aboard a newly commissioned ship. Sometimes the term *plankholder* is used interchangeably. For 1st Sgt. Travis Keen, he was the first person assigned to 5th SFAB and thus the very first person to serve in the unit.

CHAPTER 2

Breaking Ground and Eating Dirt: Finding and Hiring the Right Team

EVERYBODY HAS TALENTS, and hopefully, they can use those talents to excel in their various careers. Which makes it paramount that these people are in the right positions to use those talents. This holds true whether you are in the business world or the military. Jim Collins discusses placing the right people with the appropriate skills in the correct positions at length in his book *Good to Great*. Aligning individual talents with a job or position that values or capitalizes on those skills does not always happen in the business world or the military. Collins uses a bus analogy in his book when talking about a company. He says you need to get the right people in the key seats of the bus to make sure the bus, i.e. the company, can adapt and perform when facing uncertainty.

For those of us starting 5th SFAB, we had to go find those "right" people who were appropriate for our type of bus—an Army unit. Convincing people to be part of something new, never tested or tried before, is undoubtedly difficult. The process identifying the right people for these key positions begins during the recruiting stage. Not all Army units conduct initial screening of candidates. In fact, sometimes units are just trying to fill vacancies in their organization. When building 5th SFAB, we had to execute the hiring process differently and follow some of Collins's concepts. We had to ask the following: Are these individuals connected to our organization's core values? What is their level of expertise? Are they able to meet the expectations of the mission? How do they feel about this mission?

Recruiting: Convincing Others to Join the SFAB

Generally in an Army unit, when you need a person, say a supply sergeant, there is a process to requisition a replacement. The personnel officer or NCO in the unit sends up a vacancy request, and eventually, the Army's human resource system sends a new sergeant to the unit. Position filled. Automatic personnel requisitions are not the case for an all-volunteer unit in an all-volunteer force. Since the 5th SFAB was an all-volunteer unit, the Army human resources professionals could not simply assign an individual to our unit. Our unit was different and therefore the standard Army process would not work for us.

The most defining characteristic that differentiated the SFAB from the older SFAATs, MiTTs, and ETTs experiments was that every person in the SFAB was a volunteer. The people that wanted to wear the Brown Beret had to sign their name on a form, a 4187 in Army jargon, saying they wanted to volunteer for SFAB service. Because the person had to request service in the SFAB and sign the 4187, the volunteer status added a level of scrutiny and commitment for candidates. However, that also meant that the Army was not going to fill our ranks using its industrial-sized personnel system. Those of us in 5th SFAB, with support from the Security Force Assistance Command (SFAC), had to search for officers and NCOs to volunteer for SFAB service.

The SFAC, also known as "the Command," is the higher headquarters for all the SFABs. It's responsible for the manning, training, and equipping of the SFABs. While it technically doesn't determine how and where the Geographic Combatant Commands (GCCs) employ the SFABs, it does talk with the Army Service Component Commands to help with that process. One of its essential functions included running the SFAB recruiting program, which included recruiting visits to various Army installations and producing posters, web content, and live-virtual events to generate interest in SFAB service.

Recruiting for the 1/5 SFAB battalion began while I was still in Iraq. I was the battalion commander but had no idea how to recruit within the Army's personnel system, which dated back to WWII. The Army centralized the system within its Human Resources Command created "assignment officers" for infantry officers like me to guide career paths. Infantry assignment officers had knowledge of all the job opportunities in the entire Army for infantry officers. They were very influential on an individual's career. I remember calling my various assignment officers about job opportunities throughout my twenty-year career. I clearly remember calling and the phrase "Rowland [pause] . . . let me pull up your file," followed by some typing. Then they would say, "Let me see what's available," in a tone that (after looking at my records) meant "Let me see what's available for someone with *your* file strength." On these phone calls I always knew there were higher-quality positions that they wouldn't tell me about because they didn't think my file supported it. The Army, at the time of 5th SFAB's stand-up, was updating this legacy personnel management process to a talent management system of sorts. The idea was to get a grip on the unique talents and skills that each individual possessed and provide visibility and transparency to the entire Army job market. Now infantry assignment officers could not withhold the high-quality positions anymore. At any rate, transitioning from the old to the new took a bit of time. The Army is a large organization that can't change quickly when it comes to its hiring and personnel management system. For 1/5 SFAB, we had to navigate the transitioning Army personnel process while at the same time attracting volunteers to our new organization.

Large corporations like GE, Microsoft, Ford, and SpaceX look to recruit and hire people with passion and drive. Interviewing can be intense and go for multiple rounds—from phone calls to in-person screenings—before any candidate makes the cut. My newly assigned partner and battle buddy, Command Sergeant Major Calvin J. "CJ" Overway and I were supposed to spearhead the recruitment process, but we were yet to be assigned together. As a novice, I started recruiting with what, and who, I knew.

My early recruiting endeavors started by sending emails to fellow battalion commanders that I'd known throughout my Army career primarily focused on finding qualified infantry captains. In hindsight, these were very rudimentary emails that received the exact responses they deserved—nothing. Not a single lead for any name, number, or email address. If I did receive a response, it was usually along the lines of "Good luck with your new unit." Not exactly helpful nor even remotely the response I was looking for.

After contemplating my initial failed efforts, I asked the infantry captain's desk at Human Resources Command for a few names. I did this with my newfound comrade in arms, Lieutenant Colonel Anthony Gore. Anthony, the second battalion commander for 5th SFAB, had previously served at Human Resources Command and knew the system well. He knew the right questions to ask the desk officers and spoke the lingo to get them to provide us with a more comprehensive list of candidate names. Anthony asked questions like "Which captains are available in this and the next assignment cycle," "Who are the officers requesting out-of-cycle moves," and "Which brigades are returning from deployments that might have an exodus of officers." Questions like these helped narrow our focus as we looked at Excel sheets with sometimes more than a hundred names on them. Instead of artificial intelligence or algorithms running through potential candidates like many job placement companies have, we had two sets of eyeballs, a list of names, and an officer's record brief. The process took many man-hours of searching and screening to start targeting what we thought were the optimal volunteers for our new unit.

As Anthony and I sent emails and made phone calls, there were a lot of rejections in those first days and weeks. Some responses were simple no thanks, some discussed the other proven career path jobs they were pursuing instead, and others just never acknowledged the email at all. Many of the rejections came about because captains solicited advice from their current bosses, battalion and brigade commanders, about whether this volunteer team was a good career move or not. Most of the advice was risk avoidant, pointing to staying on the historic promotion ladder to ensure advancement within the ranks. This was disappointing, especially because we knew some of the battalion commanders providing this advice. It's challenging both in the military and civilian world to convince people that risks are worth taking. As Susan Wojcicki, CEO of YouTube, poignantly stated, "Rarely are opportunities presented to you in the perfect way, in a nice little box with a yellow bow on top . . . Opportunities, the good ones, they're messy and confusing and hard to recognize."[27]

Somehow, we had to take challenges and turn them into opportunities. For me, the most vexatious part was hearing from peers and senior general officers that SFAB wasn't a good idea. Army general officers had created these formations, SFAATs, MiTTs, and ETTs, and but they did not withstand the Army institution or processes. Many senior Army leaders knew of the scar tissue of creating small advising teams to work with foreign partners and didn't want to see good talent go to "waste," referencing the SFAAT, MiTTs, and ETTs from earlier in the Iraq and Afghan wars. The Army did not promote or select for higher command the officers and noncommissioned officers who joined these ad hoc formations at nearly the rates of their peers. I clearly remember the reaction of a senior general officer when

I first found out the Army had selected me for SFAB command. His verbal response was "Hmmm, that's interesting," but his body language said, "That's really dumb—why did you do that?" Another Army general officer asked me what an SFAB was. These were the types of people who we needed to convince that wearing a Brown Beret was a good career move and overcome a lot of biases and preconceived notions.

Fortunately, there were some believers in my peer group. Of the seven squadron commanders in the 3d Cavalry Regiment, three of us volunteered for SFAB service. Rhett Blackmon, our engineer squadron commander, would head to JBLM with me to command 5/5 SFAB. Paul, "Paully," Davis, our support squadron commander, would go to Fort Benning to command 6/1 SFAB, their support battalion. I knew I had some friends who were right alongside me in joining this adventure and the struggles that would accompany it. While there was a lot of enthusiasm and hope among these pioneers paving the way for building a new organization, there were many times in the initial stages of this start-up that felt more like eating dirt than breaking ground on the foundation of the new unit.

Arrival at JBLM: The Real Beginning

Following my nine-month tour in Iraq I returned to Fort Hood, Texas with members of 1st Squadron, 3rd Cavalry Regiment. We were excited to get back home to Texas and our families. The culmination of the return is the welcome-home ceremony, where soldiers see their families for the first time. Throughout the contemporary wars in Iraq and Afghanistan they were shown on TV and social media. As I stood in formation and scanned the crowd in the Fort Hood Abrams gym, my eyes fell on my beautiful wife, Amy. I'm sure I had a puzzled look on my face when I saw my five-year-old son Andrew sitting right next to Amy—with a plastic grocery bag in his hands. Parents and teachers recognize this tactic—she was obviously afraid he was about to puke. I thought, *That seems unusual—Amy didn't mention anything when I texted after I landed this morning.*

I didn't know it until after the ceremony had concluded, but our reunion in that gym almost didn't happen. As fortune goes sometimes with these type of things in Army life, hours before the ceremony Amy and our four kids—Zac, Abi, Izzy, and Andrew—were driving through one of Fort Hood's gates near our on-base housing subdivision. Suddenly they were struck from behind as the gate guard checked their IDs. The driver behind them wasn't paying attention and had let up on the brake, crept forward, and rear-ended Amy's minivan with everyone in it. Luckily no one was hurt, but it did take quite some time to clear the incident with the police. Fortunately, as a true testament to the Army spouse battle-buddy system that forms from years of operating as solo parents during deployments, spouse friends happened to drive by the incident and allowed Amy to offload our four children into their minivans (thank you, Micki Salge and Karin Davis) and take them back to their home while Amy spent two hours wrapping up the paperwork from the accident. As a result of this incident, the delay caused a rush of flurried activity once they finally made it home less than thirty minutes before the ceremony was set to begin.

Homecomings are nervous and anticipative times for military families following long separation periods. As a very rushed Amy was doing her makeup, our then eight-year-old daughter, Abi, informed Amy that her five-year-old brother, Andrew, had just thrown up. Now, not only were they rushed, but they were about to be late. Who wants to clean up vomit wearing a nice outfit with makeup only partially applied and three other kids to get ready? Somehow, everyone pulled it together enough to rush out the door, scramble to find parking near the welcome-home ceremony venue, and quickly walk, dare I say jog, to make it inside on time.

Oh, and I was the senior officer coming home on this particular flight, so people would be looking for Amy before the ceremony.

During the arrival ceremony at Abrams gym on Fort Hood, members of 1st Squadron marched onto the basketball court and stood in formation as we were officially welcomed back to the United States. Like all husbands and fathers and military members, I scanned the crowd for my family as I stood at attention. I was fortunate as the commander since I stood out in front and had an unobstructed view. That's when I saw Andrew holding the grocery bag in his lap. I understood what that meant. In the end, it was a heartfelt return, and our family was once again back together. Andrew never threw up, but that didn't keep Amy and I from being on edge during my long-awaited return. However, we wouldn't stay at Fort Hood long. A few months later, I turned the 1st Squadron, 3rd Cavalry Regiment over to Lieutenant Colonel Ryan Bulger and it was time for the Rowland family to drive to our next destination, Joint Base Lewis-McChord outside Tacoma, Washington, and the future home of the 5th SFAB.

Like many military families, we lived a somewhat nomadic life moving from Army base to Army base. While this is disruptive it also provides opportunities. In our case, moving from Texas to Washington State during the summer meant we could take the opportunity to see some of America's most beautiful places. Our family particularly loves America's National Parks. During this journey we were blessed to have Amy's mom, Linda Selden (also a military spouse for twenty-nine years), join us for the adventure and we took the kids to Carlsbad Caverns National Park, Roswell, New Mexico to see where aliens supposedly landed, Mesa Verde National Park, Grand Tetons National Park, and Yellowstone National Park. Amy and I wanted to stop in a few more before driving into JBLM, but the kids were worn out from being on the road.

Arriving at JBLM was like coming home in some respects. I had served at JBLM for three years as a major in 4 Battalion, 9th

Infantry, part of 4th Stryker Brigade Combat Team, 2nd Infantry Division, and the 201st Battlefield Surveillance Brigade (BfSB), and we loved the Pacific Northwest. Two of our kids, Izzy and Andrew, were born in Washington State. At the time, we routinely packed two or three of the kids into hiking backpacks (yes, one on the front and one on the back) and took them to Mount Rainier and Olympic National Parks, among other places. We enjoyed the food, the scenery, and the people.

Luckily, we qualified for on-base housing in the historic homes near the grand parade field. The house was a pretty good size, around 2,400 square feet, including a sunporch on the first floor off our quaint family room. I'd end up spending a lot of time in in that sunporch in those early days because we didn't have office space or even computers when I reported for service in the 5th SFAB. Consequently, that sunporch served as my home and work office. After twenty years in the Army, I had never shown up to a unit that didn't have physical space. I liked to compare my small sunporch office to the garages of famous start-up companies like Amazon, Apple, Google, and Hewlett-Packard. Clearly not the same, but it put me in a good mental framework. While in the sunporch, I felt the hustle necessary to recruit and build 1st Battalion. I would frequently close the door during our first summer in Washington when the kids were out of school so I could conduct phone call interviews with potential officers I was in the process of recruiting for our new unit.

The Meeting of the Minds: "Cofounders" Coming Together

Command Sergeant Major CJ Overway and I finally met for the first time in the beginning of July 2019. He swears it was the tenth, so we'll go with that. Meeting your assigned counterpart in the Army can be a little nerve-racking because the relationship between the commander and his senior enlisted adviser will set the tone and culture for the entire organization. I had seen plenty of instances where that relationship was coolly cordial, adversarial, or even toxic. In a previous assignment, one of my fellow commanders and his senior enlisted counterparts were just not a good match. I would describe the relationship as awkward more than anything else. When the commander and senior enlisted counterpart have a poor relationship, it creates tension and confusion for the rest of the unit. The result is a less cohesive and effective combat-ready unit. When I was part of, or closely observed those units, indecision was common for simple problems, decisions were unpredictable, or the organization separated into two camps—one that supported the commander and the other that supported the senior enlisted counterpart. Sometimes all these disfunctions occurred at the same time. The power of good leadership in an organization resonates throughout as well. Good leadership fosters healthy relationships, dialogue, and problem-solving. I had been blessed with great NCO counterparts for most of my career, including in 1st Squadron, 3rd Cavalry Regiment with Command Sergeant Major Kim Mendez. He taught me to listen to quality NCOs and ask better questions, and he challenged me to learn about other nuanced parts of the NCO corps, such as NCO professional development.

Fortunately, CJ Overway and I developed a great professional relationship and friendship that lasted over the duration of our command of the 1st Battalion, 5th SFAB. He was instrumental in establishing the command culture that developed and empowered our NCOs. His leadership and follow-through assisted our battalion in deployment into eleven Indo-Pacific countries a year and a half later. Much of our time was spent making phone calls and sending emails while sitting across from one another in the small office that the brigade eventually set up. There were times that I worked from home because the office was either too loud or too hot.

All the 5th SFAB's battalion command teams, consisting of the battalion commander and command sergeant major, were squeezed into a small office that eventually became the brigade S1, or personnel operations and human resources space. We had no air conditioning and the temperatures got considerably warm even by Washington State standards during July and August. Cmd. Sgt. Maj. Overway and I laid claim to the two desks next to the windows to take advantage of the sun and breeze to help cool ourselves off in the cramped office space.

I was a relatively amateur interviewer. I had picked up a few techniques that I developed into a system of sorts for my interviews with my target audience of captains and majors. Learning to interview was mostly an informal process. I had also participated as a candidate in the screening and selection process for the 75th Ranger Regiment twice, which included psychological interviews and going before an interview board. Formally, while assigned to the Joint Special Operations Command (JSOC) at Fort Bragg (today known as Fort Liberty), I attended a one-day interviewing seminar to qualify to sit on interviewing boards for new JSOC staff officers. Finally, I read or listened to a few books along the way, such as John Maxwell's *Good Leaders Ask Great Questions*, Simon Sinek's *Start with Why*, and Jonah Berger's *Contagious*. I also listened to Ken Coleman's *EntreLeadership Podcast,* which also contained some good interview techniques and tips every once in a while. But, I still wasn't quite sure how to approach the interview process in the context of the Army's personnel system and forming this unproven unit.

I was not alone in the quest to develop interview questions and a methodical process. My peer commanders in that small, crammed office felt similarly. We discussed our evolving new skills with one another and eventually compiled a series of questions that took each of us about forty-five minutes, give or take, to run through.

During the interview process I tried to get the candidates to speak about themselves as much as possible. Like many interview techniques, I started by asking candidates open ended questions like "Tell me about yourself," "What are your professional goals?" and "What are your personal goals?" Then I transitioned into the mission specific and scenario-based questions that could reveal anything of relevance on the topic of working with a foreign partner or in a small team. Some of these questions included "Provide me a nonmilitary example of a time you coached, taught, or mentored a small group of individuals to achieve a collective goal (sports, volunteer, etc.) and what surprised you from the experience," "Describe a recent travel experience to a foreign country or another place in the United States if you haven't been overseas. What did you like about it and what frustrated you the most?" and usually one that I found enlightening, "What do you do for fun?" Throughout this range of questioning, I felt I got a small glimpse into the person individually and professionally. The art of creating a dialogue was a technique that took me a while to develop.

Lt. Col. Anthony Gore had a knack for knowing what questions to ask and when. I think it came from talking with hundreds of infantry officers while he had worked at Human Resources Command. He also had a great memory about people's files, their career timeline, and details about some of their unique family situations. Anthony suggested we ask the Infantry Branch officers about each candidate's performance and potential because they had access to their entire files. This included their prior evaluation reports, which is controlled information. Anthony also asked the assignment officer questions like "Is this person on assignment instructions," "What does this captain's file strength look like," and "What other assignments is this officer asking about," to name a few. While the desk officers couldn't give all the additional details we requested, they could paint the picture that gave us an understanding of how the officer was doing relative to their peers and their general performance in their Army career.

Lt. Col. Gore also recommended that we speak to the current

and prior commanders of each candidate, i.e. references. Before 2021, officers didn't put their references into officer records briefs, which provide a simple summary of the officer's assignments and military and civilian education, among other information. Having additional information from references was incredibly helpful to me and Cmd. Sgt. Maj. Overway in determining who would be a good fit for our teams. This was innovative because it was not a standard practice in the Army at the time to talk to a candidate's previous and current commanders or conduct background checks with Infantry Branch.

While hearing from each candidate's current and prior commanders was useful for our hiring purposes, the communication also alerted the references that the officer was considering SFAB service. This backfired a few times on us. A few qualified officers who were leaning toward coming into our unit later pulled their packets after "talking to some mentors," as the rejection email usually read. We knew that meant their commanders had talked them out of joining our little SFAB "start-up." The rejections were disappointing to hear, especially when we thought we had filled critical positions in our formation. Recruiting in the early days was the hardest hurdle we tackled day in and day out.

Without the backing from the Army's Human Resources Command, and their large personnel management command, recruiting personnel for our teams would have been an impossible uphill climb. Human Resources Command did help by providing the comprehensive list of candidates and generally, without hinderances, allowed candidates to divert from other assignments to the 5th SFAB. We needed someone with authority to help us get this off the ground and lend credibility to what we were structuring, specifically the Army's future battalion and brigade commanders, the mentors of our recruiting audience. As we brainstormed on how to reach this audience, we thought about the Army's command preparation pipeline. My boss, Curt Taylor, now a brigadier general, contacted the schedulers from the Army's Pre-Command Course at Fort Leavenworth. This course trained and certified upcoming battalion and brigade commanders for their pending command assignments. Unfortunately, we were not successful in getting written into their agenda.

I would liken our lack of welcome into the Army Pre-Command Course to a new start-up company not gaining access to pitch potential investors because these investors considered the idea irrelevant with no proof of concept to date. We believed in our plan. Through persistence and determination, we would continue our pursuit of quality candidates to fill our positions. The *no's, maybes*, and occasional *yeses* created an emotional roller coaster during the recruiting process.

During my Army career I, like all officers, was typically told where to go and serve. Exceptions included joining airborne or special operations units, but that was limited to a relatively small number of people. Quality volunteers flocked to the Special Forces or the Ranger Regiment because they had tried-and-true reputations. Otherwise, accepting assignments to various places or units simply because you were told to go was part of the Army lifestyle. I never wondered what was in it for me, but now recruits wondered why they should join SFAB and what was in it for them. What could we tell them?

Thinking back, corporations like General Electric and other industry titans were once start-ups that engineers and inventors took a chance on and found their success despite the naysayers. The 5th SFAB would endure the same—or so we hoped. It was a tough sell when I was talking to many of the candidates. When General Electric was starting up, other companies were safer picks that inventors and engineers were told were better places to work and advance in their careers.

CHAPTER 3

Building a Team of Experts

RECRUITING VOLUNTEERS was certainly a challenge. Making sure the volunteers had the characteristics, skills, and attributes necessary to competently work with foreign military partners was the next step. Once our battalion had people to stand in formation, we needed to start training them to perform the SFAB mission. We started training on the basics and taking small steps toward building on our core competencies.

Assessment and Selection: Getting the Right People

As mentioned, one of the unique things about the organization of the SFAB maneuver advisor team (MAT) is the composition of the various military occupational specialties. Nowhere else could you have found a more diverse small unit: infantry soldiers, military police officers, intelligence experts, fire support specialists, EOD specialists (or combat engineers), medics, mechanics, supply specialists, and signal professionals. These volunteers came from a variety of units ranging from strategic logistic support battalions to infantry combat brigade teams. All the noncommissioned officers who filled our ranks had to attend the SFAC's weeklong Assessment and Selection Program at Fort Bragg to join the one of the SFABs.

By the time 5th SFAB started, that program was firmly in place and we began filling our thin ranks. Basically, volunteers traveled to Fort Bragg from their parent unit, conducted a PT test, interviewed with the cadre, completed some leader reaction course exercises that help assess leadership and teamwork attributes, led a small-group foot march, and finally sat in front of a panel for an interview. The program was relatively short compared to some of the other assessment and selection programs in the Army, like those in the special operations units. However, it still provided some additional information about the volunteer(s). The cadre led in-depth interviews with each volunteer primarily centered around their military occupational specialty, including a file assessment, a performance review by the current chain of command, and an attempt to understand their reason for volunteering. A military occupation specialty (MOS) designates the profession a particular officer, NCO, or soldier might belong to. For example, someone who is a 35F is an intelligence analyst. An 11B is an infantry soldier. These identifiers help determine Army force structure and strength. In the SFAB, each position is coded for a specific MOS. Therefore, SFAB leaders must recruit, screen, and hire distinct officers and NCOs from a particular specialty to fill the ranks. The file assessment consisted of reviewing their Noncommissioned Officer Evaluation Reports (NCOER). It is important to note that experienced NCOs can spot whether the evaluator has unduly exaggerated the report or has given an accurate assessment of their subordinate.

The interview panel consisted of a sitting SFAB battalion commander, battalion command sergeant major, and company first sergeant. The SFAC tasked one of the five SFABs to run two panels per assessment and selection session, which equated to one per month. During non-COVID times command teams traveled from the four other locations: Fort Benning, Georgia, Fort Hood, Texas, Fort Carson, Colorado, and Joint Base Lewis-McChord, Washington, to Fort Bragg, North Carolina, to conduct the panels in person. It took a concerted effort logistically to arrange for all these people to come together in one location for the day-long panel interviews because most leaders were busy training or building their own organizations.

It is common practice for the Army Special Operations Forces to pull battalion and higher-level leaders together for boards. This type of approach is supposed to help recruit the right people into the organization. Because SFAB teams were small and agile units, we did not want any soldier problems that could hinder our progress or relationships with foreign countries, as problems would cause us to deviate from our primary mission. As Dave Ramsey so aptly said when speaking about the interview and hiring process, ". . . you don't want crazy in the building. . ." We had no room for crazy. We didn't want people in our organization that could not handle being away from supervision in a foreign country with a significant amount of leeway. Otherwise, we would have administrative or disciplinary problems. We needed and wanted volunteers who were committed and prepared. Our reputation was dependent upon the quality of character and mission preparedness that our Brown Berets represented in the United States and to our foreign counterparts. Missteps by individual in the early build phase would significantly delay capitalizing on opportunities in the short and medium term. In doing so, those individuals could quickly shut doors and opportunities we thought were open. Quality volunteers were especially necessary as we built the 5th SFAB brand with our Indo-Pacific foreign military partners and trust with our reporting headquarters in Hawaii, USARPAC.

In 1/5 SFAB, our experience with the cadre was always very good. Before each candidate reported to the panel, the cadre provided an excellent summary of their file, including the candidate's results during the three-day testing program. During in-person and eventually virtual panels, I would split the paperwork, peer reviews during the five-day program, chain-of-command assessments, NCOERs, and other administrative paperwork among the three panel members. After that, we would ask a series of questions, each with a focus area. I typically asked candidates to explain both positive and negative comments in their peer reviews since it would be fresh in their minds. Those initial answers usually set the tone of the panel interview. Was the candidate open to criticism and feedback or were they defensive? Either the command sergeant major or the first sergeant would ask questions about their evaluations and their career history. After a few panel interviews the board members fell into our own rhythm, so we understood where questioning and discussions would flow. Once the questioning was complete, the candidate left the room. The three panel members talked about the candidate to determine whether they were a good fit for the SFAB. Finally, we voted for the various candidates, and this became part of an official record of our proceedings.

During the first year of 5th SFAB's existence, once all the interviews were complete and the candidates had been selected, the cadre went about telling them who had passed and who had failed. Notifying the SFAB candidates changed after the first year of 5th SFAB's existence. The second-year candidates returned immediately following panel deliberation and were told face-to-face by the panel members whether they were selected or not. By having candidates return to the panel, panel members were able to provide specific information to those who had not been selected without bias and how they might improve and reapply. The panel members also provided those selected for SFAB service with feedback if there were areas they needed to improve before reporting for duty.

While this assessment and selection panel process was less than perfect, it did help us to better screen volunteers and select the best candidates for SFAB service. Sometimes we would knowingly take a little risk with specialty skills we knew were understaffed in the SFAB enterprise, like communication specialist or logistics specialist. Right before panel proceedings, the cadre would pull statistics for each MOS across the entire SFAC enterprise to help us decide if we were making the correct decision. The SFAC continually tweaked the assessment and selection process to meet the needs of the force and provide the best candidates to teams.

Every organization wants quality team members, and the SFAB was no different. Our challenge was to attract people to an organization that had yet to prove itself to the Army as an institution and our future customers in the Indo-Pacific. The 5th SFAB attracted people based on our potential: what schooling, experiences, and training might be in store for them. They were certainly taking a risk joining our team. Our job as leaders was to make sure we held up our part of that informal agreement. With the resources we had at the time, that meant training or attending Army schools.

The Beginning of a Series of Firsts

By the end of the summer of 2019, the 1950s-era buildings we were assigned to were no longer in a condemned-looking status and had received a fresh coat of paint, among other improvements. All the battalion command teams, battalion commanders, and command sergeant majors moved into the first floor of what would become the 1/5 SFAB Building and had a lot more working space than in the small open space cramped inside the brigade headquarters. The additional space also gave the few officers and NCOs who had started to arrive a reasonable place to work.

During those few months, the battalion command teams got to know each other better and developed a kind of synergy. We had been somewhat disjointed working from home or, in some cases, our cars. Another improvement was having Major Tom Angstadt, the first and for a long time, the only major in the battalion, and his 1st Sgt., Travis Keen, move onto the second floor with their growing company.

By the fall after my summer arrival at JBLM, we had decided to build A Company as the first of our three infantry SFAB companies, followed in sequence by B Company and C Company. The other option we considered was to build each of the three SFAB companies simultaneously, with each company receiving personnel and equipment equally as they arrived. Instead, Brig. Gen. Taylor instructed all the 5th SFAB battalions to create small, fully functional formations within each of our organizations. To generate our first MATs meant that that the NCOs arriving after passing their assessment and selection program went to Maj. Angstadt and 1st Sgt. Keen's A Company first. Additionally, we built our small battalion staff to a basic, but functional, manning level. To meet Brig. Gen. Taylor's goal of a minimum threshold of capability, Cmd. Sgt. Maj. Overway and I had to train A Company's three MATs, the company CAT, and battalion staff to a certain standard that would prepare them to work with a foreign partner in the Pacific the following summer of 2020. We also needed to prepare to receive other multifunctional teams from the artillery, engineer, and logistics battalions. We, of course, had no idea what that might look like yet. First, we needed to work on the fundamentals that define a basic US Army organization, like processes and paperwork.

Maj. Angstadt, 1st Sgt. Keen, and the first officers and NCOs that arrived helped us develop processes and procedures to do things existing Army units take for granted. So, we worked first with what we already knew and had on hand. This included requesting simple supplies like pens, paper, light bulbs, and yes, even toilet paper. Normally items like these are available in a unit's supply room but ours didn't exist yet. We had to determine how we were going to process paperwork and receive new personnel.

Reception of personnel was especially important because it gave the new arrivals their first impression of the unit. If it was bad, then we had an uphill climb to re-establish trust between the unit and this new Brown Beret.

Another challenge was how to develop a paperwork process to send Brown Berets to individual schools like mountain warfare; air assault; or survival, evade, resistance, and escape (SERE) school. Sending Brown Berets to schooling was important because it not only increased the individual's skillset but, in most cases, it fulfilled a promise made to these soldiers at some point during the recruiting phase. Similarly, creating systems for ordering supplies and processing paperwork isn't very exciting, but it's essential when starting from scratch. Next we needed to build a secure room that turned into a sweat lodge in the battalion's building.

One essential task I had personal interest in was making sure we would have a Secret Internet Protocol Router Network (SIPR) connectivity in the building. I knew that one day most of our planning, coordination, and communication would move to this classified system. I wanted to be first in the brigade to have SIPR in my building. I looked to my intelligence officer, the competent Captain Jeff Lockwood, to make this happen. Capt. Lockwood was a young captain who my good friend Lt. Col. Dave Bowers had recommended to me. Dave and I had worked together somewhat tangentially in special operations while at Fort Bragg and had later commanded battalions (squadron) together at Fort Hood, Texas. Jeff was one of the few great officers who literally fell into my lap without me having to go on a recruiting expedition to find. I am forever grateful to Dave Bowers for sending me his application packet.

We were fortunate that our battalion barracks headquarters building already had most of the physical security infrastructure in place for SIPR access approval. Capt. Lockwood just needed to ensure a few upgrades and improvements were made, like bars on the designated windows. Of course, the downside to that particular room was that it got hot in the summer because the building didn't have any air conditioning, and they couldn't open the windows due to security requirements and the solid bars on the windows. While Washington State doesn't get very hot relative to other locations in the United States during the summer, I can assure you it got hot in the 1/5 SFAB SIPR room. When walking through the door to that room you literally hit a wall of heat crossing the threshold. The heat, lack of air circulation, and sweat mixed together created quite the aroma while trying to concentrate on reading or writing secret documents.

Capt. Lockwood's hard work and close coordination with Captain Mark Goodwin, the battalion's communications officer, proved very effective. 1st battalion had SIPR services in our building months before any of the other battalions did. It provided us with a significant amount of flexibility. Having our own secret certified building meant we didn't have to travel to other facilities on JBLM to get the secret-level work done.

By the time our first officers and NCOs signed into Maj. Tom Anstadt and 1st Sgt. Travis Keen's A Company in September and October, I had met my new "battle buddy" Com. Sgt. Maj. CJ Overway, recruited and hired the majority of the unit's officers, and Capt. Jeff Lockwood had opened our SIPR "café" in the battalion. At that point, I had been back from Iraq for nine months and, like many newly arrived SFAB Brown Berets, had moved my family from some distant Army post across the country to JBLM to embark on a new adventure. As an organization we had passed some significant milestones in the few months we'd been working together. Now we needed to start doing something besides mastering paperwork. It was time to start training on the fundamentals.

Guns and Shooting

I always thought that being in an organization that can store weapons and then use them was an inspiring privilege. Having weapons in an arms room was something I generally took for granted when I was assigned to other Army units. The weapons were always just... there. When our weapons arrived in 1/5 SFAB, there were only a handful of us on hand to receive them. The few other Brown Berets that had arrived were gone attending Army schools. But it was an exciting day in October of 2019 when our pistols, rifles, and machine guns arrived in our rented supply truck. We had to rent a truck to transport the weapons because we didn't have any vehicles in the battalion yet. Weapons arrival was a significant event for a unit in its infancy.

I will never forget carrying heavy boxes with Sergeant First Class Omar Moore, our battalion logistics NCO (S4), from the front stairs, down a winding staircase, and finally into the arms room to put our weapons into their designated storage areas and weapons racks. It was a long, tedious process because we obviously couldn't lose accountability for these things, especially when they were in transit. The weapons were also new—something none of us had ever seen before. Frequently Sfc. Moore had to tell people to keep moving because folks like Sergeant First Class Steve McNeil, our senior battalion EOD tech and a gun enthusiast, would hold up the stream of Brown Berets carrying weapons as he paused to look and admire our new weapons. Most of the time, the weapons used in an army unit have been there for quite a few years. The used weapons showed their wear with scuff marks, worn off paint, or scratches from hundreds of soldiers extending and collapsing the buttstock. The rifles and pistols we received were still in plastic wrap covered in grease straight from the factory. We found it took a long time to get that grease off the weapons. Wiping the thick grease off, however, was really an act of love by those of us who appreciated the significance of the event. These were the first weapons received by the 5th SFAB, and it was exciting to see the unit start to accumulate equipment. We were all so giddy about it that I texted pictures to Brig. Gen. Taylor with our weapons still in plastic wrapping and huge grins on our faces. We were like little kids on Christmas morning looking at all the equipment and pulling the weapons out of their packaging.

We next needed to procure ammo and all the safety equipment required to go shooting. While this is usually a routine task for most Army units, we had not done it before. You needed hazardous material and ammo transportation certifications, range safety equipment, a medical evacuation (MEDEVAC) vehicle, and general transportation to and from the range. One of our capable assistant team leaders, Sergeant First Class Nate Peno, was the man for the task. I told him I wanted to get the unit to a range and shoot before Thanksgiving. In terms of training timelines, it was not a lot of time, given the weapons had just showed up and we didn't have any other equipment to start with.

But one major lesson I learned in command of this SFAB battalion is that if you give our fantastic NCOs some predictability for planning training, they will amaze you. Predictability drives excellence. Predictability, in this case, meant assigning a specific task to a person with enough time to plan, prepare, and gather the resources to conduct a training event following the Army's eight-step training model. The Army spends most of its time training not in actual combat, so units use this model to maximize training time by synchronizing resources, preparing leaders and trainers, assigning responsibilities for tasks, and actually conducting the training. It is effective when used properly but units don't always follow all the steps and sometimes take shortcuts. When that happens, the training doesn't always achieve the desired result. All units struggle with implementing this model. The eight steps are—1: plan the training event, 2: train and certify leaders, 3:

reconnoiter the training site, 4: issue the event operations order, 5: rehearse, 6: execute the training, 7: conduct an after-action review, and 8: conduct retraining.

Providing predictability to those assigned a task is violated with regularity, but we were determined not to do so now. Sfc. Peno was extraordinarily resourceful and led the range training event, which ended up being a team effort. Our only EOD advisor, Sfc. Steve McNeil, had come from the EOD unit stationed at JBLM. Army explosive ordnance disposal (EOD) specialists are responsible for attacking, defeating, and exploiting unexploded ordnance, so they are highly trained and skilled bomb technicians. Sfc. McNeil was able to borrow some range safety boxes from his old unit that contained all the more administrative gear and small items like targets and staple guns needed to conduct a firing range. Also, Sfc. Omar Moore acquired some vehicles from the installation vehicle yard since we were still waiting for our assigned unit vehicles. And finally, due to a resourceful Staff Sergeant Jordan Blas, one of our first medics, we were able to draw our Army medical ambulance early, which was necessary to have on hand during shooting practice. It was a brand-new ambulance with some of the plastic still on the equipment in the back. The ambulance still had that "new car smell." None of us had ever seen an Army vehicle so clean. There weren't years of old dirt stuck in the cracks from various training exercises or even chipped-off paint on the side of the ambulance where the back doors open and lock into position. We almost didn't even recognize the vehicle.

On our first range day, temperatures hovered in the forties with light rain—typical for the Pacific Northwest at that time of year. Sfc. Peno and his friend and designated assistant, Sergeant First Class Ammerman, had opened the range on time and with all the items we needed to practice shooting. They had done significant research and pulled a program of instruction directly from the manual for pistol and rifle short-range marksmanship training. Early during the range opening, we even got a positive comment from the range operations inspector during his inspection. Nothing is worse than having your range shut down because of some minor bureaucratic or procedural infraction. Being a new unit on the installation, we strove to create a reputation for being organized and disciplined. In the business world this is like obtaining an Occupational Safety and Health Administration, or OSHA, certification for your new facility the first time the inspectors show up unannounced.

The first field training live-fire event for our brigade was made even more spectacular by the presence of Brig. Gen. Taylor. Protocol dictates that when a senior officer comes to a range or training event, the senior person running the event briefs the visitor and tells them what is going on. In this instance that should have been me or another officer. However, that did not occur. Sfc. Peno, who was specially selected and highly professional, was leading the range training effort and he had no need for me to brief our boss on how things had been progressing. Brig. Gen. Taylor shared with me as he left that he was pleased and impressed by our training. In that moment I could not have been prouder of my NCOs and volunteers. They were rapidly shaping up to be a great team.

Shooting that day was important, not only because it refined our shooting skills and tested our new weapons, which was inherently fun, but it also increased our confidence in our ability to properly resource and formally conduct a training event. Our unit had begun with nothing, yet we were able to meet and exceed the Army requirements to run a range in short order. Following our shooting, were happy to police up our spent bullet casings in the wet grass. We now could tackle our next series of tasks for our pending deployment.

Mission Pivot
The Unquenched Thirst for the Combat Badge

As new Brown Beret volunteers joined and participated in individual training, and new equipment arrived, the focus of the entire brigade was on our impending deployment to Afghanistan. The Army had slated the 5th SFAB for a nine-month tour of duty in Afghanistan. We were on the same page and moving with purpose in the same direction toward our shared goal. Singular focus for 1/5 SFAB's higher headquarters and its sister units kept all the leadership's energy, mental mindset, and wherewithal moving in one direction. It created a synergy that permeated throughout the organization, from the dutiful logistics advisors on MAT 5123 like Staff Sergeant Monique Richards, to the resolute intelligence analyst on the battalion staff, Sergeant Nickolaus Mickle, all the way through to the brigade commander, Brig. Gen. Taylor. Having the single mission target as Afghanistan helped us align resources, capitalize on opportunities, and, most importantly, best use people's time.

The Army developed a model for building, validating, and utilizing SFABs. It initially planned to build each SFAB, send it to Afghanistan or Iraq, refit and recover the personnel and equipment, then align the brigade against its long-term mission with one of the geographic combatant commands. The Afghanistan and Iraq deployments were to "validate" the formation as a combat unit and give the unit and people some experience. Sending SFABs on these deployments instead of BCTs was an effort to keep BCTs together for high-intensity peer-level combat training rather than breaking them apart for advise-and-assist missions. The Afghanistan and Iraq deployments would lend credibility to the SFAB concept to the Army as an institution.

SFABs would "test out" in Afghanistan and Iraq and then move on to build relationships and develop expertise with our foreign counterparts across the globe. Working this way, they could rapidly respond to threats and seek opportunities with enhanced coordination in conflict situations. The specific alignment was as follows:

- 1st SFAB aligned with SOUTHCOM in Central and South America,

- 2nd SFAB aligned with AFRICOM in Africa,

- 3rd SFAB aligned with CENTCOM in the Middle East,

- 4th SFAB aligned with EUCOM in Europe,

- 5th SFAB aligned with INDOPACOM in the Indo-Pacific.

The 1st, 2nd, and 3rd SFABs all began with this model by going to Afghanistan. The 4th SFAB sent only one battalion to the Middle East. The 5th SFAB would break this model altogether.

Going to Afghanistan and Iraq was significant for individual Brown Berets. For many NCOs and officer's, they had volunteered to be part of the SFAB to acquire some combat deployment experience and to obtain a combat shoulder-sleeve insignia for the left sides of their uniforms. They were eager to prove themselves. The combat shoulder-sleeve insignia is the unit patch the Army authorizes soldiers to wear if they served in combat with a particular unit. In Army culture, the combat shoulder patch check, when someone looks or peeks at the left shoulder of a soldier's uniform, is an informal but very real visual representation that indicates to subordinates, peers, and superiors that you have likely performed your MOS function under combat conditions. While this is most of the time very true, it doesn't always account for the variety of experiences for those that served in Afghanistan or Iraq. As an example, guarding the airfield in Kandahar was different from patrolling the mountains in Zabol Province, but in either case both individuals would wear a combat patch. For the seasoned NCOs and officers this was no biggie because they had been continually deployed since 9/11. I was once one of those young and eager officers hoping to test my training and skills, but those days were long gone as an officer that had served during the Global War on Terror. At the time of the 5th SFAB's stand-up, Afghanistan and Iraq had been experiencing troop drawdowns, so the number of opportunities for young officers and NCOs in combat situations was limited. The SFAB was one place where soldiers could get the experiences they thirsted for.

The Pivot to the Pacific

The combat experience opportunity changed six months after Cmd. Sgt. Maj. Overway and I first met and cozied ourselves next to the window in the crowded office inside the brigade headquarters. Despite the original plan for deployment to Afghanistan or Iraq in December of 2019, the 5th SFAB got orders to align immediately with the INDOPACOM and the Indo-Pacific region instead. The explanations were never explicitly laid out to us, but I believe this happened for two reasons. First, due to the reduction in the number of missions and troop strengths ordered by the Trump Administration, the requirements for an entire SFAB did not exist in Afghanistan or Iraq. Second, the National Security Strategy stated that the INDOPACOM region was the area DOD wanted to weigh its efforts, thus adjust force alignments for units like the 5th SFAB.

The Obama Administration had tried to shift the focus out of Afghanistan and Iraq and instead into the Indo-Pacific region. This was called the "Pivot to the Pacific" but it never quite got traction because there was a sudden surge of ISIS activity in Syria and Iraq that took many intelligence people by surprise. Hence, the SFABs were relegated to participate in Operation Inherent

Resolve and maintain forces in Afghanistan instead. This meant that the Army had to be prepared for any potential combat that might arise with Iran or other contingencies in the region. The Army did not deploy any additional forces to INDOPACOM after that point. Our unit was the first to be tested in the security force assistance sector in that region.

The battalion's leadership, including myself and Cmd. Sgt. Maj. Overway, expected some grumblings within the ranks of NCOs and officers who were hopeful they would deploy to Afghanistan and Iraq, but we were pleasantly mistaken. Our formation was full of intelligent people, and they understood that the Indo-Pacific was much more important at that time than ever before. Some of the more experienced officers and NCOs looked forward to our new mission. The Indo-Pacific presented unique challenges: a problem set utterly different from Iraq or Afghanistan, as well as a complete change of venue. Most soldiers were excited at the prospect of deploying to the Indo-Pacific, and some started talking of their prior experiences in these faraway places. For example, I came to find out that Cmd. Sgt. Maj. Overway had once participated as a private first class in Exercise COBRA GOLD in Thailand many years before and hoped to return with a little more freedom to explore the local area than the last time.

Searching for Proof-of-Concept Opportunities

Even before the Army made this announcement, 1/5 SFAB Brown Berets had been working with Indo-Pacific partners. When there were less than twenty of us assigned to 1/5 SFAB, just a few weeks after I arrived to JBLM, we looked for opportunities to train on the skills necessary to become an effective SFAB advisor. In the summer of 2019 we started what would become an enduring relationship with the Royal Thai Army (RTA). The RTA, in an effort to modernize, had purchased some of our Stryker combat vehicles.

As part of that process, the Thais coordinated to come to JBLM for three weeks of driver's training hosted by I Corps and 7th Infantry Division and conducted by contractors from General Dynamics. Their training coincided with our unit's stand-up at JBLM and newfound thirst for SFAB related training. It was an unforeseen, unforecasted, but fortunate opportunity for our budding unit.

Brig. Gen. Taylor and Maj. Angstadt got wind of this visit and realized it required a concerted and coordinated effort on behalf of many organizations. I Corps tasked the 7th Infantry Division to supervise and host the RTA, who in turn tasked 1-2 Stryker Brigade, who then tasked 1-23 Stryker Battalion, who passed the task to a first lieutenant and a staff sergeant. So there was a junior officer and junior NCO, motivated but inexperienced, responsible for the reception, integration, care, and training for one of our country's most long-standing partners in the Indo-Pacific. Lots of "hands were in the pot," as they say, but no one really in charge or with any authority. They needed some support.

As this national military-to-military engagement grew closer, the Corps chief of staff, Colonel Mario Diaz, held a meeting with all these organizations to do a conditions check and see how things were progressing. Sitting through the meeting that followed I was struck by the lack of synchronicity regarding the upcoming RTA events. No one person had an overall and collective view of the RTA's entire visit. This appeared to be in violation of the principles of war—unity of command. I foresaw this weakness as an opportunity to showcase our unit's value and professionalism to our foreign partners, I Corps, and the installation as well.

Start-ups must build upon their current strengths to prepare for their futures, and our unit was no different. The best preparation for a start-up is to conduct a strengths, weaknesses, opportunities, and threats analysis to help them get a handle on their current status, as well as understand and measure their business performance moving forward. Doing so assists them in meeting their business goals. We were the same. We had to take this opportunity, especially given our relatively small size and new status.

In order to properly seize the favorable circumstances, we decided that volunteering to be a sponsor gave us a definitive "in" with those we hoped to impress. Our experienced staff sergeants knew Strykers and JBLM enough to ensure that things rolled out smoothly for the RTA. Maj. Angstadt and 1st Sgt. Travis Keen and Staff Sergeants Ryan Dean and Mitchell Napier did a lot of behind-the-scenes work to simplify things by cleaning and preparing their barracks for use. They thought about the details necessary using the military RSOI framework (reception, staging, onward movement, and integration). RSOI began as soon as the RTA made it through Seattle Airport customs until they arrived at their first General Dynamics driving event. The four of them, with the help of a few others in the brigade, arranged for the RTA's transportation requirements and coordinated with the dining facility so they knew the arrival times between training sessions for the Thai soldiers and could feed them in a timely manner.

Whatever It Takes: Scrubbing and Preparing Beds to Get the Job Done

Without being asked, S.Sgt. Dean and S. Sgt. Napier swept out an entire three-story barracks building. These two made sure the bathrooms were serviceable and stocked with toilet paper (an obvious necessity), then went around checking to make sure light bulbs worked. They even went and drew the linens for the RTA soldiers and placed them on each individual's bed. Actions like these were above and beyond what anyone expected. S.Sgt. Dean and S. Sgt. Napier were awesome! These efforts paid off big time. After arriving late at night following their long journey from Bangkok, the RTA commander, whom I would come to know well, walked through and inspected the barracks before his RTA soldiers occupied them. Meanwhile 1st Sgt. Travis Keen ensured their transportation was ready and Maj. Tom Angstadt reviewed the training timeline from General Dynamics.

A "Royal" Welcome

To make sure the RTA felt honored and properly welcomed, Cmd. Sgt. Maj. Overway and I decided to act as the welcoming party and met the RTA contingent at the airport in our full uniform. We wore our "Tropical Bs" service uniforms with a white dress shirt and all our Army badges and medals. If anything, we hoped we looked the part of a proper reception party that valued the US Army-RTA relationship. With Maj. Angstadt and 1st Sgt. Keen's help, Cmd. Sgt. Maj. Overway and I were able to answer all the RTA contingent's immediate questions as they waited for their baggage at the terminal.

The integration of the RTA at JBLM went quite well. The handful of NCOs and officers assigned to the battalion built close relationships with the RTA because they were in constant contact during training. Cmd. Sgt. Maj. Overway and I would break away from our recruiting duties to check on the RTA's training. I frequently spoke to Brigadier General Pena, the RTA commander, about the Stryker training and tactics. Sometimes we talked about combat load plans for the vehicle, others it was maintenance, or just the organization of American Stryker units. But it wasn't all work. We also discussed what it was like living in Washington State, visiting Seattle, and Mount Rainier, or "the mountain" as the locals referred to it.

To help satisfy the RTA's appetite for Stryker knowledge, Brig. Gen. Taylor, a former Stryker Brigade commander, had pieced together a presentation for the RTA contingent and led a Q&A

session afterward about fighting using the Stryker formation. We talked about the range of the vehicle on one tank of gas, when to dismount the infantry soldiers in the back, and even simple concepts like how to convoy Strykers from one location to another. Personally, I found this exchange incredibly rewarding and believed the RTA was pleased with the interaction too. This meeting was the point where I realized that sponsoring the RTA may lay the foundation for a longer-term relationship with Brig. Gen. Pena's RTA infantry division. If we had failed to partake in this exchange, we may not have been fortunate enough to create welcoming working relationships with our partners and allies like the Thais in the Indo-Pacific. Just like a start-up we worked together to leverage our collective strengths, minimize our weaknesses, seize opportunities to create growth and development, and join hands to build relationships and plans for future interoperability training. This event accomplished all of that and so much more.

Gaining Traction

Following the December announcement that the 5th SFAB was to align with INDOPACOM, our brigade received an invitation to send a planner in March to Fiji for an exercise called CARTWHEEL scheduled later in the summer. This unsolicited invitation was exciting news because it was the first time that our brigade would have the opportunity to cross the International Date Line (IDL) and mingle with our foreign partners and the US Embassy staff in their home country. The invitation also indicated that people knew about our unit and were interested in what we could offer the military training exercise.

By the time we were deciding who to send to this mission in early winter 2020, we had hired most of our battalion senior leaders, but most of the officers had yet to arrive based on Human

Resources Command manning cycles. After some deliberation, we decided to send Captain Matt Orders, who served as both a team leader in A Company and battalion operations officer, to represent us in this capacity. Capt. Orders was an excellent selection. His amiability, openness, and demeanor instilled confidence in those he met and built natural relationships with all. In particular, Matt was able to build rapport with his Fijian counterparts through a tried-and-true military method—conducting physical training with them. He was able to keep up with his counterparts even after traveling across the world and dealing with jetlag. Matt later confessed to me that he was truly sucking because of the tropical heat. He never had an acclimatization period, and he had to dig deeper than he had ever had to before to not show any weakness during a few of the events. When he showed me pictures, it was evident that his PT shirt looked like it had been dunked in a bucket of water.

Most significantly, Matt was able to articulate to Ambassador Joseph Cella, the US ambassador to Fiji, how the SFAB was organized, its mission, and what capabilities it could provide while working with the Fijian military. Conveying this crucial message to a high-ranking, influential, and receptive member of the State Department greatly assisted in our campaign to educate our Indo-Pacific audiences. His professionalism went a long way toward educating USARPAC, State Department personnel like Ambassador Cella, and the Fijian Army about the benefits and good will that the SFAB could impart in their region. His interactions with these various entities precipitated a request to have an SFAB team in Fiji. This was everything we had hoped for and more. Finally, we were seen and noticed. The pictures and post-mission reports Capt. Orders produced provided a lot of visibility that had previously been missing for the brigade and the SFAC. Capt. Orders had succeeded in becoming our poster boy for the 5th SFAB and his ego got a boost from this visibility too.

Again, both cases, sponsoring the Thai Army and sending a planner to Fiji, were small steps that helped us in incremental ways tell people about our new unit and gave our tiny start-up some traction with embassies and foreign partner forces. It also allowed us to put together products, known in the Army as storyboards (pictures with a bunch of words that explain the concepts, usually on PowerPoint), to then tell the Thai Army and Fijian anecdotes to the organizational (FORSCOM) and operational (USARPAC) commands of the US Army. We hoped the anecdotes made informational impacts at all senior Army and DOD headquarters.

By the time Matt returned from Fiji in March of 2020, more officers and NCOs began to trickle in and fill the ranks of A Company. We knew we were no longer heading to Afghanistan or Iraq but instead set our sights on the Indo-Pacific region. Our partially filled battalion was about to embark on its next phase of development and collective training and had an opportunity to send more Brown Berets across the IDL—new ground for the 5th SFAB with this training and new ground for the entire SFAB and SFAC enterprise by heading west across the Pacific Ocean.

CHAPTER 4

Seed Stage: Test Runs and Trials (Beta Mode)

People and equipment arrived weekly. Their arrival tested some of our processes and systems for integrating new Brown Berets. These included ensuring their Army personnel and medical records were up to date and that they were medically cleared for deployment to an overseas location. In a small SFAB battalion I expected that I would know each of the 171 Brown Berets by name. However, with people arriving, then departing for training, and with me and Cmd. Sgt. Maj. CJ Overway both leaving for our own schooling or trips, meeting everyone did not always happen. He and I realized that we needed to make a deliberate effort to meet the new arrivals without sitting them in a theater and creating another mandatory event on the calendar. So, he and I practiced the tried-and-true leadership method known as LBWA, a.k.a. leadership by walking around. Anytime we saw some face we didn't recognize, even if we were enroute to another meeting or engagement, we stopped and introduced ourselves. We also asked them a few questions like "When did you get here?" (which helped us catch people we may have missed without feeling awkward), "Where are you coming from?" (i.e. Army installation and previous unit), "What's your MOS and MAT assignment?" and "Where is your family?" The last question helped inform us if the Brown Beret was married or had family in the area. If they did, I made sure right then and there they had access to the Soldier

Family Readiness Group (SFRG) communication app we were using at the time. In exchange I would tell them a little about me, my service history, and my family. The discussions didn't last but a few minutes, but they helped me and Cmd. Sgt. Maj. Overway get to know and understand our people just a little better.

With a small but swelling battalion, we needed to figure out how to train our people as a unit. The Army spends the vast majority of its time training and preparing so when their skills are required, units are ready to fight. When times are peaceful, people think this is a waste of time, but they forget, as General "Stormin'" Norman Schwarzkopf so aptly said, "The more you sweat in peace, the less you bleed in war." The same is true for start-ups and organizational strategy. Practice should weed out any battalion-wide weaknesses that can put the entire team at risk in a combat situation and improve combat performance on the battlefield. These are also team-building activities. A good leader will tally what tactics, strategies, and processes are successful and lead to positive outcomes, as well as see what assets the team is weakest in and adjust their training accordingly. They also need to stay abreast of the latest technological advancements and changes in how battles are fought and see how they can take advantage of those changes to make their teams more effective.

Brig. Gen. Taylor, like a smart businessman, felt strongly about testing and marketing our SFAB teams in various countries in the Indo-Pacific prior to actual rollout. This served a dual purpose of not only determining our readiness for this new role before we jumped in with both feet but also allowed for leadership to quickly note any anomalies or errors and fix them before the actual launch. Additionally, it provided an opportunity for data-driven feedback that could further leverage buy-in from other members of these and external organizations. We were conducting a mini product launch in a select market to see how it performed. We knew the important thing was to not select too large a market and to do a trial run for the entire program to get an idea of how it would fare on a larger scale.

There are numerous advantages to doing a trial run. Leadership can see how the teams perform in a natural working environment alongside the armies of our foreign counterparts and other security forces. This test can help leaders see how well they can sell it in other areas around the globe. From these tests they can get a better feel for budgets and buy-ins and make any necessary changes as circumstances might dictate. Tests can help them determine the most effective and suitable channels for marketing to their target audiences and better allocate resources and efforts in the actual launch. Leaders can also identify and build data-driven strategies and distribution channels for the real launch. Being able to see the reactions of their foreign counterparts in these real-life training scenarios is far better than any theoretical predictions and secondhand knowledge based on trends.

There can be consequences or drawbacks to testing, too, and leadership must be keenly aware of that as well. Testing costs money and time—both of which need to be spent in the wisest of ways if you wish to meter success for your project. Testing can also open the door to your competitors by revealing your combat training and engagement plans. The best advice is to weigh both the good and the bad before embarking on any test strategy. We did this through an iterative process by reading, talking to others, and watching other sister units train.

What Made Us Ready to Launch

The individual schools we were sending Brown Berets to were foundational in our quest to build capability. For instance, NCOs attending the Foreign Weapons Course familiarized themselves with the various weapons our allies and partners might use. Our medics had the rare opportunity to attend advanced medical training at Fort Sam Houston called the Tactical Combat Medical Care Course. We also worked to send all our sergeants first class to the Army's Battle Staff course, where our senior NCOs learned the basics of staffing procedures and the Army's military decision-making process, which helped with both promotion potential and their ability to work with foreign military staffs. There were also the essential, but not cool or high-speed courses that allowed our battalion to function, like the unit movement officer and hazardous material courses. Cmd. Sgt. Maj. Overway and I attempted to pair a "cool" course (like Air Assault or a weapons course) with one of our essential ones so that we worked on our overall battalion deployment capability and individual professional development at the same time. It didn't always work out perfectly, but we tried, and most of our Brown Berets were happy. Sending individuals to schools was a concerted effort that required close supervision. We had to create an Excel sheet that tracked each individual Brown Beret by day and by school to see who was available for training. The list included sergeants, staff sergeants, captains, Cmd. Sgt. Maj. Overway, and even me as the battalion commander. In some ways it was the opposite of the idea of intent-based leadership, but an understanding at this level of detail was necessary for planning and coordinating collective (i.e. group) training.

Aside from the individual training and other schooling that our Brown Berets were required to progress through, we knew they needed to develop their advisory skills and we had to find a way to bring them up to speed. Advisory skills are sometimes referred to as the "soft" skills necessary to work with foreign partners. These skills are sometimes described as emotional intelligence, understanding body language, or even elements of negotiations. The Brown Berets coming to 1/5 SFAB were clearly experts in their chosen skill set and MOS, which is why they were selected for service in the unit. What we hoped to teach or train the individuals and SFAB teams was how to identify the training needs and skills that were lacking in our foreign counterparts and how to best communicate that to them so we could help them to achieve their combat-readiness goals. Achieving foreign partner combat-readiness goals required Brown Beret MATs to strike the balance between teaching the science of warfighting and the art associated with applying the partner force's particular culture, history, and environment to combat. Many were competent army trainers in their own right, but that also came with some biases associated with working within the American and US Army-specific culture. For instance, the US Army is typically ruthless in its after-action-review process and tends to focus on what needs to be improved. In many Asian cultures where saving face is important, like Thai, harsh criticism and focusing on the negative aspects during training may actually disrupt or hinder the rapport Brown Berets were trying to build. They still needed to bring up ways to improve the partner's combat readiness, but the manner and techniques are much different from doing it with Americans. Our partner forces were different and came from unique cultures. We needed to identify some of those potential biases and adjust to them. Finding the balance between the science and art of warfighting required tailored training for the individual Brown Berets and collective training for their MATs. The SFAC, through the hard work of 1st SFAB and people like Maj. Gen. Jackson and Lt. Col. Ducote, developed the term *ASLA* (advise, support, liaise, and assess), which was used to describe the SFAB's critical mission and all the aspects of how SFAB teams would integrate with a foreign partner force.[28] We would use the ASLA framework to develop training that reframed biases while still building our own combat capacity.

Our core mission began with advising. Advising meant just

that. We acted very similar to a consulting firm for the Army, except making less money than my West Point classmates who work for McKinsey and Company like Andy Caine and Aaron Bailey, or Jennifer Zais (DeBruin) at Booz, Allen, Hamilton. Based on previous experiences, we were expected to give our foreign partner force our best military advice on training, organizing, conducting an attack, and providing logistic support to their own units. We found using the term "advising" was a bit of a challenge since our INDOPACOM partners in many cases were from experienced armies in their own ways. What advice could we provide that they did not already know? To work with partners such as these, we needed to build trust and demonstrate expertise in our profession. The "Advisor" tab we wore over our unit patch was also very controversial. But that was a sensitivity that was best addressed by our senior Army generals.

The second core mission was supporting our partners. Support meant that we needed to provide them with functions or capabilities they lacked. Our teams needed to fill in our partner's gaps so they could perform their essential combat mission to the best of their ability. Supporting our partners could incorporate a wide range of options. For example, I realized I had supported a foreign partner force as a squadron (battalion) commander while in Iraq, working with the Baghdad Operations Center for nine months. The mission included, but was not limited to, providing releasable intelligence and joint fires, including bombs from airplanes or missiles from drones. We were also able to leverage one of the DOD's major strengths in logistics to move foreign partner force equipment from one location to another as long as we had the authority to do so. Our teams needed to be able to perform similar functions with their partner force. It could be as simple as having a trained and qualified medic on hand or flying their small unmanned aerial surveillance aircraft overhead to view the terrain in front of them.

The start-up's third function, liaising, meant we needed

to establish a trusting working relationship with our foreign counterparts and their armies so we could cooperate and work together on combat training maneuvers. Much of liaising meant passing along information between US forces and the partner force. The most basic liaise function is passing the location of units between each force during combat operations. The more advanced level is understanding a commander's intent while planning for future operations. When US personnel liaise with foreign militaries, like in Afghanistan and Iraq, understanding what the Afghan or Iraqi commander was thinking before an operation allowed US commanders to best determine how to support them by aligning intelligence, surveillance, and reconnaissance, as well as strike capabilities. Essential for liaising with a foreign military is developing trust. Trust, built through competent leadership and teamwork, directly relates to a team's ability to carry out their mission(s). Leadership provides a clear vision and a strategy for everyone to move in the same direction toward their shared goal. Teamwork allows all team members to share their talents and energy to accomplish those goals. This requires focus as well as having the right priorities. Sometimes while conducting Security Force Assistance (SFA), MATs could conduct their support and liaise functions at the same time.

Along with building trust, good communication is paramount when supporting or liaising during coalition warfare. Our maneuver teams had a robust suite of communications equipment due to some excellent foresight to accomplish these tasks. Having such equipment meant that an MAT could plug into a foreign partner force battalion, brigade, or division and provide real-time information back to their US counterpart, whether a US Army brigade, division, or even a Marine Corps unit. We could more effectively fight alongside each other at the tactical level using the MAT's communications equipment, including things like a tactical voice bridge (TVB). As an example, with this piece of equipment we could connect our foreign partner's radio to the TVB and a US radio, allowing us to talk with each other on separate radio frequencies in real time. As training progressed, the Royal Thai Army company commander was able to speak to the US battalion headquarters using Thai radios to coordinate attacks with the Joint Readiness Training Center (JRTC).[29] The MAT developed trust with their RTA counterparts and provided the means, which in this case was the communications equipment, to execute their support and liaise missions.

The SFAB's last core function, assess, involves providing feedback for each task or element from the platoon through the brigade task force. Businesses do this too. They use what they call *key performance indicators*. The Army calls them *after-action reviews*. They both serve the same purpose: to improve performance and increase personal and professional development. These AARs can be applied to a host of scenarios selected for integration with any branch of our military, as well as civilian roles and foreign host nation players, nongovernmental organizations, news media, insurgents, and terrorists. After-action reviews are mission specific. Basically, our teams could come to a unit or institution, understand how they operate and train, then provide feedback to our allies and partners on what they observed and potentially what could be done better. Many of our observer-controller/trainers (O-C/Ts) at the Army's combat training centers (CTCs) do this all the time with US combat units. At the end of a training rotation, the senior O-C/T would provide an assessment using the warfighting functions framework on how the organization performed during simulated combat.

We found ourselves doing a lot of assessments with many military institutions in places like Thailand and the Philippines. While attending US military schools and conducting AARs we usually didn't realize how innovative our Army truly is. The US Army changes and adapts based on feedback from combat units in the field. This impartial feedback encourages interaction and discussion among units regarding their various strengths and weaknesses. This critique includes all members of that unit. O-C/Ts are able to not only pinpoint the weaknesses, but also select who is going to fix it.[30] Not all armies do that.

Through leadership and teamwork, our SFAB teams needed to be able to advise, support, liaise, and assess with their foreign partners. That was our start-up's mission going into the Indo-Pacific. We needed to take the individual Brown Berets, and their CAT or MAT, from their current level of expertise to a place that built confidence in these new skills. How exactly to do that was the next challenge. It would require some research, some creativity, and even a little role playing.

Testing Ourselves: Beta Testing

Discussions between the Army and SFAC determined that the SFAB's would be charged with advancing America's foreign partnerships across the globe. Specifically, they were to create trust and collaboration during the competition phase over the spectrum of operations. In crisis situations, SFAB teams should be able to respond better and faster by working together with interagency teams and task forces. When in conflict, they would need to coordinate efforts with our foreign partners and allies to leverage US capabilities.

Knowing the specific SFAB mission helped us determine what skills we needed to emphasize. The first four SFABs had already trained and certified for missions in Afghanistan and Iraq. Therefore, the 5th SFAB had the added benefits of using their existing data to learn from and train with, even though our mission was different in the Indo-Pacific. Maj. Angstadt and I spent many hours reading AARs and training concepts from other units and conducting follow-up phone calls to best understand what to do.

In the business sector this would be similar to industry research on best practices. Best practices are the ethical guidelines and working standards that provide direction for specific courses of action given any situation. These best practices, in essence, form benchmarks for creating reliable results.

In February 2020, First Sergeant Chad Workman from B Company and I traveled to Fort Carson, Colorado to observe the 4th SFAB go through their team training exercises. The commanders were great hosts and provided open and honest feedback on what they did well and what they could have done better. Being able to actually see something in action helped us to crystallize how we might duplicate these operations at our home station. We saw how the 4th SFAB commanders developed scripts for role players, the tangible setup of mission-support sites in the bitter Colorado cold, and how they brought in observers and coaches from 1st and 2nd SFABs to leverage their experiences. 1st Sgt. Workman and I saw how the commanders physically separated each team during the training, so they tested independently without much foreknowledge. The training was as simple as it was complex. My biggest takeaways were that we needed a simple yet well thought-out scenario, rehearsals with the role players and support staff, and a basic live-fire scenario. No reading, phone calls, or even live video can make up for seeing something in person. It was good old-fashioned field research.

To make the first collective training event happen, we needed leaders who could dive into the details and turn our brainstorming ideas into a concrete sequence of events that trained and tested our teams. We had framed our problem and needed to create solutions. We had two people who could be our solution creators. 1st Sgt. Workman's Ft. Carson experience observing 4th SFAB coupled with Capt. Orders's Fiji experience provided keen insight into what we hoped to put together as a training-and-evaluation scenario for the few 5th SFAB teams we had in preparation for

A Company's deployment to Thailand in the summer. Earlier, Brig. Gen. Taylor had assigned 1st Battalion the job of sending folks to Thailand as part of the brigade's beta test deployment. The battalion's deployment would be the first to a foreign country for the brigade and the first for the SFAC into the Indo-Pacific region. We expected to be a very minor contributor in a US-Thai exercise called HANUMAN GUARDIAN in Thailand. Our small group of sixty to seventy people would be dwarfed compared to the thousands of BCT soldiers and hefty 7th Infantry Division and I Corps staffs also scheduled to participate. We had work to do to make ourselves valuable and known during HANUMAN GUARDIAN.

Creating a situational training exercise (STX) can be relatively simple or extremely complex. Training for all the tasks that we thought might be relevant to this mission and to the achievement of our goals made us realize that we could use some extra depth to our actual scenarios. We needed a fictitious conflict, fictitious enemy, and fictitious friendly-partner force. The scenario had to test internal security, military decision-making process competencies, and the team's communication systems. However, we would still have limited personnel to perform all the backside support such as role players, medical coverage, and simulating a higher headquarters. We turned to 1st Sgt. Workman to help us devise such plans.

1st Sgt. Workman was an experienced NCO. His time as a Ranger instructor in the prestigious Airborne and Ranger Training Brigade gave him the background to develop a robust training environment consisting of an overall scenario, a simulated foreign partner force, an attack scenario, and reaction to enemy contact that hit all our primary training objectives with relatively minimal resources and requirements from other parts of the unit or others in the brigade, known as the backside support. It was a team effort across the brigade's battalions. To maximize the benefit of the exercise, we used Thailand's equipment pack-out certification process so that the teams were both training and conducting a real-life pack out simultaneously.

The training for the A Company teams going to Thailand started as planned. The scenario tested the teams' abilities to set up basic security, link up with a partner force, set up communications, conduct detailed mission planning, and develop relationships. The weather in the Pacific Northwest was perfect, clear blue skies and temperatures in the seventies. 1st Sgt. Workman excelled in his dedication to the training and attention to the smallest details. His performance made my job easier.

Managing COVID Risk

Things were moving right along until COVID happened. Little did we know just how much COVID would affect our brigade as we began to see more and more positive cases in the United States and throughout the world. There was no contingency plan in place for a worldwide pandemic. This threw a wrench into our training exercises. We needed to ensure, to the best of our abilities, that these positive cases did not further jeopardize our entire mission for Thailand. We were afraid we were too late.

Businesses use what is called a risk assessment to help minimize the effects of potential threats. The strategies used to mitigate or overcome these effects vary depending on the likelihood of those potential threats. COVID was not a threat that anyone on the planet had aptly prepared for, and as such, many scrambled to do what they could to remain safe and keep their businesses open. Based on the timeline identified by our medical professionals, a single positive test would jeopardize our entire mission to Thailand.

The 5th SFAB was no different from a business. There were

rumors circulating about units being redeployed from ongoing exercises and those on official travel being recalled from various Indo-Pacific countries due to the COVID threat. Our brigade was fortunate to have the fewest number of positive COVID cases on JBLM. However, the relatively small number of COVID cases weren't enough to alleviate our concerns that our opportunity to participate in the Thai-hosted HANUMAN GUARDIAN exercise wasn't at risk. We fretted that it may be canceled, or we wouldn't be able to attend due to a positive COVID case in our formation. It was a turbulent time in our unit with significant uncertainty, just like everyone else in the world experienced at the time. We needed to reduce face-to-face interactions as much as possible if we wanted to remain safe. This was our last chance to showcase our team across the IDL during the summer 2020 season before our brigade initiated its large training exercises. We just didn't know whether it would happen or was destined to be scrapped.

Shortly after we started 1st Sgt. Workman and Capt. Orders's training exercise to validate our teams, we learned that HANUMAN GUARDIAN in Thailand was getting canceled for all the US participating units and the Thais were scaling back their own training as well due to COVID. Miraculously, discussions between Maj. Gen. Braga, the USARPAC deputy commander, Col. Bartholomees, USARPAC's operations officer, and Brig. Gen. Taylor, plus our conversations at the battalion level with mid-grade staff officers in the US Embassy in Thailand, preserved the idea that the US Army could send a token US force to Thailand to conduct some sort of training with the RTA under the umbrella of HANUMAN GUARDIAN. 1/5 SFAB would be that token force. We needed to preserve the health of the force as medical professionals across the globe tried to understand the COVID pandemic.

COVID forced the entire military to rethink how we trained and how to stifle the spread of COVID cases among the ranks.

The overall US Army's idea was to create "training bubbles" that grouped units together for set periods of time and isolated them before, during, and after training events. In 1/5 SFAB, we decided to implement that at our micro level as well. Cmd. Sgt. Maj. Overway and I decided to split the unit into two parts: those being deployed to Thailand and those not going. This was not an easy decision to make, but one we made with a cautious eye on what COVID had already done across the world. Splitting the unit was hard because of our limited resources, the most critical being personnel. We had consolidated the battalion for the ongoing certification exercise for those going to Thailand since we were still a fairly newly formed unit at about 50 percent strength. Battalion consolidated training for such a small exercise would have been unusual anywhere else in the Army. However, we were new and needed to do things differently.

Change is never easy but change we must. It was oftentimes a last-minute reaction to transition through this process of rigorous medical protocols and ensuring training was being attended to. Maj. Roland Salazar, our battalion physician's assistant (PA), had our medics take temperature readings every day before we started training, we wore uncomfortable cotton facemasks in the unusually warm PNW days, and awkwardly attempted to keep six feet apart when possible. The ingenuity and talent of our officers and NCOs helped make this transition possible. Creating a training bubble in the field was one thing, but we decided to take it a few steps further. For instance, we decided it would be best to split the unit barracks and office spaces according to those being deployed and those not being deployed to further safeguard our mission. The bottom two floors were restricted to the Brown Berets that were being deployed and were distinguished by muted American flags on their uniforms. The bisection was Cmd. Sgt. Maj. Overway's idea, and it was a good one! Those who were not being deployed wore the brightly colored American flag on their uniforms. The pressure for zero COVID cases for those individuals going to Thailand was tremendous.

USARPAC took significant risk telling the Thais the US Army could safely send an army unit across the Pacific and not spread COVID. While sending our SFAB teams was a risk, it was one worth taking on behalf of USARPAC's higher headquarters, Indo-Pacific Command (INDOPACOM). By doing so, the US demonstrated commitment to its partners and demonstrated to our adversaries the US Army's ability to operate in an ambiguous and medically challenging environment. Brig. Gen. Taylor talked to Maj. Gen. Braga daily about what protocols we had implemented to mitigate risk. Brig. Gen. Taylor talking to our Army Indo-Pacific higher headquarters every day meant I in turn talked to Brig. Gen. Taylor every day describing how we were alleviating COVID concerns. It was a necessary form of micromanagement not normally practiced by these two leaders who I knew very well.

Completing our first battalion-level collective training exercise was a significant accomplishment. Doing so in the COVID environment with zero COVID cases was an added distinction. But we couldn't rest on our laurels long because we were about to embark on another first for the brigade. We needed to deploy the 5th SFAB's first team off the continental United States for an exercise before heading to Thailand ourselves.

Test Team

In the 1940s General George C. Marshall, chief of staff for the US Army, thought there could be an advantage to fighting a war with a faction of airborne soldiers. Jumping out of an airplane had never been done before. The US War Department approved the formation of a "test platoon" under the Army's Infantry Branch.

One hundred and eighty men volunteered to join this platoon. Of those 180 who had volunteered, two officers and forty-eight enlisted were chosen. They became the 29th Infantry Regiment.[31] The test platoon evaluated new parachutes, helmets, and assorted equipment necessary for airborne operations. They assessed airborne insertion concepts, troop assembly procedures, and follow-on attack capabilities of airborne troopers. The US Army used the lessons learned by the test platoon while fighting in World War II, including the now memorable D-Day airborne drop into Normandy, France.

The 5th SFAB had our own test team that validated equipment, verified movement requirements, and assessed employment concepts as we methodically trained and developed our capability as a battalion. Our test team partnered with the Royal Thai Army in Hawaii, just under a year after Major General Pena and his soldiers had conducted Stryker driver training at JBLM. Our test team worked with a composite RTA infantry company during one of 25th Infantry Division's exhaustive exercises in Hawaii. It was an opportunity to work with a partner force in large, well resourced, combat-simulated environment that tested our people, equipment, and methods. The exercise was also an occasion to demonstrate to senior US Army leaders how a SFAB MAT could enhance the value of a foreign military unit working alongside a US force.

The purpose of the 25th Infantry Division's exercise, called LIGHTNING FORGE, was to validate one of its BCT's combat readiness before it went to the Joint Readiness Training Center (JRTC) in Fort Polk, Louisiana (today known as Fort Johnson) in October 2020. JRTC served as Forces Command's (FORSCOM) certification exercise for the brigade, 2nd Brigade, 25th Infantry Division (2/25).[32] Our role was to make sure the RTA integrated with this BCT as well as possible since the RTA would also accompany it to JRTC. Unfortunately, previous RTA elements that had participated in past Lightning Forge exercises had been relegated to the rear area, a secondary role for the exercise. Secondary roles did not take advantage of the RTA's strengths or capabilities and didn't facilitate US Army-RTA relations. With an SFAB MAT participating in Lightning Force, the RTA company became an integral element that was "plug and play" with the organic US elements. Major General James Jarrard, the division commander, welcomed the opportunity for an SFAB MAT to partner with the specially selected RTA composite company coming to participate in such a large-scale exercise like LIGHTNING FORGE. This was an important milestone in our evolution as an Indo-Pacific focused start-up.

I chose MAT 5113, led by Captain Mathew Brown (yes, that's spelled correctly—Mat with one "t"), and Sergeant First Class Jeromee Javar to execute another inaugural mission for 5th SFAB. Both had served in Hawaii and were highly familiar with the requirements and resources necessary to transport equipment and personnel to the remote training areas of Hawaii where exercise LIGHTNING FORGE took place. We planned on shipping some of our equipment but didn't remember everything and neglected smaller but necessary items. These included things like the suite of cable adapters required for our new communications systems, which were unfamiliar to everyone in the SFAB. Their previous knowledge and connections inside the 25th Infantry Division allowed them to borrow many of these and other small items they overlooked from friendly and sympathetic professional counterparts in Hawaii. Irritating lessons like these helped us update and refine our packing list. Luckily Mat and Sfc. Javar's team was resourceful.

In the truest sense, I gave Capt. Brown an intent-based order— very broad guidance and purpose. It was simple: get to Hawaii, link up with the US brigade and RTA, be value -added to both the RTA and 25th Infantry Division during the exercise, and come back. In most US Army organizations, a captain and sergeant first class that got such broad guidance would respond with hundreds of questions. Instead, these two departed and started doing their own in-depth research and work. I couldn't offer them a battalion staff that had all the answers to their questions. I barely had much of a staff, let alone the resident knowledge to provide detailed guidance and advice. Nor could the brigade staff help much other than giving lines of accounting, i.e., money and points of contact to get equipment moved. Maj. Angstadt and 1st Sgt. Keen were able to provide some behind-the-scenes work to coordinate and move the small team to Hawaii. However, mostly MAT 5113 did everything themselves.

COVID guidelines appeared to be in constant flux during this time period. The capricious mandates created some obstacles to get our team COVID-free from JBLM, Washington to Hawaii. We originally thought we needed the team to drive from JBLM to Travis AFB in California, which is more than a seven-hundred-mile drive, to remain in a COVID-free "training bubble," one military base directly to another military base. I frantically called the Army's Battlefield Coordination Detachment (BCD) commander, a colonel, in Hawaii about getting MAT 5113's personnel and equipment onto an Air Force aircraft at the last minute without high priority orders. Before that incident I didn't even know what a BCD was nor that it even existed! Meanwhile Capt. Brown and Sfc. Javar were trying to find vehicles they could rent to drive their team's personnel and equipment to California. It was hectic for certain, and, of course, all on a Saturday. Eventually, at the last minute, someone said flying "bubble to bubble" wasn't necessary and we scrapped the Travis AFB idea and had MAT 5113 fly commercially out of Seattle-Tacoma International Airport. It was a rough time.

The team arrived safely in Hawaii and immediately began working with the RTA. They were able to put their equipment in use. The US battalion commander in Hawaii began to realize he had a competent team that could help maximize the use of the RTA company. Right from the start Capt. Brown and MAT 5113 assisted the RTA through the US operations orders process and helped them prepare for backbriefs and the detailed rehearsals with their US counterparts. The leaders of 2/25 realized the RTA company was filled with motivated and competent leaders and soldiers. The result is that 2/25 used the RTA company in a complex attack against a trench system following a five-kilometer movement over difficult terrain at night. The RTA's role in the attack was disparate from the rear security role from previous Lightning Force exercises. MAT 5113 demonstrated that by performing advise, liaise, and support functions using a small team, they could enhance a foreign partner force's contribution to combat operations. The exercise was a win for the 5th SFAB.

We also learned a lot about our equipment and how to organize for such a mission. We found that maintaining satellite communications with voice and data through our Scalable Class of Unified Terminals (SCOUT) system was difficult to use partnering at the company level since establishing connections took too much time when the RTA infantry company was frequently moving. Also, we needed to make sure our vehicles and generators had enough fuel to run and charge the multiple batteries and electronic systems the MAT had at its disposal. Some such lessons we would learn again as a brigade when we went to JRTC.

Because MAT 5113 was with the only foreign military unit in the exercise, there were a lot of VIPs coming to see how things were going. The visitors were primarily interested in observing the Thai Army but also watched our team too. During these visits, our team had the impression that our Army senior leaders weren't sure about the SFAB, yet. Nevertheless, the team's results were commendable and made the rest of us proud of its accomplishments. Our first mission into the Pacific Arena was a success.

The Battalion's Minimum Viable Product

Our team was in Hawaii working with the RTA. Those that were being deployed to Thailand were working on crystalizing their mission so they could head to Thailand. This took some convincing and coordination. USARPAC desk officers worked with the Defense Attaché Office (DAO) in Thailand to help persuade the US DAO to allow our small group into their country for an undefined mission, though associated with the barely existing HANUMAN GUARDIAN exercise. Usually such military-to-military engagements are planned a few years in advance. We were trying to get this done inside of three months, which was when the HANUMAN GUARDIAN exercises would begin. HANUMAN GUARDIAN typically involved a corps headquarters, a division headquarters, and two seven-hundred-person infantry battalions training in Thailand. The exercise was part of USARPAC's larger Defender Pacific exercises that occurred throughout the region during the summer. Unbeknownst to us until later in the summer, these exercises were getting canceled. Getting to Thailand required many late-night phone calls and VTCs (video-teleconferences) across the ocean.

With regard to our mission in Thailand, the battalion's fortunes improved in three significant ways. First, everything about the HANUMAN GUARDIAN exercise was canceled except our newly added SFAB portion. Keeping the SFAB part of the exercise was in large part the work of Maj. Gen. Braga, Col. Bartholomees, and Brig. Gen. Taylor. Otherwise, if the general officer headquarters, corps and division levels, participated in the exercise, they would have received higher-priority attention than our small contingent. We would have been lost in the shuffle of hundreds of US soldiers and units descending on Thailand for the exercise. Instead, with those US Army units removed from the exercise, the DAO and Joint US Military Advisory Group Thailand (JUSMAGTHAI) instead focused on our country-entry bureaucratic requirements and partnership activities.

The subsequent two fortuitous assets we had were experiences and previous relationships established by two of our people. The second resource was leveraging Maj. Tom Angstadt's unique work experience to our advantage. Maj. Angstadt had been at JBLM for longer than any major I knew and had served in several positions that facilitated personal connections at I Corps and USARPAC. And in Thailand, he was able to navigate the usual bureaucracy to get Brown Berets into Thailand. An added perk was that Tom had worked the Foreign Military Sales case that eventually persuaded the Thai government to purchase the Stryker combat vehicle. Tom was invaluable throughout this whole process and was the person who conceptualized the ideas that became the plan we executed months later. Tom's initial concept, developed after a few conversations with staff officers in JUSMAGTHAI, was simply to send our SFAB teams to work with RTA institutional schools and RTA operational units. We worked out the details as the departure date approached. It also helped that Maj. Angstadt genuinely believed in the SFAB mission and dedicated many evenings and late nights talking with people in Thailand fourteen time zones away while at his home and during his personal family time.

The final resource hinged on Maj. Scott Orr, who was instrumental in making this entire ordeal happen. Maj. Orr was the second major assigned to the battalion and served as the battalion's operations officer. He arrived in the battalion less than four weeks before departure. Maj. Orr was a Special Forces officer with extensive experience with the 1st Special Forces Group in the Indo-Pacific. He had recently been to Thailand before joining 1/5 SFAB and knew the people, the culture, and the bureaucratic terrain.

Scott had a thorough understanding of the funding, authorities, and requirements to move US forces into foreign countries, how to train with allies and partners, and knew the limitations on what we could and could not do. His knowledge influenced the brigade over the coming year. 1st Battalion, 5th SFAB would not have been able to accomplish all that it did without the assistance of Maj. Orr.

I was not aware of how much effort it took to move a unit to train in a foreign country. I had personally crossed borders to train in Singapore, South Africa, and Germany and been stationed in and trained in South Korea and Italy. The unrelenting work by members internal to the brigade, USARPAC, and the JUSMAGTHAI allowed us to make it into Thailand. Even so, obstacles still appeared right up until the last minute. For example, we were forty-eight hours out from boarding our contracted aircraft and nobody had thought to secure an alternate state quarantine location in Thailand. This was required prior to the Thai government approving our country's entry. I was on the brink of canceling the mission due to this obstacle when Maj. Angstadt convinced me to hold on for twelve more hours. I held off, predominantly due to the time differences between Washington State and Thailand. JUSTMAGTHAI and our team resolved the final ASQ issue just in time to be part of this special opportunity, for which I am eternally thankful.

As I left the office that day, I did a virtual high five with the battalion's newly arrived executive officer and chief of staff, Maj. AJ Vogel. He had recently arrived at JBLM from Fort Polk, Louisiana, and we didn't have a face-to-face meeting because of our internal COVID protocols. It was a strange way to greet a new team member who had no idea who anyone else was in the organization. Even more odd was that most of the battalion staff was going with me on that mission.

Deploying on our next inaugural mission were the battalion headquarters (BAT 510), a company headquarters (CAT 5110), a company's three MATs (5111, 5112, 5113), a field artillery team (FA-AT 5421), and a logistics team (LAT 5611). We were a relatively small contingent tasked with going to multiple locations at the request of JUSMAGTHAI and the RTA. This deployment was slated for two particular purposes as sketched out by Maj. Angstadt earlier. First, we would work with their institutional schoolhouses: infantry, cavalry (armor), and field artillery. Second, we would work with their combat or operational forces in the 11th Infantry Division, including the newly formed 111th infantry regiment (light infantry), the 112th Stryker Regimental Combat Team, and their logistics battalion. The deployment to Thailand gave us some keen exposure and experience, which would serve us well in future Indo-Pacific missions.

Once the standard country clearances and any additional COVID-related clearances and tests were done, we boarded our aircraft. While uneventful for the most part, our trip did allow for a few humorous stories at our stopover in Hawaii. First, in usual Air Force fashion when it comes to the Army, they allowed our aircraft to park next to the terminal while it refit, refueled, and changed crew, but wouldn't let us in the actual terminal. Our guys and gals had to stand around on the tarmac watching the activity and hoping the rain clouds in the distance didn't approach our location. The Air Force liaison, a young airman who really acted like a scrutinizing chaperone more than anything else, wouldn't let us into the terminal no matter what logic we used about comfort, the weather, or simple convenience. It wasn't until Maj. Angstadt explained to the airman that they could either let us use the restrooms in the terminal or we were going to start peeing along the fence line. Eventually, the airman called a supervisor in some remote portion of the expansive airfield, and they begrudgingly allowed us to use the bathrooms. Of course, we still had to wait outside on the tarmac.

Second, during this lengthy six-hour delay it was noted that our young Brown Berets were hungry and found the airplane food seriously insufficient. Who could blame them? We had been there longer than we had expected, and these young, fit people have substantive metabolism rates. Many of them began to order food from delivery services to thwart that hunger. Delivery people were coming right up to the chain-link fence line and tossed the food over or pushed it through small gaps between fence posts. Eventually, and thankfully, our plane was ready for departure, and it was time to board. Most of the Brown Berets were eager to climb the stairs and plop back into their seats. But not all. Right up until the last minute, Cmd. Sgt. Maj. Overway was ushering people to the plane minus a handful who snagged their final food deliveries and trotted to the plane. There were, however, two still lingering by the fence staring at their phones, Staff Sergeants Justin Deberg and Rafael Soto. These two waited until late in the layover and had ordered and paid for chicken nuggets and fries, but now the plane was ready to leave. Cmd. Sgt. Maj. Overway hollered at them to hurry up and get on the plane; we had only been waiting for over six hours. Then, at the very last second, the delivery driver arrived and heaved a large bag over the fence as an eager Deberg caught it. The two of them then sprinted toward the airstairs and bounded up with huge grins on their faces. They were so famished that they ate all fifty nuggets before the plane was airborne. Shortly after takeoff, with full bellies, they were fast asleep.

In-processing in Thailand was slow due to COVID. We arrived at a military-civilian airfield and once again stood outside while we waited for processing. Not only did the Thais need to check our typical entry requirements like visas and passports, but they also verified COVID tests, took temperatures, and made us fill out medical questionnaires (all before COVID vaccines were available). Then there were loads of Thai officials making sure everyone and everything was going according to established procedures. I don't think I've ever waited much longer to process through an airport.

But it was worth it because the Thais, at the time, were the only foreign military in the Indo-Pacific allowing travelers, especially military, to enter a host country. Just arriving successfully, COVID-free, was a win for the 5th SFAB and USARPAC. We had to savor the small, incremental victories.

After a longer-than-expected bus ride where I watched jetlagged heads bob up and down and in and out of consciousness, we eventually made it to our hotel, where we would quarantine for fifteen days. It was pretty odd for all of us to get treated liked infected patients as we went through the whole COVID screening process while arriving in an exotic foreign country. Plus, there was the unusual way we checked into the hotel and received yet another COVID test. First, each of us had to sit separated in individual seats on the bus and were called into the hotel one by one. Some, not all, of the hotel staff were outfitted in protective suits, and it seemed like everything was covered in clear plastic. The whole process seemed calculated and rushed at the same time. At one point I was having my temperature taken by someone with a thermometer gun (I never did get used to having someone point a gun-like object at my head), then I was signing for my room, and all of a sudden, I was in a freight elevator. Scenes from the 1982 movie *E.T. the Extra-Terrestrial* where astronauts and G-men in hazmat suits invaded Elliott's house came to mind during the process. It seemed like in a flash I was on one of the upper floors getting my nose swabbed by what I thought were medical personnel in yellow contamination suits. Before long, I was sent up a plastic-lined elevator and walked down a plastic-lined hallway that squeaked as my foot struck the floor to my room. Once the hotel door slammed shut, I studied my room to see where I would eat, sleep, exercise, and work for the next fifteen days.

As I walked around the room, my initial thoughts were, *This is pretty nice—good view. Wow, that's a big bathroom*! Then reality set in. The room was also the only place I was allowed to be for the next 360 hours, fifteen days! I knew I had to organize both my physical space and my daily routine. I rearranged some furniture so that I ate in one spot, did my SFAB office work and VTCs in another, and situated a chair specifically for recreational reading. I reserved the bed for sleeping—no TV watching and no reading in that. I also arranged my day, something I learned after reading Father Walter Ciszek's books *With God in Russia* and *He Leadeth Me,* about his experience sitting in the Soviet Union's Lubianka Prison in Moscow for five years. I set aside time for recreational reading, VTCs, work emails, calling home, eating, and exercising on a calendar. Keeping seventy US Army officers and NCOs for fifteen days in a hotel room was a significant price to pay in terms of time and money, but it was clearly worth it to support INDOPACOM objectives of working with partners and allies during such a challenging time like the uncharted COVID epidemic.

Our team did not waste the time in alternate state quarantine. We still had a lot to do. Because of the accelerated timeline, we missed many steps usually taken before going into a foreign training exercise, including the critical pre-deployment site survey (PDSS). A PDSS would answer many questions we still needed to answer, like where teams would sleep and eat, the detailed agreed-to activities between the SFAB and RTA, and the contracting requirements (transportation, food, linguists, etc.), to name a few. Now that we were in Thailand, most coordination requirements happened virtually, over VTC or phone, or through a messaging app service. An advantage was that there was no longer a fifteen-hour time difference. Regardless, it was a frenetic time for all involved. We had the good fortune to have selected the right people for this mission. They knew how to ask the right questions and find the proper people who had the authority to respond to those questions.

After fifteen days and three more COVID tests, we were free

to leave. However, leaving was not as simple as walking through the front doors. We had to be sensitive and sensible about our presence in Thailand—politically and militarily speaking. As such, we departed through a service entrance and left at regular intervals so as not to attract any attention. It felt like we were sneaking around the country. Teams that had to travel the farthest departed first and the remainder of us walked over to the US Embassy and JUSMAGTHAI to partake in some briefs in person. It was at the JUSMAGTHAI where I would meet a character right out of Hollywood, Colonel Wayne Turnbull, who was the senior ranking, cigar-chewing military official in-country. An Army foreign area officer (FAO) by trade then, he oversaw all military activities in Thailand for the United States. He showed us around the compound, but it somehow felt phony and put on. It made me uneasy and, as it turned out, my "Spidey senses" were spot-on when I observed him at a later senior leader engagement.

Getting to all the locations went well, and the RTA were great hosts and happy to work with us. COVID restrictions were problematic because they limited our ability to complete the full range of our mission. Cmd. Sgt. Maj. Overway and I spent a lot of time on the road meeting with senior RTA leaders at each location and checking on how our Brown Berets were working with our partners.

We were able to showcase our adaptability and flexibility when the 11th Infantry Division requested through the RTA headquarters for one of our teams to switch from working with one of their military schools to work with the RTA's 111th Infantry Regiment on small-unit tactics and air assault training. The 111th Infantry Regiment had not previously been designated as a partner unit during planning, but Major General Pena and the RTA's G3 staff asked if we might accommodate. To that end, we sent Capt. Matt Orders and Sfc. Chris Avila's team, MAT 5111, from the infantry school mission in the south to perform this new mission in the central part of the country. This gave them some incredible training experiences to build upon and even garnered some story-worthy commendations. Working with the 111th Infantry Regiment (RTA), the team trained on small-unit tactics, air assault and helicopter operations, and close-quarter combat, also known as going to a *shoothouse*. While much of the training I would describe as "hip-pocket" due to the short planning timeline, the Thai officers and soldiers appreciated the training. Luckily the local RTA training areas were available and the 111th RTA officers and soldiers had the opportunity to show the team where they routinely train. Our Brown Berets were also happy to perform the mission and tasks they signed up for when volunteering for the SFAB. Again, our teams exhibited superlative agile practices in this change of direction with regard to the unplanned training exercises. This is a characteristic that is embedded in the DNA of most start-ups. They proved they were able to move fast and respond and pivot in this ever game-changing environment and do so with flair.

Our field artillery team had a great relationship with the RTA's artillerymen. I'll never forget when Cmd. Sgt. Maj. Overway and I walked into the classroom to check on Capt. Chris Kosmyna and his team. Our NCOs were huddled together with the RTA artillery officers talking about the process for calling for artillery fire. This is termed the *sensor-to-shooter* process and involves following the science of getting some sort of effects on a desired target. The most basic is having an artillery observer on the ground see the enemy. The observer requests artillery from his higher headquarters, who verifies the information, checks friendly positions, and sends the request to an artillery unit. The artillery unit then fires and talks to the observer to adjust the rounds as needed. The sensor-to-shooter process becomes much more complex when using unmanned sensor systems and other aircraft or naval gun fire. While the process is simple in concept, it's challenging to make sure all the communications work, there is a verification process for the target, and the appropriate munitions are selected.

From where I stood, it appeared to be a very intense discussion. The Brown Berets and RTA students were scratching on pieces of paper and drawing diagrams to show who would need to talk to whom in the sensor-to-shooter process. I heard them talk about whether 82mm mortars or 105mm artillery would be appropriate for their fictitious scenario. I never did catch the answer. Later, my RTA escort told me that the students thoroughly enjoyed the lively discussions about US Army artillery tactics. The discussions were important, and obviously thought provoking, because our Brown Berets addressed the topics the RTA instructors and students wanted to understand about US artillery operations and not a pre-planned agenda. The Brown Berets of FA-AT 5421 were competent and skilled in their chosen profession and could discuss the sensor-to-shooter process and a variety of other artillery specific topics as necessary. Because of their training, they demonstrated to the RTA their agility and adaptability. Ultimately, Capt. Chris Kosmyna and FA-AT 5421 met the needs of their customers.

Cmd. Sgt. Maj. Overway and I also got to see a state-of-the-art artillery gun simulation center, which is something I had personally never seen before. It was a full-size mockup of a 105 mm artillery tube with training rounds, canisters, and everything else you would see during a live-fire shoot. The RTA used it as a low-cost but realistic way to train their gunners without the cost of firing live ammunition. I was quite impressed and learned a lot during that short visit.

With the RTA's 7th Infantry Division, the Stryker training was one of the most important aspects of the entire mission. It was important because the Stryker training complemented the sale and delivery of the US Army's Stryker vehicle to the RTA as part of the Foreign Military Sales program. The MATs and LAT were able to apply lessons learned from their previous duty stations where they served on the Stryker platform and trained with the RTA. Sfc.

Javar and Staff Sergeants Brandon Gallup, Joshua Eckhardt, Tylor Williams, and Jose Brambia from MAT 5113 partnered with the 112th Stryker Regimental Combat Team (SRCT) for a combination of classroom discussions and tactical field training.

The most significant benefit of this interaction was the trust and mutual respect built between the RTA and SFAB Brown Berets, both at the personal and organizational levels. My own experience working with Maj. Gen. Pena, commander of the 11th Infantry Division (RTA), although short, was one I'll never forget. I enjoyed our conversations about organizing units, planning training, and even the specifics of US Army Stryker fighting. We also talked about leadership and inspiring other officers to better themselves within the framework of Army life, including self-development and study. As I watched him with his men, it was obvious Maj. Gen. Pena got around to see his formations and talk with his officers, NCOs, and soldiers frequently. It wasn't a show for us, either. Based on the reactions of those groups, he knew them, and they were familiar with their division commander. Finally, in confidence we even talked about the challenging domestic politics in both Thailand and the United States. This led to richer conversations on international relations and how domestic politics impacted those relations. I certainly enjoyed my time with him.

But nothing is ever entirely roses. Along with the good there is inevitably a little bad. That said, it pained me to observe one of the most awkward key leader engagements between a senior foreign officer and our senior military representatives I'd ever witnessed. Col. Turnbull's interaction with Maj. Gen. Pena was the worst interaction I've ever seen in my entire life between two military officers, and there was nothing I could do about it. The meeting occurred the last day with our RTA counterparts and was supposed to be a friendly culmination discussion highlighting US-

Thai military relations. During this whole interaction, Maj. Gen. Pena's body language read, "Get me out of here." The cadence of their conversation was strewn with awkward silences and pauses. Responses from Maj. Gen. Pena to Col. Turnbull's questions were short one-sentence replies or a simple yes or no. It reminded me of watching a D grade movie where neither actor really knew their lines or cared. This was in such stark contrast to the conversations that I'd had with Maj. Gen. Pena about Army life, training, organizing staff, and the current state of affairs for the RTA and Stryker tactics. I found Maj. Gen. Pena to be quite engaging and personable with the Brown Berets, and he was very immersed with his staff and subordinates too. Unfortunately, that wasn't the case during this Pena-Turnbull engagement on our last full day with the 11th Infantry Division (RTA). One of my takeaways from this engagement was that our Brown Berets needed to develop their emotional intelligence and ability to read body language. I wasn't sure how to train on such skills, but I knew they were important to develop trust with our foreign partners. One of our teams, Logistics Advisor Team 5611 was doing an admirable job developing rapport and trust with their RTA counterparts.

LAT 5611 worked with the 11th Maintenance Battalion of the RTA 11th Infantry Division as it was transforming into a brigade support battalion to support the 112th SRCT. Because they were living and working on the RTA's compound, they had more opportunities to interact with each other. Assistant team leader Sfc. Robert Hilton was working with an RTA soldier on proper tie-down procedures for a Stryker vehicle to ensure safe transportation to a training exercise. He did this after his morning workout and realized he could teach our partners a better way to secure the vehicle. Working together and collaborating to make this transport safe and easy was a smart way to boost creativity, productivity, engagement, communication, and efficiency. It is sometimes these unforeseen opportunities to connect that give us the most purpose and ability to showcase our competitive advantage to other teammates.

Traveling and seeing our teams work with their RTA partners was important for me and Cmd. Sgt. Maj. Overway. Seeing the Brown Berets in their operating environment helped us determine if our preparation and training had, or had not, prepared them for their mission. We weren't sure what our future Indo-Pacific deployment would look like the following winter and spring, so the Thailand experience might be the only opportunity to evaluate our training and operations. We observed MAT 5111, MAT 5113, and LAT 5611 working with Maj. Gen. Pena's 7th Infantry Division (RTA), MAT 5112 at the Armor/Cavalry schoolhouse, and FA-AT 5421 at the artillery school. That left Maj. Angstadt and 1st Sgt. Keen's CAT 5110 at the infantry training center last on the list.

Our challenge with seeing CAT 5110 was the five-hour drive time between the infantry center and the 7th Infantry Division (RTA) in Chachoengsao. Eventually Maj. Angstadt and 1st Sgt. Keen convinced us to make the trip, which ended up being an out-and-back in one day. We didn't see much due to time constraints and spent more time driving than anything else, but between talking with the team members on CAT 5110 and seeing their reports, we knew the SFAB team composition was the correct one. The variety of military occupational specialties, coupled with the right personalities, created strong synergy inside CAT 5110. Diverse teams are important to businesses because they offer up new perspectives and ideas as a result of coming from different walks of life. Our teams were filled with professional diversity, and this added value to the performance of them as a team, in this case CAT 5110. One such example of diversity was CAT 5110's senior medic. S.Sgt. Blas demonstrated his physical prowess and earned the respect of the CAT's RTA counterparts while negotiating their infantry obstacle course. A popular photo of him emerged while swinging across a large mud pit on a thick twine rope, all while wearing his distinctive Brown Beret. What the photo doesn't capture is the commendable medical instruction he gave to the RTA infantry students. I believe it was well received by them because he could do all the physical tasks associated with Thai infantry training but also demonstrated his deep knowledge of the medical profession.

Recording and communicating the lessons we learned while in Thailand was not only important for our battalion and brigade, but SFAC and USARPAC as well. By writing down the details, we could refer back to them to make our organization better for the next rotation into the Indo-Pacific and publicize to USARPAC that we were having the strategic impact it desired. Gathering and disseminating this crucial information fell on the shoulders of the 1/5 SFAB staff. While validating some of our reporting procedures and communications, we came across some gaps in task execution that needed to be addressed. Gaps identify points where training or retraining are required. The battalion operations section, which mostly consisted of Captains Josh MacKenzie and Josh Henry, was constantly working with the teams to refine reports and help troubleshoot communications equipment. I know Sgt. Leslie Demalla, our satellite specialist, was up at all hours of the night on the phone with the Regional Hub Node in Guam trying to figure out how to configure our equipment to operate between the Pacific and Ft. Lewis. I had no idea the amount of cumbersome precise data entry necessary to make our SCOUT terminals work.

One of the most awesome things about collaboration and teamwork is that both parties end up learning a lot from one another in the process. I know this is exactly what occurred between us and the RTA. Our primary mission was to preserve the relationship, even with a severely reduced scope, between the RTA and the US Army. We were also challenged to conduct exercise-related training for the HANUMAN GUARDIAN at both RTA institutions and with tactical units while deploying and redeploying our entire unit. We were experiencing the best type of on-the-job learning in this environment. We now had a better understanding of how to engage foreign partners as it related to institutional schools like at the RTA's infantry, cavalry/armor, and artillery centers and what it meant to live and train with a mixed and maturing organization like the 7th Infantry Division (RTA). Other important, and much more critical lessons, included how to set up life support contracts and secure billeting, and testing the limitations of some of our communications equipment. A significant bout of learning occurred across the force in a short amount of time.

Reluctantly, the moment had come for us to leave Thailand. Leaving, as in coming, required a detailed and well-coordinated effort to move the people and equipment from five different locations simultaneously to the vicinity of our departure airfield. Thanks to the hard work of the battalion's logistics officer, Captain Pete Smith, we had barracks, showers, and food available for our teams as they arrived. He even organized a beach party to allow individuals to have some rest and relaxation before we departed after an intense month.

Writing daily reports, being always "on" with our partners, and leading the other Brown Berets could eventually reduce a soldier's focus, which we could ill afford. Moreover, we still had to contend with the strict COVID medical protocols the Thai government and US Army required. Making it to Thailand and working with the RTA was like knowing you finished the season and made it to the finals. A significant amount of work was complete, but we had further to go. The teams desperately needed a break, a little fun and levity before rejoining the rest of the brigade and preparing to ramp up for our "semifinal" training in Fort Polk, Louisiana. (I'll reserve the term "Superbowl" for getting our teams into the Indo-Pacific working with foreign partners.)

One of our most valuable paybacks for the brigade and

USARPAC was our detailed after-action review report that captured all the lessons we learned about deployment, entering a foreign country, training, and safely returning home. We dedicated a full day of talking among ourselves over the weekend before flying back to the States about what went right and what needed improvement during the time before and in Thailand. The after-action review process is how the US Army gets better and passes lessons learned to sister and follow-on units. The output was a lengthy document that I pulled out midway through our rotation the following year to evaluate our ability to learn. Some of the lessons we took to heart, others received less attention since we then focused on other training priorities leading up to our JRTC rotation. Unfortunately, we did have to revisit and relearn some lessons—but some of that is simply par for the course.

Our excursion into Thailand was an accelerated test run of our whole SFAB concept working in the Indo-Pacific. Our SFAB was the only battalion that placed teams into countries the summer of 2020. Other battalions would do virtual engagements from JBLM, and the 2nd battalion would eventually get a team into Indonesia, but we were the only ones able to execute the mission entirely. It was undoubtedly a team-of-teams effort from individual Brown Berets making sure entry paperwork was correct, strong advocacy by Brig. Gen. Taylor, and support from USARPAC staffers (whom I called "SFAB believers") including Col. (soon promoted to brigadier general) James Bartholomees, the G3 operations officers, and Maj. Gen. Braga, the deputy commanding general. Everyone had done their homework, made the necessary phone calls, and allocated time and money to our success.

In the business arena this can be called due diligence. What due diligence involves is ensuring that your investors or stakeholders are comfortable with your plans moving forward and have all their questions answered sufficiently. For instance, have you secured all the intellectual property rights and created all of the necessary corporate documents? Who is responsible for what? And more. When Apple designed the iPod, it was on the heels of the Walkman. There was nobody out there who was doing anything remotely similar. Steve Jobs was taking a big risk, but he had a vision and imagined that it would fill a niche that had not existed previously. Not unlike that example, our teams in Thailand did their due diligence, or market research, on their foreign partners, USARPAC, and the country team as part of the US Embassy. We foresaw that our services would also fill a valuable niche in helping to make the world a safer place with strong US partners and allies.

There was little time to relax and reflect upon our return from Thailand. The brigade was moving forward with its large training exercise at the Yakima Training Center in eastern Washington State and teams were already in place prior to our departure from Thailand. We had new Brown Berets to integrate into our formation and preparations to make within the battalion before we could press onward. We needed to organize the staff to conduct command and control of subordinate units in a field environment. We had new team leaders arriving, such as Captains Brenton Clark and Matt Thimble. Most significantly, Maj. Morgan Maier had been assigned to the battalion and was now taking command of C Company.

BUILD STAGE | 103

Joshua Eckhardt works with his RTA counterpart at the Joint Readiness Training Center, Louisiana. 5th SFAB photo courtesy of Mat Brown.

Mat Brown talks with his RTA counterpart during 1/5 SFAB's first Indo-Pacific partnered rotation at the Joint Readiness Training Center, Louisiana. 5th SFAB photo courtesy of Mat Brown.

From left to right, Steve McNeil, Troy Cherry, Omar Moore, and Brian Hall help bring 1/5 SFAB's brand new weapons into the arms room. Notice the weapons in plastic." Photo courtesy of David Rowland

The original commanders of 5th SFAB. Standing from left to right, Rhett Blackmon, Anthony Gore, Marty Wohlgemuth, author David Rowland, Tim Ferguson, Jeremiah O'Conner. Kneeling Deputy Commander Andy Watson and 5th SFAB Commander Curtis Taylor. Photo courtesy of the author.

Jordan Blas, medical NCO from CAT 5110, demonstrates his skills on the RTA's Infantry School's obstacle course. Jordan Blas, medical NCO from CAT 5110, demonstrates his skills on the RTA's Infantry School's obstacle course. US Army photo courtesy of Pietro Dimaria.

Early members of 5th SFAB pose for a photo following their brown beret donning ceremony on July 16, 2019 at Joint Base Lewis McChord, Washington. Kneeling from left to right: 5th SFAB commander Curt Taylor, deputy commander Andy Watson, and command sergeant major Rob Craven. The author, Dave Rowland, is standing center right. Photo courtesey of 5th SFAB.

PART II
THE TRAINING CYCLE

CHAPTER 5

Prelaunch (Growth Stage)

OUR SMALL CONTINGENT was flying back to the United States at the same time that the 5th SFAB was driving to a training area on the eastern side of the Cascade Mountain range in Washington called the Yakima Training Center (YTC). The YTC is situated along the Columbia River. The Columbia River region is both dry and arid, which makes it especially good for cultivating grapes and producing wines. Washington State is known for having good wine. It was not the wine that brought us there to train, however, but the terrain. As with all growth spurts, there are often accompanying growing pains and stretch marks, and we experienced both during that training cycle. Our time at YTC was certainly a refining process that exposed not only our Achilles' heel—our communications systems—but also several chinks in our armor: battalion command post processes, small unit personalities, and understanding internal team dynamics.

While most of the battalion headquarters, Cmd. Sgt. Maj. Overway and I, and A Company had been busy in Thailand, our B Company had simultaneously conducted internal weapons and communication training in Yakima. 1st Sgt. Workman and Captain Danny Garcia, the OPNS advisor who commanded B Company before Maj. Chris Wallgren arrived, had planned this training event as another rehearsal for the entire brigade. We had to learn some relatively simple lessons to resource and set up the shooting range at a more remote location. We had been the first to conduct a shooting range with our brand-new weapons at our home base on JBLM but heading to Yakima forced us to stretch our legs a little and do something more challenging. Hence, B Company had to learn to deploy an SFAB company from one side of Washington State to the other. It may, on the surface, appear straightforward—and it was for the units who had done this previously—but without that prior knowledge for which processes and procedures were necessary, it was a semi-daunting task.

Maj. Wallgren and 1st Sgt. Workman kept everyone up to date with feedback from Yakima with regard to requests for highway march credits, the authorizations by the state of Washington that allow us to transport military vehicles on public roads and move live ammunition. Maj. Wallgren and 1st Sgt. Workman also had to coordinate with the YTC facilities management regarding their arrival times, barracks request, and range facilities. We also tested our communication equipment by communicating from Thailand to Yakima with both voice and data over tactical networks, another significant achievement for 1/5 SFAB on behalf of the 5th SFAB. B Company's training at Yakima served as another rehearsal before the brigade embarked on its first major training event. While small in number, it helped identify shortfalls in planning, account for equipment readiness, and served as an opportunity for those who had never seen or trained at Yakima an opportunity to view the facilities firsthand. Following their successful return, Maj. Wallgren and 1st Sgt. Workman's Brown Berets formally briefed brigade staff officers and informally discussed their experience with fellow Brown Berets from across the brigade who were preparing to go to Yakima as part of this major training exercise. We had proven our mettle in Thailand and, with company-level training at Yakima completed, entered the next stage of training.

Brigade Training

Taking a company to training is one thing, but taking an entire brigade with additional helicopters, role players, observer/controller-trainers, and all the logistics associated with that takes a lot more effort and planning. While those of us who conducted the Thailand mission were still airborne returning from across the Pacific Ocean, the brigade was pushing units through the Snoqualmie Pass, which travels along I-90 through the Cascade Mountain range. Lucky for the brigade, it was September and not winter, so there were no concerns about the pass being closed due to snow or avalanche risk. The Brown Berets who conducted the Thailand mission throughout the month of August needed to quickly recover from the jetlag and join the rest of the brigade on the eastern side of the Cascades for the training event, named Vanguard Focus.

The most significant change for the 1st Battalion as part of this training was that we needed to coordinate things more closely with the brigade headquarters and the other supporting units to ensure cohesion. It was a leap forward in complexity because not only did we have to do "standard" Army training, which usually includes movements and maneuvers, weapons, and command and control training, but we also needed to create an in-depth scenario that would challenge every Brown Beret on the team. Besides creating the scenario, the role players needed to be briefed with deep knowledge about the depicted unit, country, and mission. Typically, this is handled by the combat training centers in Fort Polk, Louisiana; Fort Irwin, California; or Grafenwoehr, Germany. The CTCs have a very seasoned staff that write the scripts that replicate the situational templates and background scenarios that challenge Army leaders. They also have a professional opposing force and regular role players who portray other characters. We had none of that to assist us in this training exercise and as such had to create something from scratch.

Brig. Gen. Taylor also stressed our enabler battalions—fires (artillery), engineers, and sustainment—outside their standard functions. In order to accomplish the added pressure on the enabler battalions, he took one company from each of the infantry battalions and a troop from the cavalry squadron and sent one each to the fires, engineers, and sustainment battalions. Normally, these battalions did not have maneuver companies working for them. They had to figure things out for themselves how to command and control, sustain, and employ these added units. Our enabler battalion staffs were not built to fulfill such a role.

For this exercise Brig. Gen. Taylor added some professional embassy staff role players—not just any role players, but a retired ambassador to change things up and reinforce their critical thinking skills under stress. It's one thing to role play through a scenario with a peer or someone similar, it's another when conversing with someone with years or decades of experience who also carries the gravitas of the role. SFAB leaders had to walk into those engagements well-prepared and able to react to unanticipated questions or challenges. Part of the mission was to allow every team member and two select persons from their team an opportunity to go to the embassy to conduct a series of meetings. This proved to be a beneficial scenario, as many of the young leaders had no previous contact with working near or next to an embassy. Several confessed they had never even been to a US Embassy. This dynamic allowed them to learn the different jargon and to coordinate between our DOD entity and the Department of State. Some found this a real challenge.

Every leader needs to push their staff to achieve their organizational goals. These are commonly called stretch goals. A good leader will know where to draw the line. Realistically, these stretch goals should take them somewhat out of their comfort zones, but not to a place where they become discouraged and unable to focus. This can sometimes be a delicate balance. As senior leaders in the 5th SFAB, it was our job to develop these younger leaders to the best of their abilities. Not every leader was the same, so we had to encourage their strengths and help improve on their weaknesses. Observing the interactions between our

Brown Beret leaders and role players like the former ambassador helped identify these strengths and weaknesses.

At one point a commander exhibited what some felt was rude or aggressive behavior toward the role-playing ambassador. To resolve this situation and keep the peace, Cmd. Sgt. Maj. Overway and I went down to meet with the retired ambassador and get the background story about what had gone awry. I later had to sit down with my commander and explain to him that the military can't go into a country where there isn't a declared conflict and attempt to demand things nor tell the ambassador how things were going to run. As it turned out, this was not an individual lesson, but one that the entire brigade needed to learn. Many leaders found that they needed to purge their old operating value system that had been so ingrained during their time in the Middle East, especially Iraq and Afghanistan, otherwise those attitudes risked polluting our plans for our Indo-Pacific mission. In this instance, the military was not in charge, like they were in the Middle East regions. We wanted the ambassadors and their staff to see the value of having the SFAB as a partner for their military training in-country and as such, needed to approach this training with the utmost sensitivity and respect.

Brig. Gen. Taylor placed heavy emphasis on using our communications equipment during this exercise and we certainly did not want to disappoint him. Our MATs had almost thirteen different ways to send data and voice messages, and he wanted to use and validate every single one. The challenge for us was that this equipment was relatively new and none of our Brown Berets had any prior experience with every system. As such, this took a concerted effort to master. As we dove headfirst into this learning, we noticed it was taking as much time and effort on the team's behalf to setup and validate their communications equipment as it was for them to plan and prepare for the training scenario. For instance, instead of doing an in-depth terrain analysis in preparation for meeting the role-playing partner force, some teams rushed through the analysis and had to help troubleshoot problems with the SCOUT (Scalable Class of Unified Terminals) system and the vehicles' FM radios, as well as set up the high-frequency radio antenna. Understanding and troubleshooting these systems fell on the shoulders of our young communications NCOs, and there was only one on each MAT. While many of them were good at their job, none of them could troubleshoot all the systems as each required very specific technical knowledge. Humorously, the teams' communications team members became touchy and freaked out at the mere mention of the communications systems.

Our communications NCOs, which were 25Us (pronounced "twenty-five uniforms") were signal support specialists primarily trained to work with radio equipment but were expected to understand the suite of a very of different signal systems. They were a bit overwhelmed by their momentous tasks. I might liken their frustration to someone asking a computer coder who is familiar with the various coding languages to suddenly be asked to fix someone's car radio experiencing static or a loss of signal. It was all new. We routinely asked our SFAB communications experts to work on entirely different systems like this daily and expect those assorted systems to function. This was a stretch goal if ever there was one. We endeavored to find a match between the challenge and their abilities that helped them to become a better version of themselves by praising their efforts and allowing them to successfully build up some creative tension. It was definitely an exercise in patience that we hoped might boost motivation and foster learning from mistakes. Despite all of this extra time and pushing, they never quite mastered every system.

It was not just our team that struggled with the communications gear. Most of the other 1st, 2nd, 3rd, and 4th SFAB commanders confessed to having similar issues with their teams. The other commanders told us the anticipated problems, so we generally understood what they were. We mitigated some of this risk by sending some of our infantry and field artillery NCOs, among others, to SCOUT or AN/PRC-148C Improved Multiband Inter-Intra Team Radio specific training, but it was still complicated. We also lacked the hands-on expertise at the operator level to make them all work. We realized all thirteen systems couldn't be operating simultaneously with a team of only twelve Brown Berets, and we needed to establish communications time windows to transmit information. Unfortunately, the desire for perfect information at any given time created a lot of friction throughout the chain of command. We would struggle with communications gear and systems for the rest of the time I served in the SFAB. It was quite honestly something we became "good enough" at managing and had to move on to other required tasks.

For many of the 1st Battalion teams, the Yakima training was the first time they worked together as a collective group. In addition to that hurdle, many members of B and C Company command teams were at individual schools just before the exercise or were new arrivals at the unit. In some ways this reminded me of a pick-up basketball team going into their regional or divisional playoffs. We had to bridge the gap. The individual members were good at their jobs, but they had never worked as a team together. Living and working together intently in such close quarters created a crash course in internal team dynamics, but we needed something else to build some trust and mutual respect.

In my experience, live-fire shooting was an extremely good way to foist cohesion among soldiers. Throughout my Army career nothing created the stress, tension, and fear which then created the bond in a unit more than when using live ammunition and maneuvering through a training area. No one wants to get shot or hurt, but at the same time, it's an adrenaline rush. Whatever the level—squad, platoon, company, or even battalion—live-fire events always ended up being a milestone for the unit members. For a new unit like ours, especially in 1st Battalion, completing such an event was like a shotgun wedding for the new Brown Berets, no pun intended. To that end, Lt. Col. Anthony Gore and his 2nd Battalion team put together a great scenario that integrated all our assigned pistols, rifles, and medium to heavy machine guns on behalf of the brigade. It included inside-building shooting, long-range shooting, and large vehicle targets. Most importantly, it was incredibly scalable. Scalability for a live-fire event meant that if a team was doing well on the dry or blank fires, the senior trainer could add complexity to challenge the leaders. Conversely, if a team was struggling, some things could be removed, and the team could continue to work on the basics. Identifying the training strengths and weaknesses of each team made them better as they progressed through the entire exercise.

Some of our infantry Brown Berets said they did not believe the live-fire exercises would be challenging enough to the various shooters. Cmd. Sgt. Maj. Overway and I reminded them that some of their teammates, specifically the mechanics, intelligence analysts, and logisticians, had never participated in any close-quarters or maneuver-style shooting previously. There were even some artillerymen who had not partaken in this type of exercise. Once the infantry Brown Berets got into the live-fire scenario, they realized that these exercises were hard and that a dress rehearsal before the real thing makes them better prepared for the real-life scenarios they might face. In many cases it was a good opportunity for team level self-reflection as they found out they weren't as good as they thought they were, and that everyone has areas they could stand to improve.

Our brigade was forging a new generation of medics, communications specialists, intelligence professionals, and other experts through their SFAB learning progression, as well as increasing their individual combat, medical, and shooting skills. Toward this end we sent NCOs like Staff Sergeants Andrew Locke (medic, 68W) and Jesse Enebrad (artillery, 13F) to the 75th Ranger Regiment's Marksmanship Program and Staff Sergeants Shawn Fox (communications, 25U) and Justin Deberg (artillery, 13F) to the Army Marksmanship Team's training when they arrived at JBLM as preparation for live-fire training. These two programs helped establish the foundations for future SFAB training events. Between these critical shooting programs and their experiences in unique SFAB training events, they were prepared combat ready leaders for their future Army formations who would in turn train their soldiers on the same combat skills. There isn't anywhere else in the US Army where large numbers of those noninfantry NCOs can get such excellent training and take it back to the larger Army force. The live-fire training scenario in Yakima validated and solidified these skills.

One disadvantage of putting some of my SFAB infantry companies under the command of the other enabler battalion commanders during the training exercise in Yakima is that Cmd. Sgt. Maj. Overway and I didn't get an opportunity to work with them and get a firm understanding of their strengths and weakness, team personalities, or a sense of the team's internal dynamics. Just like a professional sports team understands their fellow teammates' moves, strengths, and weaknesses, we needed to understand that about our individual teams. Such insights help match temperaments and skillsets with anticipated challenges or delicate personalities.

For instance, I felt Team 5122 was a "quiet professional" team. Captain Greg Lentz and Sergeant First Class Jamaal Kennedy were methodical, well-read on Army doctrine, and directed very precise roles and responsibilities for their team. Both of them were also literally soft-spoken, and I never heard either of them raise their voice. It was evident they had a great team when Cmd. Sgt. Maj.

Overway and I had the opportunity to visit with them for a short afternoon after they had just initiated their training scenario. Their MAT command post had a dry erase board up on the wall by the time we arrived with a timeline, specific tasks assigned to each MAT Brown Beret for setting up the site, and the anticipated foreign partner's mission. There was a hum of activity, but it wasn't rushed, and everyone seemed to move about with a purpose.

One of the other teams in the same company, Team 5123, led by Captain Oleg Sheynfeld and Sfc. Nate Peno adhered to a different leadership style. During this exercise, Oleg led the team more like a quarterback on a football team. He was more dynamic and outgoing, complemented by Sfc. Peno, who was also up front and very active in everything the team was doing. Capt. Sheynfeld directed his MAT Brown Berets with specific instructions in a very active manner as he prepared to meet his role-playing foreign partner force commander. Sfc. Peno was working side by side with their communications NCO to get their SCOUT system up and running while simultaneously discussing internal security requirements with Staff Sergeant Hunter Livingston, his military police NCO. There was a feeling of hustle and liveliness with MAT 5123 that was much different from Capt. Lentz and Sfc. Kennedy's MAT 5121. Neither was better than the other, but it was a stark contrast in personality and temperament.

Understanding these leadership styles and team dynamics was key for any upcoming training at JRTC, as well as for team deployment into Indo-Pacific partner countries going forward. Ideally, we needed to match the team's strengths with the culture and problem sets they would encounter during their deployments. Unfortunately, we missed some of this because teams were spread out across the large training area and doing different things at different or the same times. Though Cmd. Sgt. Maj. Overway and I personally hired all the captains and sergeants first class in the battalion, it helped to see them in action in an SFAB-specific scenario. Whatever shortfalls we had we made up for by observing the training lanes and going to the live-fire lane when we weren't in training ourselves.

The company CATs and MATs were not the only training audiences for Vanguard Focus. The battalion headquarters trained and was tested as well. Our portion of the exercise placed us into a thirty-six-hour scenario. For the scenario, the 5th SFAB HQs required us to establish a mission command post (MCP), communicate with our assigned teams and brigade headquarters, and work with our own foreign partner force. Conceptually it was straight forward, but just like some of our MAT's overconfidence in their abilities on the live-fire range, we had our own opportunity to look in the mirror and see our shortcomings. We were a little overconfident in our abilities since we had just completed the 5th SFAB's first mission in Thailand. Not all of that experience would translate into easy successes at Vanguard Focus.

The first task we had to accomplish was setting up our MCP. I decided to motivate the staff and headquarters Brown Berets by challenging them to meet a timing goal, called *a time hack*. Someone noticed during rehearsals before the scenarios started that we could probably get the secret line up in about an hour after the last vehicle came to a stop at the MCP site. This became our benchmark. Sergeant First Class Dave Nagle, our senior medic, was the timekeeper. First Sergeant Richard Lane and his headquarters team had briefed and rehearsed the staff to accomplish the one-hour time hack. Each person had an assigned task, and everyone worked, which made the entire process move along faster than I had seen with larger regular line infantry battalion and brigade tactical operations centers (TOCs). Usually, traditional line units, including the one I had previously commanded, struggled with getting the tents, generators, and communications equipment up on time. Establishing the MCP was an underappreciated, thankless, and sometimes disorganized show. Usually there was only one, two, or maybe three people that knew what was going on and likely one person trying to orchestrate every minute detail and problem, usually a very senior NCO (like a master sergeant/E8 or sergeant major/E9). Many times junior NCOs and officers from the staff stood around waiting to be told what to do.

Our experience for the SFAB MCP setup was completely different. Instead, Cmd. Sgt. Maj. Overway and I were taking commands from one of the headquarters medics, Staff Sergeant Javier Brambilla, on how to lay out the tents and where to start staking them in. 1st Sgt. Richard Lane, as the senior person in charge, was still giving directions, but everyone knew their role to play. As I watched everyone from the 1/5 SFAB staff—NCOs and officers alike—move from one piece of equipment to the next, pulling it out of labeled bags and setting it up, or running multiple cables from one place to the next in a methodical fashion, I realized I was the one out of place and didn't know what to do. While I was out observing training as our MATs went through the scenario or conducted the live fire, the battalion staff and headquarters section had done their rehearsals, and I had missed them. Cmd. Sgt. Maj. Overway was much more experienced with some of the hands-on setup and fell right in. Instead, I was used as 1st Sgt. Lane's extra person for manual labor. My highlight during the setup was pounding tent stakes in with a sledgehammer. In any case, I was pleased to see the battalion headquarters staff work together. To my delight, right before the one-hour mark and before the tables, chairs, maps, and generator were up and running, Sergeant Angel Mercado, our network systems specialist, handed me the secret phone. I was on the line with the brigade's battle captain. The battalion staff and headquarters section had met the one-hour challenge. We were off to a good start.

But despite meeting the one-hour goal with the secret line, we noticed we had also forgotten some essential items. It was our first bite of humble pie during our short scenario in Yakima. We noticed we had misplaced, overlooked, or forgotten some parts to one of our large multifunctional antennae that held most of our line-of-sight communication equipment. This state-of-the art antenna normally towered some thirty feet in the air with outstretched branches at the top from which multiple receivers were placed. When we had received and tested the antenna system back at JBLM it looked sleek, efficient, and professional. Having such a piece of equipment that no one else in the Army was using at the time made us feel special and part of an exclusive group. As I looked up with other members of the battalion staff and headquarters section at the mast holding our antennae and sensors, we did not feel the same pride and inspiration. Instead, our state-of-the art antenna looked like a sad telephone pole that was leaning to one side after a storm with cables drooping along the top. Its beams looked like a bunch of high schoolers had toilet-papered a tree in someone's yard but were able to get the rolls to stay snugly in the branches with only a few sheets dangling in the breeze. We had overcome our missing parts with a "field expedient" mix of zip ties and duct tape—the old military standbys for fixing just about anything. We were certainly in need of them. The antenna mask circumstance wasn't a big deal overall because we were able to make it all function, but it highlighted a chink in our armor. It also wasn't the only chink.

Even though we had experience together in Thailand working as a command and staff, we still struggled with many of the same issues other Army headquarters grapple with. Over the next thirty-six hours, we confronted difficulties with the knowledge management of information coming from our subordinate teams and identified what relevant information to display in the MCP. While it's something all units struggle through, having a small staff exacerbated the situation and the fact that we hadn't worked together in this way before, even in Thailand or in our other training scenario. Reports from our subordinate teams came in continuously, providing information and asking for guidance. Our simulated higher headquarters also requested additional details on the situation and fed us numerous intelligence reports. Finally, the battalion headquarters simulated partner force wanted to meet and discuss tactics, support requirements, and the enemy. To say we were flooded with information and requirement would be an understatement. The training scenario did exactly what Brig. Gen. Taylor had wanted it to do—test and evaluate our people and our processes.

A few times in this short time period, Brig. Gen. Taylor and Command Sergeant Major Rob Craven swooped in on their UH-60 Blackhawk helicopter to check on us. Before talking to us, they paused as the helicopter rotors stopped spinning and making some noise and called back to the scenario exercise command post. The scenario writers and monitors gave them an update on what our battalion MCP should be tracking, what was happening in the scenario in real time, and what actions we should be anticipating as part of our planning process. Sometimes we were on point and up to speed, which made us feel good about ourselves. Other times Brig. Gen. Taylor would start asking us leading questions—the type a parent might ask when wondering if their child took out the garbage by stating, "I wonder what should be at the end of the driveway right now?" It was evident that he was doing so because there was information we had not learned from our subordinate teams or weren't anticipating something as part of the scenario. Overall, it was a humbling learning experience for the entire battalion staff. The most important aspect of it all was that we learned we were relying too much on the high-quality talent present in our staff NCOs and officers to overcome our failures to establish processes and procedures. These young NCOs and officers could gut out thirty-six hours of continuous work to complete the mission. However, they wouldn't be able to sustain such a tempo for days at a time at JRTC. We were glad we'd had this experience before heading to the brigade's crucible training event at JRTC. Even with all this stress, however, we were still able to have some fun, or at least some humorous moments.

One exciting event that made its way through the headquarters and eventually the battalion involved one of the simulated attacks on our command post. Probing attacks were designed to test our security, responses, and add a little stress to the mock battle environment. The Army Special Forces master sergeant who was our lead O/C-T, recommended that the MCP needed to struggle a bit without my direct intervention as the commander. The solution was that I would become a casualty during a particular attack, thus taken out of the MCP and used as a training aid for our medics. Two problems were solved at the same time: battalion staff got some training repetitions in the MCP as recommended by our O/C-T and the medics had an opportunity to treat patients, especially our most junior medic, the newly promoted Sergeant Richard Duran. I got a little more out of this deal than expected.

The attack started with artillery simulators—large and loud cherry-bomb-type pyrotechnics that whistle and explode like incoming artillery—going off around tents and vehicles. Staff NCOs and officers grabbed their gear and took defensive positions or manned the MCP to assess and respond to the attack. I, for my part, cowardly flopped to the ground in the middle of the position and wailed, "I'm hit!" Cmd. Sgt. Maj. Overway played my rescue buddy in this particular scenario. He performed simulated initial medical treatment, called for assistance, and dragged me, combat gear and all, to the aid station. Once there, Cmd. Sgt. Maj. Overway and Sgt. Duran went through the treatment process, pulling off my gear while assessing the situation. Sgt. Duran, since this was a simulated environment, would call out to Sfc. David Nagle what he was doing and checking. Its hard work and even in the cool air, Sgt. Duran started to sweat. Eventually I was bandaged up and wrapped like a mummy in an army space blanket unable to move or raise my arms. Then to my horror, Cmd. Sgt. Maj. Overway whispered to Sfc. Nagle that "the commander probably needs an NPA." Sfc. Nagle, normally very stoic, grinned ever so slightly and agreed that my injuries necessitated a nasal pharyngeal (NPA)—a five-to-six-inch-long plastic tube used to keep a patient breathing. It is stuck up the patient's nose and back into the throat to maintain the airway. I was familiar with the procedure because I had done it before in training. Receiving an NPA is uncomfortable, causes your eyes to tear up (at least mine do), and makes you cough when it's eventually taken out. Oh, and in a real-life situation, the NPA is typically only used when the patient is unconscious. However, in this case the medics didn't have the surgical lubrication to make the NPA insertion process tolerable for a conscious training patient. I was undoubtably conscious for this discussion. I looked at Sfc. Nagle and said, "Seriously, you guys don't have any lube?" So, I ended up taking the nasal pharyngeal with just my saliva. Sgt. Duran was a little nervous giving his senior commander the NPA, but he did a good job. Receiving it without the lubrication was extremely uncomfortable, and sometimes I think it was Cmd. Sgt. Maj. Overway's fun idea to torment me a little. Naturally the story that the battalion commander took a NPA spread like wildfire in the headquarters and eventually to others in the battalion. I, of course, was the brunt of some friendly pokes from my fellow Brown Berets. I was reminded of this episode while in Mongolia several months later when I watched Sgt. Duran describe, demonstrate, and train Mongolian officers and NCOs on medical tasks such as giving a nasal pharyngeal. He had come a long way as a much more confident and articulate NCO.

The battalion headquarters part of Vanguard Focus was a relatively short run-through of our core competencies and tasks. However, it was an essential practice before heading to the brigade's culminating training event at JRTC because it highlighted whatever weaknesses we had that required more training. Identifying strengths and shortfalls occurred at the battalion then went through the company to MAT levels. We all learned something. I was happy to see that all the leaders in 1/5 SFAB were able to humbly take feedback from multiple sources and have a good holistic view of their team or teams. Understanding where you truly stand in terms of combat readiness, not where you wish you were, is the first step in becoming a stronger, more effective organization. As a whole, the battalion was shaping up to be quite a cohesive unit. Teams were now minimally manned and had reached their desired size by being filled out with the essential personnel required to operate efficiently. The battalion staff had also filled some essential billets with both our officers and NCOs. However, training for JRTC at the Yakima Training Center in eastern Washington during Vanguard Focus was only one of two critical tasks our battalion was asked to do. We also had our had our eyes fixed on a purpose beyond success at JRTC—we needed to make sure our Indo-Pacific mission became a reality.

Generating Business and Demand: The Start of Double Work

While our sister battalions and the brigade headquarters exclusively focused on the training at the Yakima Training Center (YTC), the 1st Battalion simultaneously tried to determine how to get teams into the various countries in the Indo-Pacific. This proved to be another long and challenging process that no one in the SFAC or SFAB enterprise had done before. Adding to that challenge was the fact that our operational headquarters, US Army Pacific (USARPAC), also had never deployed Army units into the Indo-Pacific in this manner before. The staff at USARPAC always tended to tie Army units to some sort of exercise. The units then rotated in and out of a country for a specific event and limited duration. We were doing something different. The 5th SFAB proposed going into Indo-Pacific countries outside of exercises for longer durations with initially imprecise training objectives. While we concurrently supported, trained, and learned during the Yakima exercise, we began to feel the influence of what I would call the "tale of two bosses." Our problem was unique because we were doing something for the first time outside of exercises and outside of armed conflict or a named operation, which gives the military the authority and funding to deploy troops to a specific area to conduct operations. Named operations can occur outside of armed conflict. Operation Atlantic Resolve in Europe is such an example.[33]

The US Army routinely trained and prepared units for deployments to Iraq or Afghanistan during the War on Terror. Many of the Brown Berets in the 1st Battalion were a product of those years and had lived the repeating cycle of train and then deploy. For the Army, US Army Forces Command (FORSCOM) is responsible for manning, training, and preparing units for utilization by the geographic combatant commands (GCCs). The DOD divided the entire globe into five major commands of responsibility: Southern Command (Central and South America), Africa Command, European Command (Europe, including Russia), Central Command (the Middle East), Northern Command (North America, including Mexico, the United States, and Canada), and finally INDOPACOM (the Indo-Pacific region). These commands had authorities and responsibilities to conduct military operations as designated by the president and supported by Congress. While we were in training and in the United States, the 5th SFAB was assigned to FORSCOM. So, through SFAC, the FORSCOM commander was our boss. FORSCOM designated the tasks we were to train on, helped field necessary equipment, and provided the personnel through our assessment and selection program. The culminating certification event for a brigade in FORSCOM was a rotation to JRTC or NTC, and until that certification was complete, nothing else mattered.[34] Our brigade designed our training at YTC, so we were prepared for our pending rotation at JRTC. The issue here was that there were different requirements and preparatory work for SFAB teams to deploy into the Indo-Pacific. Our quandary was whose training and preparatory work should we accomplish, FORSCOM's or USARPAC's? Mind you, both commands were commanded by Army four-star generals. We were physically in Yakima but had to cast our eyes on the Indo-Pacific.

As we gazed at the Pacific Ocean on our map, the first problem we had to solve was a legal one. So, in between going to ranges in Yakima, preparing for scenario training, or one of the other miscellaneous tasks necessary for training, we had some staff work to do. Major Scott Orr, based on his previous experience, led the battalion staff and company commanders through a process to determine how 5th SFAB teams could legally deploy teams into INDOPACOM, the geographic combatant command (GCC). Of course, this was not a problem in a declared theater of war like many of us had experienced in the Global War on Terror in Iraq and Afghanistan. So much of our hard-won knowledge didn't directly apply to this legal problem. The August 2020 deployment of A Company, our enabler teams from the other battalions, and elements of the 1/5 SFAB headquarters to Thailand also didn't apply because ultimately USARPAC allowed us to go under the guise of HANUMAN GUARDIAN. Instead, we were embarking on a new type of deployment where the GCC and its Army Service Component, USARPAC, didn't know exactly what it wanted from the SFAB teams. The foreign security forces didn't know we planned to come, nor did the US ambassador. This was a classic example of the tail wagging the dog. Many times the Department of Defense and the Department of State have dissimilar goals for a particular foreign country. As such, we needed some guidance.

Navigating this web of who had the authority to do what in various countries throughout INDOPACOM was a challenge, especially since we did not plan to enter the country as part of an exercise. Exercises were usually designed one to three years in advance. Typically, multiple planning interactions occur between US, foreign, and ally representatives during these extended times. The product of these interactions is the "agreed-to activities" for each participant's role in the exercise. It is a lengthy process, and we were already in September 2020 trying to make something happen by January 2021, just five months later. And that five-month window included Thanksgiving and Christmas, neither of which were the most productive times for most organizations, including the Army. How could we make it happen?

We were told that the USARPAC commander wanted us in the Indo-Pacific "now," which meant as soon as possible. But what we learned is that they didn't exactly know where or how we were supposed to do that. We needed a place and a purpose. Most importantly, we had to determine the funding and authorizations to go anywhere. These conundrums became our battalion's problems to solve. For the funding, we had to link what we were doing to a congressional fiscal approval that allowed us to pay for our teams to go into INDOPACOM. Furthermore, we needed to apply to the appropriate statutory authority for the authorizations to train our teams with foreign partners. In combat, like in Iraq and Afghanistan, the president, with the consent of Congress, has the authority and funding to send US service men and women. In INDOPACOM, a US Army Military Advisor Team (MAT) couldn't just show up at the airport in, for example, Jakarta, Indonesia with all their military equipment—including weapons and night vision devices—and say, "Hi there Indonesian Army! We are the US Army's SFAB, and we want to train with you." That simply was not possible. I mention this a bit tongue in cheek because some people thought we could go and do precisely that. Instead, it would require a lot of planning, research, and communication with many other stakeholders who had an interest in our deployment.

Luckily Maj. Scott Orr had done this type of staffing during his time in the Special Forces. Special Forces are specifically designed to work with foreign security forces (primarily other special forces) and must routinely go through the process of deploying to a foreign country outside of conflict; usually, they do it six months to a year in advance of any bilateral training event. I remembered hearing from my SF buddies about their trips to South America or Africa, but I never gave a thought of how that process happened. All of us in the 1st Battalion were about to find out.

Once we had identified the proper operational and fiscal law appropriate for our deployment, we did something that would become a consistent theme in the 1st Battalion—we decentralized as much as possible. The biggest asset the SFAB had was the talent on our advisor team of sergeants and staff sergeants led by an experienced captain and sergeant first class. They were bright and could easily execute tasks once we gave them some basic guidelines. To distribute the massive workload, we assigned companies specific countries to prepare the necessary initial paperwork that commenced the entire process for these types of activities under the appropriate fiscal law. The baseline document is called a Concept of the Operation (CONOP), which explained what the SFAB teams were going to do in comprehensive terms. These CONOPs were basically PowerPoint presentations that in very generic terms described what an SFAB team, or teams, would do in a particular country. They included the mission; tasks to be trained; operational, statutory, and fiscal authorities; and a cost estimate. It was important for these documents to tie what the SFAB team would do to the INDOPACOM commander's priorities and the ambassador's Integrated Country Strategy (ICS). These documents were then processed through the USARPAC and INDOPACOM headquarters and forwarded for approval to the

Joint Staff in the Pentagon. A rough analogy is a business proposal a local mom-and-pop shop might write to secure a loan from a bank. We were the business asking INDOPACOM, the bank, to fund our ideas. Each country required a different proposal. The INDOPACOM area of responsibility consisted of thirty-six different countries, and we weren't sure at the time which were interested in partnering with us. Obviously, the People's Republic of China (PRC) was off our list, so that made it thirty-five! Toward this end there was an interactive and iterative discussion between Brig. Gen. Taylor and the 1st Battalion staff, and between Brig. Gen. Taylor and the leaders at USARPAC, primarily the deputy commander, Maj. Gen. Jonathan Braga. All of us were attempting to chart out the process to get the CONOPs approved. Maj. Orr understood the process through the Special Operations Forces chains of command, whose staffs and commanders understood it as well. However the USARPAC staff did not, nor was INDOPACOM yet comfortable with the new SFAB concept. Learning and sketching out this process required significant staff work in the midst of sending teams to weapons ranges, going through the Vanguard Focus training exercise, and supporting the exercise with role players and O/C-Ts ourselves. It was a demanding, stressful time for members of the battalion. As the commander and unit's leader, I had to balance how much I was asking everyone to do without breaking their motivation and morale.

Part of the battalion's challenge was that USARPAC didn't necessarily tell us what to do and where to go. During the Global War on Terror, units knew months in advance where they were going in Afghanistan and Iraq and could plan against a particular mission. Sometimes, the senior military commander in Afghanistan or Iraq issued additional guidance to forces back in the United States so they could best understand their pending mission. For INDOPACOM we had no idea and did not receive such direction, so we put together CONOPs for every country to which we thought we might go. This was good because it provided the command with a variety of destination options. The downside was that the battalion had to put all those requests together and track them through the exhaustive staffing processes in USARPAC and INDOPACOM's headquarters and the Joint Staff located in the Pentagon, many tiers above our small tactical formation. It was a bit like the mom-and-pop shop in your local town asking the CEO of Bank of America if they had processed that business loan or not. The CONOPs also had to get approved by the defense attaché office and security cooperation office located in each of the embassies. In other words, the Department of State also had to agree that it was a good idea for Army SFAB teams to come into the country and work with the foreign military. It added an extra layer of complexity to the whole process. Now the mom-and-pop business loan had to get reviewed by a couple of government regulation agencies. We would eventually find that no one had ever done this before with conventional units like the SFAB. Therefore, no one really knew who was responsible in the USARPAC headquarters for helping track any of this or guiding the documents through the various headquarters.

Oftentimes, it felt like those service calls you make when you have a question about your bill. You know the type—you make the call, get asked a lot of questions and are routed to what you think is the right department or person to help you, but then you get rerouted to yet another department or person and you never quite find the real person or response you needed, or your call simply gets dropped. We have all been there, sadly. At the end of this tunnel to nowhere you realize that an hour has gone by and there is no resolution. This was exactly how we felt. Col. Bartholomees worked to bring clarity to the CONOP approval process, but he was also working multiple other tasks inside the USARPAC headquarters and was only one man.

Brig. Gen. Taylor was a decentralized type of manager whereby he shifted a lot of authority to us to make decisions. His guiding principle was to "assume the yes." It meant assume at some point the defense attaché office, embassy staff, and designated partner force would say agree to our Brown Berets coming to the country and conducting combined interoperability training. Assuming the yes allowed us to simply continue planning. As such, we progressed and conducted a more detailed plan to be better prepared should our team be able to get access to any of the multitude of countries. This framework carried the battalion through many challenges up until the last team arrived in Japan in June of 2021. The idea of "assume the yes" helped us reframe Army force employment in the Indo-Pacific away from the exercise mentality, somewhat singularly focused on year-to-year bilateral training with foreign ally and partner armies, which was found in the Army of the Pacific as well as with the attaché offices in countries like Thailand, the Maldives, and Fiji. Our small tactical battalion formation from Washington State helped reshape some of our bilateral military-to-military relationships in many Pacific countries from an episodic short-duration series of engagements to more long-term persistent engagements with partners and allies. No one had done that before in the Indo-Pacific, not even our colleagues in the Special Forces, except for some specific efforts in the Philippines.

Breaking new ground meant doing something different. In the business world, it's called disruption. "Disruption describes a process whereby a smaller company with fewer resources is able to successfully challenge established incumbent businesses."[35] Furthermore, "In the case of new-market footholds, disrupters create a market where none existed. Put simply, they find a way to turn nonconsumers into consumers. These eventually replace the older, outdated models."[36] We had a lot of noncustomers in the Indo-Pacific who didn't know we existed at the time. The video industry is an excellent example of disruption. Netflix and Hulu changed how we consume video. No one waits in lines or visits Blockbuster video stores or even receives DVDs in the mail anymore like many of us did in high school and college. Now we can stream just about anything, and it all started with Netflix.

Our "assuming the yes" attitude and being a disruptor in a sizable organized bureaucracy like the Army also had some downsides. Bolstered by this attitude, SFAB officers tended to be aggressive with USARPAC desk officers and country teams. This caused a lot of frustration and friction between 1st Battalion, 5th SFAB, and just about everyone else, which wasn't always good considering another battalion rotating in after us would be doing the same exact partnership training.

Brig. Gen. Taylor and Colonel Andy Watson, the deputy brigade commander, mitigated this by hiring a liaison officer that worked inside the USARPAC headquarters located at Fort Shafter, Hawaii. Sending liaison officers to other units, higher headquarters, or with allies or partners is a common practice in the Army. When selecting a liaison officer from your headquarters staff, it should hurt a little to lose that person. That means you know you are letting a high-quality officer or NCO go, and you're going to lose some capacity in your own headquarters. Brig. Gen. Taylor and Col. Watson learned they needed someone who went to the internal staff coordination meetings at USARPAC and could listen to the staff and commanders discuss what was happening in the Indo-Pacific. That would in turn help the brigade identify opportunities we would otherwise not know existed. They ended up hiring a senior master sergeant named Mary Rose. She had worked in Hawaii for several years in the public affairs offices, which allowed her to travel and interact with many senior leaders on the island. Master Sergeant Rose became one of the busiest people in the 5th SFAB since she had to interact with multiple staff sections in the USARPAC HQs, Brig. Gen. Taylor, the 5th SFAB brigade staff, the 1st Battalion staff, and nine to twelve individual team leaders who were talking with country desk officers. She also had to keep up with all the emails associated with such tasks. Part of her learning and education process was understanding what the SFAB was, how it was organized, and what it did.

Besides telling people who we were in the Indo-Pacific region, we also had to identify which countries we really needed to go to. That in turn was largely dependent on what perceived problems there were in that country or region. Some questions we had to respond to in order to dial into this process hinged on the following: where did our leaders want us to go (we had a broad operations order from USARPAC), where did we think we should go based on our organization and availability, and where could we go based on access and partner force availability? To answer these questions, we had to create what the Army calls an operational design concept. The purpose of the operational design is to bridge the gap between the strategic documents published by the geographic combatant command, in this case INDOPACOM, and the USARPAC headquarters. These were big-picture-type general guidance documents that we needed to translate into simplified and specific language that our officers and young sergeants could use at the tactical level and turn into actions on the ground. Luckily our intelligence officer loved to read, or should I say *learned* to love to read all these strategic documents. Capt. Jeff Lockwood had to comb through multiple documents with annexes and appendixes to simplify it into something understandable. It also helped that Capt. Lockwood had routine access to SIPR, where those documents resided. Looking back on our first draft of our operation design, we realize it wasn't nearly as good as the "final" draft we produced six months later sitting in Mongolia, but it was a good start. Our company commanders, Maj. Tom Angstadt (replaced by Maj. Dan Ludwig), Maj. Chris Wallgren, and Maj. Morgan Maier, were then able to use Capt. Lockwood's operational design to focus their efforts on the right things since we only had limited time. I often remember walking past the "vault" on my way home (our name for where our SIPR lines and secret computers were in our headquarters) and popping my head in and asking Jeff what he was doing. His response, usually with an energy drink in his hand, was that he was reading, and I could see he was reading those strategic documents. I would tell him not to stay too late, but I know he didn't listen to me and stayed there engrossing himself in his task. Jeff was highly dedicated to the SFAB mission and was driven to make it succeed. Our success was a team effort, and he was a critical member of the team.

The Pitch: Becoming a Salesman

A significant hurdle to getting our teams into countries was that no one really understood what the SFAB was or what our teams were capable of. Every team leader, battalion staff officer, and individual Brown Beret had to describe to someone what we did and the value we could provide. None of us had really had to do that before in any of our previous units or assignments.

Brig. Gen. Taylor was an expert, and also quite influential, in opening doors into the Indo-Pacific. He was the one who initiated contact with various defense attachés in every single country in the region. As previously mentioned, defense attachés are the US military's senior representative to both the ambassador and foreign army in a particular country. They could be Navy, Air Force, Marine, or Army officers ranging from the rank of major to colonel, depending on the size of the embassy. Brig. Gen. Taylor dove in fearlessly. He began with cold calls and emails absolutely unannounced. He described the SFAB in detail and how it could benefit the host country. He was the best salesman the Brown Berets could have asked for. He was passionate about helping them to succeed.

Above all, Brig. Gen. Taylor believed in the SFAB mission. No one could ever doubt that from those that worked with him in the 5th SFAB. He even helped design the distinctive flash (the embroidered cloth patch shaped like a shield and sown on every US Army beret) with its deep blue color, three red diagonal lines, and five horizontal notches signifying the 5th Security Force Assistance Brigade. These are the same colors you can see in the USARPAC insignia, which is not a coincidence. He was also responsible for the crest found on every NCOs beret. Brig. Gen. Taylor devised all types of designs for the 5th SFAB. This paraphernalia is used in Army units much like big corporations put their logos on coffee cups and pens, etc. The crest was striped with a diagonal alternating green, blue, and silver with a sword, a tribute to the SFAB lineage of military advisors in Korea and Vietnam. The colors and designs were selected to stand the test of time. The most commonly used item out of all the things made was the commander's challenge coin, seen frequently in military circles. The brigade's coin easily fit in the palm of my hand and was in the shape of a shield with the unit's colors. Frequently Brig. Gen. Taylor and Cmd. Sgt. Maj. Craven gave the coins to 5th SFAB Brown Berets for achievement or recognition for a job well done. Graduating top of the class at a military school, best shooter at a range, or organizing a brigade-wide leader professional development class were among many reasons why someone might be awarded the coin. We also eventually presented the brigade's challenge coins as tokens of appreciation to USARPAC staff officers for their assistance to hopefully keep our unit top of mind when wading through their workload. Brig. Gen. Taylor's dedication and passion were contagious. He truly wanted to showcase the mission of the Brown Berets in the Indo-Pacific.

Brig. Gen. Taylor started the SFAB sales pitch as a one-man show. Typically, Army divisions and corps staffs reach out to country teams in foreign countries. The US Army doesn't usually allow tactical units to potentially shape foreign military policy by engaging with foreign militaries. To change this paradigm, Brig. Gen. Taylor knew he had to reach out to many different people. He spent countless hours on the phone late at night in Washington State contacting embassies on the other side of the international date line. The emails that preceded these phone calls and the phone calls themselves were the 5th SFAB's first proposal (a "pitch") to these foreign area officers to get them to say yes to Brown Berets working with their country's military. The first versions of this pitch were very focused on what the SFAB was, how it was organized, and our people's experience and credentials. In essence it told people who we were. Later we revised this to explain what we could do for them, which better resonated with our target audiences. Over thirty-six countries reside in the INDOPACOM area of responsibility. Brig. Gen. Taylor could not manage all those relationships alone; it was a daunting task. He needed multiple salespeople to assist him in this endeavor. Tackling such a problem meant decentralization with these salespeople constantly engaging the lower-level staffs that were instrumental in shaping the decisions made by senior US Embassy and foreign military officers and officials.

The most consequential operational decision Brig. Gen. Taylor made to ensure that all of 1st Battalion successfully deployed into INDOPACOM was to decentralize our engagement strategy with embassy country teams, defense attaché offices, and the USARPAC country desk officers. Letting go of these relationships and control was an epic decision! I remember being in his office with Maj. Scott Orr and explaining that he had to hand over all those defense attaché office relationships to my team to release him to work on other problems and relationships only *he* could do as the senior SFAB representative and commander for the Indo-Pacific. I explained to him that he had unlocked the doors that others could go through, but there were too many for him to address by himself.

My battalion staff and team leaders would only come to him if there was a problem or needed some senior-level advice or guidance. His hesitation was palpable as he pondered this momentous decision. I could tell by his uncomfortable body language and pursed lips that he was wrestling with the decision internally and likely calculating the downside risks if it went sideways. In essence he had to trust a bunch of captains and majors in military-to-military interactions on his behalf and that of the US Army to do things that they had never been formally trained to do. We could also mess it up by mismanaging a relationship, agreeing to something we weren't authorized to do, or damage our burgeoning positive reputation. But, as difficult a decision it was for him to make, he realized he could not do everything that needed to be done on his own. He needed our help.

Brig. Gen. Taylor set about teaching twelve to eighteen people how to replicate his "pitch" for the SFAB. The initial pitch deck consisted of a PowerPoint presentation that spoke about the various opportunities that these host countries could reap from working together with the SFAB face-to-face in these training exercises. The presentation described the 5th SFAB's task organization and the experience level associated with our seasoned officers and NCOs. Brig. Gen. Taylor talked about methods to communicate the information and some of the questions or concerns he had confronted thus far in the marketing process. The PowerPoint presentations themselves may have been a bit rough to begin with, but by the fall of 2020 they were polished and professional and ready for us to use in person as we approached the various embassies and other foreign partners. In our updated 5th SFAB pitches we talked less about ourselves and more about what we could do with the partner force, highlighting some specific examples from our time with the Royal Thai Army (RTA). In some cases we provided an example training calendar. By the fall of 2020 our team leaders and company commanders were ready to discuss the 5th SFAB with the staffs at USARPAC and in the embassies. Many of these staffs had a specific type of officer assigned to them called a FAO, pronounced "fay-oh."

The Army Foreign Area Officer (FAO) program takes officers from their basic branches (like infantry, field artillery, logistics, etc.) and puts them through two years of country- and region-specific training where they learn to be a kind of soldier-diplomat. Usually this means that the FAO is out of the tactical and operational Army for the rest of their military service, never to return. Typically, they serve in embassies, on three- and four-star equivalent staffs, in the Pentagon, teach at the service academy, or a variety of other smaller assignments. So, by the time our SFAB officers talked to the US Army FAOs at USARPAC or in the Indo-Pacific embassies, the FAOs had been out of the tactical Army for three, four, five, or up to ten years and didn't know what an SFAB was.

FAOs, by the nature of their functions and activities, actually work for the embassies and not the US Army. The FAOs that work in the attaché offices have different roles, responsibilities, and, most importantly, authorities derived from various places, laws, regulations, etc. Since our formation was so new, we had to educate the FAOs on what the SFAB was and what it did, as well as, how it could further the mission of the embassy. We also had to help them translate the information we presented to them into something that sounded appealing to the partner force or ally. We immersed many of the FAOs so much into the SFAB pitch that they were able to speak proficiently to our foreign partners on this topic. We also had to be very precise regarding the language and culture of these places. One misstep could ruin our training possibilities with that country.

I remember trying to help Capt. Matt Thimble and Maj. Morgan

Maier set up a meeting with the defense attaché officer and office of defense cooperation in Malaysia to discuss the SFAB. It was another late night sitting in my JBLM house on the sunporch with the kids heading up to bed and me on a Microsoft Teams meeting. I sat in to help provide oversight in case I needed to help clarify a point or provide context. Matt had gone through the briefing, and some of the US Air Force and Navy officers were asking questions about the SFAB. One Navy commander (O-5 rank) asked what a brigade was, and I realized immediately we had begun the brief from the wrong starting point! Not only did we need to overcome the idea of a new employment concept for an unfamiliar Army unit, but we also had to overcome interservice language and cultural barriers between the US Army, Navy, Air Force, and Marines. I quickly attempted to recall Navy organizations and command structures and made some analogies, trying to relate to their equivalents. I explained to the Navy commander the task organization of a brigade combat team (BCT) and how the SFAB drew a majority of its people from a BCT. Therefore, our Army organization was filled with very experienced people and, should an SFAB team come to Malaysia, it wouldn't be filled with young seventeen-to-twenty-one-year-old soldiers, which I think was the Navy commander's concern. Young soldiers, sailors, marines, or airmen can sometimes get into trouble in foreign countries during their off time. If they do, the military embassy staff and foreign area officers, must smooth things over with the local authorities and foreign military counterparts. For me, this was an aha moment. We needed to understand what experiences and concerns our pitch audience had so we could determine the appropriate starting point for our discussions.

    Other times we weren't able to quite explain the benefits that we could provide to the host country's armies and security forces. Somehow our message was getting muddled or misunderstood. We were receiving a lot of polite rejections from a few embassy foreign area officers and staff officers, a few suggesting we try again in a year or so. My sense from these interactions was that they didn't want to try something new. There were even a few who asked if USARPAC or INDOPACOM knew what we were doing. It was downright confounding to us that we could not get a sympathetic ear. Anyone who has ever done sales as a profession knows that it is a numbers game, and that 20 percent of the salespeople make 80 percent of the sales. Given that it was a highly competitive environment, we needed to learn what we could do to better engage them in this conversation so they could see the benefits of having us to train their foreign partner armies.

It always helps if everyone is on the same page. We found through interfaces with our defense attaché offices that we were not discussing the same timeframes. For instance, in the 1/5 SFAB we believed that we could effectively plan six months to a year out. Conversely, the defense attaché offices were thinking about the long-term strategic relationship two, five, and ten years down the road. In many cases their responsibility was to maintain the status quo and overall partnership with their particular country, keeping the military-to-military relationship with the existing planned exercises, exchanges, and military sales. There wasn't any incentive or benefit for them to try something new and take a risk on an organization such as ours. It became obvious that our timeframes were much different. The defense attaché offices did not want a somewhat unproven tactical formation to come into their country that might endanger their strategic relationships. It's much easier to cruise through familiar territory than divert into uncharted waters.

So, of course, "assuming the yes" only got us so far. The military embassy staff in countries like Brunei, Papua New Guinea, Timor Leste, Vietnam, and Burma gave us firm rejections, with no encouragement to try again in the future. When the 1st Battalion team leaders who were working through these relationships came and told me the responses, my first response was a little anger and frustration. Inwardly I thought, *How could these people be so small minded? I have this great capability to come work in their country, pursue national objectives on behalf of the United States, and I'm serving it to them on a platter with zero strings attached.* However, after my initial reaction I regained my composure and told the team leader that I would try to reach out to them as well. The decentralized approach only worked so far, so now it was my turn. During the course of some of these conversations, I learned that many of the countries had small defense attaché office staffs that couldn't handle anything outside the norm. Some would like to attempt working with an SFAB team but couldn't due to their workload or the status of US military-to-military relationships with the host country at the time. Many just didn't want to try anything new. Both they and many USARPAC staff exercise planners had become complacent in their work after decades of routine. The USARPAC planners were used to the "rinse and repeat" of the exercises in their countries of responsibility year after year. Our proposals meant change, and they were not eager to change. We had to convince them why this change was good for their assigned country.

For our part, we also had lessons to learn. We experienced again and again that we, as an Army enterprise or even a Department of Defense enterprise, didn't know what to do with this brand-new unit we had built. Brig. Gen. Taylor used to say, "We have this Ferrari in the garage. Still, no one wants us to take it out to drive it." Sending SFAB teams to Iraq and Afghanistan was easy because of the ongoing mission requirements, which were well-established and acknowledged. Achieving each geographic combatant command (GCC) commander's intent to build relationships with partners and allies in the region was a little vague. We had pulled a lot of experienced NCOs and officers from other assignments they would generally have gone to in order to make this venture a reality.

As volunteers in the SFAB, we all had presumed that if the Army built this thing called an SFAB, then they (foreign partners, Army Service Component Command, headquarters, and defense attaché offices) would come, to paraphrase the quote from the movie *Field of Dreams*. Or in other words, they would be inclined to accept the services and value that we offered. However, if we wanted to be successful selling our services, we needed an entrepreneurial mindset. This meant persuading these embassy staff members and foreign partners there would be a worthwhile return on investment in terms of time, effort, and money by allowing an SFAB team, or teams, into their country. Specifically, we had to build brand awareness, educate our potential foreign partners better on the impact we could make, and engage them in this process. We had a lot more to discover about national strategic-level relationships.

As we continued to learn, we found that the Napoleonic organizational charts that are standard in military briefs did not resonate with our military diplomats or our foreign army counterparts. Those charts did not convey in human terms what value the people and their experience would bring. We also had to explain that the captain wasn't going to bring 150 infantry soldiers with him, which was somewhat shocking to many people when we talked about our organization. Many of those FAOs and even many of the foreign military partners, weren't interested in one hundred young seventeen-to-twenty-one-year-old infantry soldiers. The FAOs might be concerned with the life support and potential trouble they could get into, and the foreign partner forces would want more advanced training in areas like engineering, intelligence, logistics, or communications. Instead, we would bring a small twelve-person team with a variety of specialties that could adapt to the requests of the partner force.

Additionally, we had to explain that we were not Special Forces. People often saw the "S" and "F" as part of SFAB and assumed we were a Special Forces unit. We continually had to explain that we were just a normal conventional force— but brand new—designed analogous to SF to work with foreign security forces, yet not Special Forces. Special Forces in the Indo-Pacific were working primarily with foreign special forces counterparts and also came in small twelve-person elements. The Special Forces had built a strong reputation in the region and foreign military units viewed working with them as a qualitative badge of prestige. Surprisingly we encountered this misnomer over and over even after we arrived in our designated countries. Captain LeShaun Smith and his team that eventually went to Indonesia repeatedly explained to their Indonesian Army counterparts that they were not Special Forces but part of a new unit called an SFAB. Our conventional SFAB teams were ideally suited to work with other conventional foreign military units. Clearly, staying consistent with our message was of the upmost importance.

As the battalion struggled and negotiated through initial engagements with defense attaché offices and USARPAC desk officers, we were still working through the CONOP approval process we had started during September's Yakima training. The CONOPs were the documents that describe what an SFAB team would do in a particular country and how it tied into the INDOPACOM and USARPAC commander's plan. With little knowledge or guidance from our higher headquarters, we had created a CONOP for twenty-five countries in the Indo-Pacific. It was sort of a shotgun blast because we didn't know where we would eventually go. As we navigated the unfamiliar territory of funding and authorities, we knew that we needed the explicit permission of the geographic combatant command, INDOPACOM, to do activities with ally and partner nations in their area of responsibility. INDOPACOM also had to inform the Joint Staff in the Pentagon so it could officially notify Congress that we were doing some sort of military activities overseas. While our teams were not engaged in combat operations like in Iraq and Afghanistan, the military still needed to inform

Congress as dictated by law what we were doing. The CONOPs served these purposes. Even though we sent CONOPs up the chain of command to ask for permission to engage in partners activities, some notification had to come back to us that approved our requests. Eventually most of the request were approved. However, just because the requests was approved didn't mean the US Embassy or defense attaché office would authorize Brown Berets to enter the country, as we would soon find out. While the tail wagged the dog, eventually the dog had to come back and wag the tail.

Another line of effort we had to complete in our administrative checklist was receiving an operations order from USARPAC that told the 5th SFAB to do something in the Indo-Pacific. Brig. Gen. Taylor and Major Liam Walsh, the brigade operations officer, worked with a select few supporters on the USARPAC staff to generate an Army operations orders that directed 5th SFAB to partner with the militaries in INDOPACOM. Brig. Gen. Taylor and Maj. Liam Walsh helped write most of the operations order that USARPAC that would use to approve our request. I know that might sound backward, the subordinate unit helping write the higher headquarters order, but that is precisely what we were doing. Conjointly, Capt. Jeff Lockwood, through parallel staffing channels, sent the operational design we presumed made practical sense when it came to placing specific teams in specific countries. However, with all the work Brig. Gen. Taylor, Maj. Walsh, and Capt. Lockwood did, it was only a draft product. It wasn't official or approved until published by the USARPAC headquarters. After the 5th SFAB gave input, the draft operations order went through the USARPAC bureaucracy to provide us with the approved priorities. When we heard the operations order was finally published, we excitedly ran to our SIPR computers and logged on. Our anticipation as the computer when through the bootup cycle was the same high-school students feel when opening the envelope from the college admission office. What was it going to say? Did they accept our input? Was there something in it we didn't anticipate? Once we opened it and started reading, we could see the approved countries in their priority order. The priority list gave us what we really needed to focus our remaining limited time and manpower on. For example, we knew that Timor Leste was less strategically important to the US than, say, Indonesia. Thus, Capt. LeShaun Smith spent less time emailing and calling the defense attaché Marine lieutenant colonel in Timor Leste and more time working with the deputy Army attaché in Indonesia. This was a relatively simple matter of prioritizing, and soon we were gaining steam.

Initially, the brigade wanted us to report every email and phone call contact with defense attaché offices and USARPAC desk officers in an excel spread sheet. I believe Brig. Gen. Taylor requested this type of information to reduce risk as he decentralized and delegated much of the relationship building to those of us in the 1st Battalion. Attempting to update this document daily proved to be not only unwieldy but also just impossible. Decentralization helped us get more done as a battalion. However, part of the decentralization process also caused me, the battalion, and brigade staff to lose control of information. Decentralization caused a lot of discomfort for commanders like Brig. Gen. Taylor and me because we had limited knowledge about what was being said and communicated between 5th SFAB, USARPAC staff officers, and embassy country teams at any given time.

We had to balance the need between reporting too much information, which took a significant amount of time, with not reporting enough but leaving leaders without the data necessary to make timely or accurate decisions. Without real-time information on the status of deployment negotiations or the last time someone in the 5th SFAB had any conversation with Hawaii or across the IDL, Brig. Gen. Taylor and I felt a little in the dark sometimes. It was a position no leader wants to be in. When I felt uncomfortable with a lack of detailed knowledge for a particular country topic, I thought about some advice another leader had previously given me. Gen. Thomas, retired SOCOM commander, told me as a young officer that you "need to be able to delegate tasks until it becomes uncomfortable for you to not have full understanding or control of the tasks. At that point, you probably have it about right," or something to that effect. This mindset also meant that one was relinquishing a bit of control and visibility with regard to what was going on. In order to strike a balance in this regard, Maj. Scott Orr and I decided we would send reports weekly outlining what the team leaders were doing in each country. We called this the DIRLAUTH or direct liaison authority report. It was helpful and struck a balance between reporting requirements from subordinate captain team leaders and keeping essential parties informed of progress. Trust in our young captains and staff officers in the SFAB allowed our unit to follow Gen. Thomas's delegation principle.

Trust was at the foundation of the culture ingrained and emphasized by Brig. Gen. Taylor at the brigade level and me within the 1st Battalion. Everything we did involved trust. We were moving at the speed of trust, whatever that might be. Brig. Gen. Taylor had a tremendous amount of trust in the 1st Battalion. Because of his trust, we could move more quickly and were allowed to operate in a decentralized manner. We formally reported to him on a weekly basis, and this freed us up to work on our relationship building and negotiation plans for entering our partner countries to train. If this trust had not been extended, things would have progressed far more slowly. I had tons of trust in my officers and NCOs in the battalion.

In many ways, individual team leaders and the battalion staff were like small franchise restaurants drumming up business for their particular locations then reporting the information on what was happening to the corporate headquarters. What it comes down to is planning. Businesses usually conduct some market research prior to selecting their franchise locations. You want a spot that has high visibility and high traffic so you can make money. You strategize and do some financial forecasting to ensure you have the best spot you can afford. Then, you draft your plan, revise and proofread it, and implement it. Each team in the battalion was at a different stage of this process. But before we could forecast which countries our SFAB teams would go to in the Indo-Pacific or even when they would leave, we had to spend a month training in the swamps and backwoods of Louisiana and say goodbye to someone important to our organization.

Our First Loss: A Plankholder Departs

While we had been training in Yakima in September and initiating our staff work to coordinate entry into countries with the decentralized version of the SFAB pitch, we lost a crucial member of the 1st Battalion. We learned that our first company commander in the battalion would leave us for another assignment. Maj. Tom Angstadt had been a pure godsend! He had served multiple roles in the battalion as it grew from a four-person team to a full-strength unit. He had been instrumental in developing many systems and processes for us and responsible for our successes, especially going to Thailand.

We lost the "godfather" of the 1/5 SFAB when Maj. Angstadt moved on. The infantry branch at Human Resources Command had heard that the chairman of the Joint Chiefs of Staff was considering Maj. Angstadt for a speech writing position. This was seriously the major leagues. After several emails, a few phone conversations, and a panel interview by a member of the chairman's staff there was no response. We thought the matter had died. However, while we were in Yakima Tom got a surprise call to interview with General Mark Milley, chairman of the Joint Chiefs of Staff. It progressed, they interviewed, and the conversation lasted way beyond the time they had allocated. Everyone knew this was an omen that Tom was leaving. Our loss was now the Pentagon's gain.

Tom's exit left a gap in leadership since he was a key person in our ongoing planning efforts. However, we knew it was for the best, and Gen. Milley would have an officer on his staff who had trained and deployed in one of his SFAB formations. We would sorely miss Tom's sense of humor. He often found funny things to say in our most frustrating moments. This levity helped to keep things light. When we complained about all of the work we had to do with JRTC and INDOPACOM he would say, "Nobody pays to watch somebody juggle one ball." Then if he was trying to relay the response of some other nameless Army or DOD entity that was not helping us the way they should, he would summarize their response to us as "That's a good-looking question—I've tried nothing and couldn't figure it out." When we questioned why the Army or our chain of command told us to do something we didn't quite understand or agree with, he would quip: "I've done a lot of silly things in my life in the name of freedom." It always made us laugh.

Tom had made a lasting impact on the 5th SFAB, and his presence would be truly missed. Soon after his departure it became evident that he was whispering to other officers on the Joint Staff what the 5th SFAB was doing way down at the tactical level, which in turn was having a strategic impact. And we needed everyone to hear those whispers.

Now the time had come to fill Tom's big shoes within our battalion. The search for Tom's replacement had started that September after his interview with Gen. Milley while we were in Yakima. We knew we needed to replace him before JRTC in November. In a demonstration of complete selflessness and commitment to the overall brigade mission, Lt. Col. Tim Ferguson, our 3d Squadron commander, nominated two majors he would be willing to give up to fill our personnel gap. When the SFAB struggled to fill officer positions, offering a field grade officer was a big deal that would get repeated by the squadron as we filled other holes in our formation at the sergeant and staff sergeant levels. Tim would go to JRTC without a replacement for his vacant position. Eventually, Brig. Gen. Taylor approved Maj. Dan Ludwig for the command position, and just before the battalion was to head to JRTC in late October, Dan and Tom switched out. Dan proved to be a great teammate in the coming months with 1st Sgt. Travis Keen—the original plankholder in the brigade.

CHAPTER 6

The Final Test: The Brigade's Big Exercise

THROUGHOUT THE EARLY fall of 2020 while members of the 1st Battalion were making late-night calls trying to generate missions, i.e., business, for their teams, the rest of the brigade was focused on our culminating event for a US Army brigade, a rotation to a combat training center. For 5th SFAB, that meant the Joint Readiness Training Center (JRTC) at Fort Polk, Louisiana. We had two missions on our minds.

Walking the short two-to-three-minute walk between the 1st Battalion headquarters and the 5th SFAB headquarters doesn't seem like a long time. However, for me it was a brief moment to think about what the priority mission for my officers was and what the priority mission for my NCOs was. Brig. Gen. Taylor and my fellow battalion commanders primarily wanted to talk about JRTC prep during Brig. Gen. Taylor's weekly commander's huddle, but it wasn't always top of mind for me. In the 1st Battalion building, I frequently roamed the hallways to talk to the team leaders and company commanders and elicit informal updates on how coordination was going with their prospective countries. I'd ask Major Morgan Maier or Captain Chuck Spencer if the defense attaché in Fiji had responded to the email they sent. Or if Matt Orders had heard from the Bangladesh Embassy about our training proposal with the Bangladesh Army. Did Maj. Chris Wallgren or Capt. Greg Lentz think the 8th US Army in South Korea would allow Greg's Maneuver Advisor Team (MAT) 5121 to work with the Republic of Korea (ROK) Commandos when they went to the National Training Center (NTC) in Fort Irwin, California? The short walk was a mental transition where I recalled many different conversations with the battalion's NCOs. Did Sfc. Omar Moore, our battalion logistics NCO, believe we had all the block and tackling necessary to load our vehicles and equipment onto railcars for transport? What was S.Sgt. Demella's assessment of our SCOUT system's configurations to connect to the satellites from Fort Polk? Or was Sergeant Major Doyle, our operation sergeant major, comfortable with our plan to command and control (C2) the movement-control hubs for all the people, approximately four thousand in number, transitioning across the continental United States from Washington State to Louisiana?

The standard operating procedures for our organizational efforts had been split between two bosses within the Army. USARPAC wanted to place emphasis on the Indo-Pacific while FORSCOM believed we should concentrate on the JRTC. Luckily, we had the internal talent to do both. I further delegated to the battalion's officers that I wanted them to focus on our long-term mission in INDOPACOM because it required many late-night calls and lots of coordination between the various offices and agencies to ensure that we could deploy our teams in three short months. In my opinion, this was the mission with the most risk because if we didn't achieve it then we would fail to meet the INDOPACOM commander's intent. Conversely, I told our NCOs they were responsible for preparing their teams for JRTC and doing all the work necessary to move our personnel and equipment across the United States and conduct all the tasks associated with starting a combat training center (CTC) rotation. The JRTC mission was the most impactful for us in the short term. It seemed like a natural choice to divvy up the various tasks between the battalion and organize people for specific tasks. However, this was not typical of how the conventional US Army unit worked. Most of the time, the entire organization, "Lottie, Dottie, everybody," as the military jargon goes, would focus solely on moving to and preparing for one of these CTC rotations. Moving in one direction includes all the task organizing, briefings, conditions checks, and rehearsals associated with these rotations. This had long since been established because rotations cost millions of dollars and require many different units to come together. It is a use of a precious resource, both in terms of time, money, and the training centers themselves. There are only three CTCs and around thirty-one US Army brigade combat teams spread out between the United States and Europe. We also share some of the rotations in Germany with our NATO allies, which means not every BCT goes to a CTC.

Organizing the way I did was a professional gamble for me as the commander. It was never spoken out loud or written in any official documentation. Still, a brigade and battalion commander's "report card," i.e., evaluation report, is primarily based on how they and their unit perform at a CTC rotation. The FORSCOM commander, corps commanders, and division commanders, i.e., the senior leaders of the US Army, closely follow these CTC rotations. CTCs, especially for battalion commanders, are where senior officers decide whether they get promoted and move on. . . or not. You cannot do both. I wasn't just gambling my battalion's reputation, but I was gambling on my Army career. But, at that point, we knew in the battalion what needed to get done to be successful.

Therefore, the mantra we used was *Determine your embarrassment level and stay above it*. I think my father-in-law, Colonel George Selden, had mentioned that to me at some point. While ill-defined, it did set the tone for the battalion and how we were to conduct ourselves. What we really needed was a switch in our heads so that we could go back and forth between JRTC and INDOPACOM—that way we could remain focused like a laser on what we needed to accomplish. While the mantra applied to everyone in the battalion, I believe it applied and impacted our small battalion staff the most. Normally, for a CTC rotation the battalion intelligence section, called the S2 shop, conducts a full intelligence preparation of the battlefield analysis of the enemy and the terrain we were to face, which would include lots of charts, pictures of enemy equipment, and maps with detailed terrain analysis. It's a significant amount of work, to say the least. Instead, I asked Capt. Lockwood, Sfc. Murphy, and Sgt. Mickle from our intelligence section to simply provide an overview of the scenario, general enemy organization, and find some 1:25,000 scale maps. We could learn the rest along the way and assume some risk in our in-depth knowledge of the JRTC scenario. Instead, their focus during that time period was to shepherd our official passport paperwork through the application process. Capt. Lockwood frequently fielded phone calls from JBLM's passport office about typos and missing documents and would need to track down the offending Brown Beret. Making sure each Brown Beret in 1st Battalion had their official brown-jacket passport was critical in our planning timeline. They weren't all required, but due to the numerous unknowns we were dealing with, we wanted to be ready. Applications sometimes took eight to eleven weeks, plus depending on which country the Brown Beret went to, they would need to submit for visas. Visas could take another four to eight weeks. Altogether, the entire process had the potential to take three to five months! JRTC preparation was important, but so was our INDOPACOM paperwork.

For the 5th SFAB's JRTC rotation, the 5th SFAB needed a partner force. The Army needed a unit to replicate a foreign partner force in some type of crisis or conflict. Typically, according to Army doctrine, a company advisor team (CAT) led by an experienced infantry major would partner with a foreign partner brigade, and maneuver advisor teams led by a senior captain would partner with a foreign infantry battalion. Finally, the SFAB battalion advisor team (BAT), which included me and a selection of people on the battalion staff, would partner with a foreign division headquarters.

If that math were to hold true, the 1st Battalion alone would need to partner with a division headquarters, three brigade headquarters, and nine different battalions. Where would the Army find such an available organization and multiply it to meet all the partnership requirements throughout the 5th SFAB? It couldn't. It was unrealistic to expect the US Army to use one of the eleven active-duty divisions or create an organization to replicate one given the limited physical geographical space at JRTC. Instead, FORSCOM decided that the 5th SFAB would partner with 1-2 Stryker Brigade Combat Team (SBCT) colocated with us at JBLM, Washington. 1-2 SBCT, nicknamed "Ghost Brigade," was a 3,600 person Army brigade outfitted with the eight-wheeled Stryker combat vehicle. The brigade has three infantry battalions, a cavalry squadron, artillery (fires) battalion, engineer battalion, and sustainment battalion assigned to it. Assigning such an organization the mission to replicate a foreign partner force for the 5th SFAB may not stress all the SFAB people and systems, but it was a way to resolve the training partner requirements and complete the event. In the short term, the Army was able to adapt this SFAB-BCT model to both certify the SFAB for combat readiness and deployment and train one of its BCTs. It was as if the Army was getting a two-for-one training event. Not a bad investment in terms of time and money.

The first thing we did to "stay above our embarrassment level" was to meet with our counterparts in the battalion that would replicate our foreign partners inside 1-2 SBCT. Our assigned role-playing foreign partner force would be 1st Battalion, 23rd Infantry Regiment (1-23 IN), the "Tomahawks," commanded by Lieutenant Colonel Sean Lyons. Coincidentally, Sean lived four houses down from me in the battalion commander housing area on JBLM. Occasionally we exchanged pleasantries, but our paths just didn't cross much, for one reason or another.

On the other hand, Cmd. Sgt. Maj. Overway knew the 1-23

IN command sergeant major, Joe Nicholson, better than I did. Cmd. Sgt. Maj. Overway also shared Tomahawk history. Before becoming the command sergeant major of 1/5 SFAB, he had been the command sergeant major of the 4th Battalion, 23rd Infantry Regiment (4-23 IN). 1-23 IN and 4-23 IN were stationed on JBLM but assigned to different brigades. However, they shared a common history and lineage with the 23rd Infantry Regiment. Each of the units held some of the historical lineages of the 23rd Infantry Regiment as passed down from official Army historians. It was natural to feel some sort of connection for Cmd. Sgt. Maj. Overway.

The SFAB company commanders and I decided it was best to travel to the 1-23 IN headquarters at JBLM and meet our counterparts on their home turf. In our eyes it set the tone for the relationship—we were there to help and support them. I came to find out I passed the 1-23 IN headquarters building every day on my way to the 5th SFAB but had never realized it. It was just another discreet beige Army building on JBLM to me. Lt. Col. Lyons told me the entry to the parking lot was tricky, but I didn't believe him until I tried to turn in and found myself embarrassingly driving back and forth on the main road a few times. After struggling to find the awkward entrance into the parking lot, I met our team outside. Either Maj. Dan Ludwig or Maj. Chris Wallgren asked me immediately before we were about to walk into the building which company he was going to partner with. I stopped in my tracks and looked at Maj. Scott Orr then my company commanders. Oh shoot! I realized we hadn't thought through a very basic, but critical aspect of our new relationship with 1-23 IN. How were we going to align our company headquarters? I made a hasty and uninformed decision. We simply paired our A Company with their Apache Company, our B Company with their Bandit Company, and our C Company with their Comanche Company. We didn't take into consideration personalities, unit strengths or weaknesses, or experiences from either organization. I consider this decision a minor failure on my part. Luckily, Maj. Dan Ludwig, Maj. Chris Wallgren, and Maj. Morgan Maier were all very experienced and professional. After a short round of introductions, the company command teams paired up. Majors Ludwig, Wallgren, and Maier smiled and shook hands with their newfound partners and started to talk. All of them set up future appointments to introduce the SFAB team leaders to the 1-23 IN platoon leaders.

I believed our partnership with 1-23 IN was an excellent opportunity to develop some Army mentorship along with combined combat training. Our seasoned majors who had already served as battalion or brigade operations officers or executive officers, as well as successful infantry company commanders, had the chance to work with new captain company commanders during a significant training event. Our major-led company commanders had between six and ten years of Army experience over their captain counterparts. Likewise, our SFAB team leaders, all post-company command infantry captains, became mentors for the young infantry platoon leaders. The 1/5 SFAB team leaders had anywhere between six and eight years of experience over the lieutenant platoon leaders. It was a great lineup for our officers to practice the tenants of advise, support, assess, and liaise with the Tomahawks.

Unfortunately, 1-2 SBCT, "Ghost Brigade," did not see this as a training opportunity with the experienced officers and NCOs found in the SFAB, but instead took it as a "tasking" or required duty that did not follow their planned training schedule. That it took place in November, with the units finishing training at Fort Polk over the Thanksgiving weekend, added to the negativity. SFAB Brown Berets and Ghost Brigade soldiers, NCOs, and officers would have to spend Thanksgiving together in the field on the last day of training instead of being with their families. I have never understood why the Army has NTC and JRTC rotations on

Thanksgiving, a clearly predictable holiday. Morale is negatively impacted. Suffice it to say, I've never heard anyone say it's a good idea.

The deviation from what 1-2 SBCT wanted to do caused them to view supporting the 5th SFAB's rotation as a nuisance—something they begrudgingly had to do. This attitude prevailed at all levels of the brigade, down to the squad leaders and squad members and manifested into a lack of action once we started the actual rotation in Louisiana. It would take time for our SFAB team members to demonstrate "value-added" to the Ghost Brigade soldiers. An indicator that we had broken this attitude came after the JRTC rotation when some of the Tomahawks expressed interest in volunteering for the SFAB. In many ways their initial attitude reflected what many Army leaders felt: the SFAB was not worth the investment in people and equipment and was a distraction from near-peer combat preparations. Overcoming such a sentiment was, in some ways, good preparation and practice, as we continued to work through hesitant Indo-Pacific foreign partner forces who weren't too sure of the SFAB either. For our forthcoming JRTC rotation, we would need to translate the pitch we'd given the Indo-Pacific US Army foreign area officers and others into actual practice for our newfound friends in the Ghost Brigade. Before we could do that, we needed to do one more practice before the big exercise.

Step 1: Pretraining

Going to a combat training center training rotation like JRTC begins before units enter "the box," which is the terrain in which the live-simulated environment occurs. At Fort Polk, the box line is literally marked on the road as you drive in. I remember seeing the sign at a four-way intersection in the cantonment area while sitting in one of our fifteen-passenger rental vans. Across the road from me stood one of those ranch entrance gates I frequently saw in Texas. Instead of *Welcome to Such-and-Such Ranch* across the top it read *Welcome to the Box* and there was a yellow painted line on the road to indicate the physical border. As a member of the rotational unit, peering across that intersection felt like peering into the unknown. I felt a small knot in my stomach as my experience indicated the amount of stress these rotations can induce on its leaders. I had seen this imposing sign while on our trip to Fort Polk for Leader Training Program (LTP). The Joint Readiness Training Center designs LTP to give commanders and staffs the opportunity to train without other distractions and is intended to allow them the chance to plan for the initial phases of the simulated battle in the box. Thus, the 5th SFAB brigade and battalion commanders and staffs all flew from Washington to Fort Polk during last week of September 2020 immediately after returning from Yakima to attend the week of LTP just a few weeks before the JRTC rotation itself.

After consulting with Cmd. Sgt. Maj. Overway, Maj. AJ Vogel (our battalion XO), and Maj. Scott Orr, (the battalion operations officer), we brought the entire 1st Battalion staff to Fort Polk's LTP to stay above the "embarrassment level" and left the company commanders and first sergeants back at JBLM to recover from the training out at Yakima. Not all the 5th SFAB battalions and squadrons took all their staffs. We did. The Leader Training Program for the battalion allowed the staff to run through the military decision-making process (MDMP) and refine planning skills while working as a team. It was something we, both me as the commander and the staff, really needed, especially given the quick transitions from Thailand to Yakima and the planning for our Indo-Pacific mission in between. We had not had time to focus on the staff's ability to work together in a simulated training environment fighting against a peer-competitor over an extended period of time, so this was another decision we had to make. Thirty-six hours of battalion-level training in Yakima, plus the bonus of a non-lubricated nasal pharyngeal for me, wouldn't suffice to prepare our staff and headquarters company for replicated continuous simulated combat conditions when faced with the professional opposing force and environment JRTC presented us.

Compared to maneuver infantry battalions, SFAB staffs don't have a lot of personnel depth to them. For instance, an infantry battalion intelligence section might have five or six people, the SFAB had just three, Capt. Lockwood, Sfc. Murphy, and Sgt. Mickle. In our case, they had to do all the other Army-directed administrative requirements, including physical security, arms-room inspections, and periodic security clearances, to name a few. I also had our folks running down all our official passports.

The LTP provided an excellent opportunity for the battalion staff to focus on the JRTC mission and some recycled simulated training scenarios. We were fortunate to work with a retired former battalion commander, pulled up a few historical scenarios, and worked through tactical problems and briefings. I recall Sfc. Murphy from the intelligence section and Sfc. Omar, our experienced senior supply NCO from the S4 section, debate about the task and purpose for our simulated friendly forces during one of those practice scenarios. They would talk about the effect they needed to achieve then look up Army doctrine to determine whether they were using the right terminology. Capt. Josh Mackenzie, a recent Maneuver Captain Career Course graduate, looked on and helped them along to accomplish an endeavor for which they were not prepared. For some others on the staff, it was the first time going through an infantry unit's tactical challenges. Practicing such a scenario was necessary because it best prepared the staff to tackle correlative problems our role-playing partners from 1-23 IN would face during the FORSCOM-directed rotation. To advise or assess the Tomahawks, we needed to be experts ourselves, especially at the battalion staff level. Focusing on the JRTC rotation and the infantry tactical scenarios was extremely beneficial to the battalion staff officers and NCOs to build the expertise.

However, in the mist of tackling the tactical scenarios we still found ourselves working on USARPAC challenges as well. I recall chatting with Cmd. Sgt. Maj. Overway in the hallway outside our battalion staff's planning bay toward the end of the day and watched as the other brigade and battalion commanders and staffs slung backpacks over their shoulders and made their way to the exits. We ended up being envious of them as they chatted about what they were doing for dinner. We were staying. The 1st Battalion staff stopped working on FORSCOM and JRTC tactical problems around 5:00 p.m., then transitioned to working on our CONOP and decision briefs for Brig. Gen. Taylor about moving forward on advancing teams into the Indo-Pacific countries. There was still staff work to be done, phone calls to make, and emails to send. In addition to those requirements, we brainstormed about what Brig. Gen. Taylor might do to help alleviate some of the bureaucratic staff hurdles and barriers that may be encountered at the various echelons or Army departments. Our briefings to him morphed as we learned what information was relevant and how he could help. During this phase of the INDOPACOM planning, we ended up using a "stoplight chart," which listed all the countries in the Indo-Pacific down the lefthand column and various staff requirements or coordinations necessary along the top such as "CONOP Submitted," "DAT Concurrence," or "USARPAC Approved." We then filled it out with red bubbles, which meant the item was not approved or not complete, yellow bubbles, which meant the action was in progress, and green bubbles—everything was good to go. After gathering all our information, it was a mixture of greens, yellows, and a lot of reds. The first time we briefed Brig. Gen. Taylor and described a particular obstacle, he asked, "Who do I need to call?" After an initial pause as everyone on the battalion staff looked at each other, befuddled, we finally provided him a name and phone number. The following day at the end of the brief we laid out the top three "targets" requiring his action. The targets had a name, phone number or email, brief description of the problem, and the decision or answer we needed from them to move forward. Our extra INDOPACOM work continued every day for the five days of LTP training at Fort Polk. Doing both sets of work was mentally, and sometimes a little physically, exhausting.

We spent a lot of time in our battalion planning bay. It was just a square box of a room about fifteen-by-fifteen yards in size, if that, with no windows. At one point, Cmd. Sgt. Maj. Overway and I noticed Jeff Lockwood and Josh Henry, two of our young captains, were discussing how to secure more energy drinks and sugar-laden snacks. They weren't the only ones thinking about food and caffeine, everyone else was as well. The meals ready-to-eat (MREs) for lunch and the hot food "mermited" in for breakfast and dinner were not cutting it. Mermites are the insulated food containers that the Army uses to ship food from a food preparation location to troops that cannot get to the dining facility.[37] MREs were prepackaged, nonperishible food packs designed for troops engaged in combat who require high caloric intake. We weren't burning that many calories, and the taste is never what anyone would call good. The mermite food was usually, not always, similar to the sad and pathetic food you would see at a third-rate hotel during their complimentary breakfast: powdered eggs clumped together that were sometimes eerily hard and only made palatable with a heavy dose of ketchup and hot sauce. There was much to be desired. Because the amount of work was so taxing on everyone,

Cmd. Sgt. Maj. Overway and I made a commissary run (military grocery store) early in the week. We bought the sugary snacks young people desire, which in turn gave them the boost of energy needed to carry on and satisfied their cravings. We also grabbed a variety of caffeinated drinks. What surprised me and Cmd. Sgt. Maj. Overway was the astronomical rate at which our officers and NCOs rapidly ran through our purchase. I guess we were willing to compensate them with snacks and energy drinks to get the double work out of them.

Aside from being cooped up in the LTP training center, Cmd. Sgt. Maj. Overway and I had the opportunity to spring free to see some of our Brown Berets who were also at Fort Polk but not slugging it away doing staff work. Capt. Mathew Brown and Sfc. Javar from Team 5113, who had previously worked with the Royal Thai Army (RTA) during their training mission in Hawaii, were also at Fort Polk. They were there independent of the rest of the 5th SFAB preparing to enter the box with their RTA counterparts as a component of 2-25 Brigade Combat Team's JRTC rotation. Many, but not all the RTA officers, NCOs, and soldiers they were working with had participated in the Hawaii training. The RTA had put together a composite company of soldiers, NCOs, and officers and sent them to Fort Polk to participate in this capstone training event. The participation of MAT 5113 with the RTA during the JRTC rotation was the first-time members of the 5th SFAB had partnered with an Indo-Pacific Army unit for a CTC rotation.

When we arrived at their mission prep site in the cantonment area, it was a satisfying sight to see. S.Sgt. Eckhardt was mounting their .50-caliber machine gun on their vehicle and making sure it functioned correctly. S.Sgt. Williams was checking their radios inside the truck and Sgt. Grace, their communications NCO, was validating their SCOUT equipment. They were doing exactly what they were supposed to be doing without anyone looking over their shoulder or telling them what to do. Accompanied by Brig. Gen. Taylor, Cmd. Sgt. Maj. Overway and I went in to find Capt. Brown. We found him typing up a report to send to the 2-25 BCT headquarters to let them know how things were going with the RTA. Again, exactly what he needed to be doing. He promptly took us outside to meet with the RTA company commander. The RTA commander was almost as excited to meet a US Army general officer as we were to see him and some of our Brown Berets working together at one of the Army's premier training centers. We enjoyed the brief, but very positive, interaction with the RTA and MAT 5131. Perhaps it was the most important meeting we had while at Fort Polk during LTP.

In true 1st Battalion fashion, Capt. Brown and his team broke some new ground for the 5th SFAB. They established a baseline for the unit to determine exactly how an SFAB MAT would support and liaise with a Thai Army unit during simulated large-scale combat operations. The first lesson involved using some of our specialized equipment. The tactical voice bridge (TVB) and the end-user devices—small smartphone devices with encryption and map sharing software—were found to be essential equipment that allowed the US infantry battalion that MAT 5113 worked with to both communicate with the Thai company as well as know its disposition, or location of subordinate units and combat power. The Thai company performed exceptionally well and eventually executed a company-level live fire at Fort Polk. This was a big deal for the Thais and JRTC. During previous rotations, the O/C-Ts hadn't allowed the RTA to shoot live ammunition because there wasn't a way to ensure everything was done safely. With MAT 5113 there were safety mechanisms in place which made those responsible for the live fire feel comfortable. This simple training event made big headlines in Thailand across traditional and social media venues. We believe that MAT 5113 was a significant contributor to the Thai company's success.

After we completed LTP and 2-25 BCT's JRTC rotation started, the Thais had the opportunity to experience Louisiana weather. Hurricane Delta swung up from the Gulf of Mexico and dumped rain and brought strong winds to Fort Polk. Luckily JRTC only paused training briefly during the storm. Nothing prevents a CTC from proceeding, not even Mother Nature.

During LTP, time quickly passed between MDMP classes, tactical practical exercises, various JRTC briefings, and our INDOPACOM work. The day before the brigade and battalion staffs departed, we issued our operations order over a secure video telephone conference link to our subordinate companies still at JBLM. Regrettably, it was a pretty thin order given the magnitude of the training event we were about to begin. It was missing the tactical details that units at combat training centers usually have going into the first "battle" of the rotation. Normally following a leader training program at a CTC, the order is rich with particulars that include routes, task organization, specific missions, areas of operations, timelines, and external resources the battalion and companies will receive to execute their missions. During our staff brief to the company commanders, the commanders, who were all experienced battalion and brigade-level officers, asked many pointed questions that neither the staff nor I as the battalion commander could answer. It wasn't quite embarrassing, but it was uncomfortable. Both the battalion staff and I regretted the lack of details we provided for the briefing given all the staff work and training we had done over the previous week.

The reason we were delivering an inferior product to our subordinate commanders was a little outside our control. The JRTC script and scenario writers had not finished developing and writing the scenario that would combine previous decisive action rotations for conventional brigade combat teams with the historically used SFAB scenarios that were counterinsurgency focused in preparation for deployment to Iraq and Afghanistan. Nothing like what we were doing existed yet. Additionally, FORSCOM wanted to test an Indo-Pacific-based scenario that had not been used before at a CTC. There wasn't one on the proverbial shelf the script writers could just pull up. Given all that required input, the JRTC staff was behind schedule and didn't have the information necessary to provide the planning details and background to put the 5th SFAB and 1-2 SBCT into the first battle period.

Scriptwriting is exceptionally challenging for the Army because you want to test all sorts of systems, processes, and the warfighting capabilities of the Army units in a controlled manner. The scenario script must be extremely detailed when between 4000–6000 soldiers, NCOs, and officers with numerous subunits that must be tested on these various tasks. Combining a professional opposing force (OPFOR) acting as a live-thinking enemy with limits during the fight gave the scenario developers significant, sometimes conflicting, requirements to think through. In some ways, I sympathized with them.

Leaving Fort Polk after LTP I felt satisfied that the staff had the opportunity to train on MDMP, frustrated we had to do the double FORSCOM and INDOPACOM work, happy we had made progress with the INDOPACOM planning, and proud to see MAT 5113 working with their Thai partners. I guess my emotions were all over the place. With LTP in the rearview mirror, though, and with many questions still unanswered with regard to our JRTC rotation, we departed Fort Polk, Louisiana on the eighth of October 2020. Since the script was not complete and our planning process for the scenario rotation was only an inch deep, we would need to improvise or do some crisis planning when we returned. That would happen a mere four weeks later when we stepped foot on Fort Polk again with the rest of the 5th SFAB and our assigned partners, the Ghost Brigade.

The Crucible

The time in October 2020 immediately preceding our JRTC rotation was a flurry of activity that included packing equipment, loading vehicles onto railcars, overseeing individual administrative and medical preparation, conducting planning calls with Indo-Pacific country teams, and switching out Majors Tom Angstadt and Dan Ludwig in command of our A Company. To say a lot was going on would be an understatement. We even found time to squeeze in a trunk-or-treat Soldier Family Readiness Group (SFRG) event.

One area that remained a challenge was building the community of families within the organization. Building a family network in a new unit requires a deliberate effort and is difficult. COVID made it even harder. The SFRG for the US Army, as outlined in regulations, is a company commander's program designed to keep the spouses and families of their soldiers informed. While the program is formal, many commands use it to develop informal support networks among the spouses and families of service members. It was extremely effective during the height of the Global War on Terror when units had casualties. This network helped assist those family members affected by the trauma. The Army has since changed the FRG to SFRG, Soldier-Family Readiness Group, to reflect the requirement to support single soldiers as well. [38]

In the best cases, the SFRG becomes an informal social network that spouses and families can use to bond while a unit is gone on a deployment. It takes considerable effort to create this environment where people can rely on each other in the event of a crisis or incident. During the Global War on Terror years, the FRG, as it was called then, proved to be an essential network that spouses and families depended on when times were tough, and when Army families lived far away from their typical familial network. Army families had to rely on each other.

Because of COVID restrictions, we couldn't create the network and bonds between families that we wanted. However, in a rare window of opportunity, the 1st Battalion did a little something before heading to JRTC. While somewhat of a standard for many American communities, the Tiger battalion dressed up our vehicles and put together a trunk-or-treat. It was amazing to see the creativity of many of our Brown Berets and their families. I'll never forget S.Sgt. Amber Heintz, one of our intelligence NCOs, who really got into character and displayed a fantastic fairytale-land spread around her vehicle. S.Sgt. Heintz called it "Candy Land." She even wore a Cinderella-style dress. As my wife Amy and I watched the kids come and go to her station it was obvious she enjoyed what she did, and the costumed kids loved it too. She won first prize among all the impressively decorated vehicles! It was great to see many of our battalion families interacting with each other while still following COVID protocols. The rare social opportunity gave Amy and me the chance to meet one of our newest battalion members, 1st Sgt. Duane Bochman, his wife Kimberly, and their three kids. They arrived just a week before the trunk-or-treat. 1st Sgt. Bochman was the newly assigned first sergeant for our C Company, paired up with Maj. Morgan Maier.

The excitement, joy, and relaxation we enjoyed during our family event was temporary and fleeting. Immediately following the event, we sent our advanced elements to Fort Polk merely three weeks after we had departed following LTP. Our 1st Battalion was responsible for commanding and controlling the personnel movement control nodes at JBLM and Seattle-Tacoma Airport in Washington and the other at the Alexandria, Louisiana airport, called the Arrival/Departure Airfield Control Group, for all the 5th SFAB and 1-2 SBCT units arriving. Capt. Matt Orders and Sfc. Avila from MAT 5111 were responsible for accountability, briefings, and bus transportation. It wasn't a complicated mission, but it did require coordination and synchronization.

A few days later, Cmd. Sgt. Maj. Overway and I departed on one of the last main personnel flights from JBLM to Fort Polk. Doing so allowed us to squeeze out a few more days of work for our Indo-Pacific mission. We knew once we arrived in Louisiana, we would be swept up in the JRTC rotation requirements. During our daily touch points prior to our arrival, Maj. AJ Vogel and Sgt. Maj. Doyle, the battalion XO and operations sergeant major respectively, told us about the conditions in the cantonment area. They told us of overcrowding, congestion, and soldiers skipping meals because of chow lines that required them to stand in line for over an hour before getting served. There was simply too much work to do to just stand around. I took these comments with a grain of salt and based on my experience, didn't think it could be as bad as they said. I was wrong.

When I arrived I found people piled on each other in large festival-type tents in rows after rows of the olive-green Army cots. I didn't dare venture into the row of portable toilets standing outside. The overwhelming smell indicated overuse and underservicing. When I found Lt. Col. Tim Ferguson, the SFAB cavalry squadron commander, in one of the fests tents, he was sitting on the end of a cot trying to type something on his computer. His hunched over posture and the awkward positions of his legs while balancing the computer on his lap were clearly uncomfortable. When I asked him where his troops (companies or subordinate units) were, he smiled and started pointing in various directions. Then in typical Tim fashion, he mimicked the scarecrow from *The Wizard of Oz* and pointed in multiple directions. There wasn't enough work or living space for everyone to conduct their final preparations effectively and efficiently for the rotation.

The billeting arrangements were the first challenge the combined 5th SFAB and 1-2 SBCT units encountered at Fort Polk. Because this was such a new type of training rotation, the facilities were unable to house such a large number of people. The 5th SFAB, the designated training and certifying unit for the rotation, was responsible for piecing this all together. Therefore, as the 5th SFAB commander, Brig. Gen. Taylor was responsible for everything, even though he was commanding the smaller of the two organizations. We wanted to help our SFAB headquarters solve this problem. Maj. Scott Orr reached out to his Special Forces contacts and identified Special Operational Forces (SOF) specific spaces we could occupy. There weren't any Special Operations units participating in the exercise, therefore their buildings and billeting were unused and available. The disadvantage was that the buildings were far away from most of the meeting locations and life support facilities, even the mess hall. Still, they were a little nicer because they had actual hardstand bunk beds and more individual and company space to work in. We were happy, and so was the brigade. And to avoid the long trek to the mess hall and bypass the lines, we coordinated mermite deliveries of our food to our companies' barracks area.

The next challenge was getting those thirteen different communications systems to operate and talk to each other. Getting them to work was our number-one priority and proved a more significant hurdle than expected. These various systems provided us with reliable options for encrypted communications across short and long distances using radio waves, cell towers, or satellites. Brig. Gen. Taylor had directed that we validate every team's communications systems through the brigade's signal company. That meant over twenty-five MATs and nine CATs from the maneuver battalions, plus six company-level advisor teams (artillery, engineer, and logistics) and their twelve subordinate teams for a total of fifty-two different elements (MATs 5113 and 5213 were not included because they had worked with the Thais and Indonesians during 2-25 BCT JRTC Rotation).

The Rotational Unit Bivouac Area (RUBA) is the staging area where units go when they arrive before going into the box and starting their combat training center (CTC) rotation. The other commonly used term is the *cantonment area* because of the life support facilities located there for the rotational unit. The RUBA simulates how a combat unit might arrive in a foreign country to prepare for operations. The administration and logistics requirements to bring personnel and equipment together in a short four-to-seven-day timeframe is challenging for every unit that goes through a CTC. Additionally, as the unit conducts its reception, staging, onward movement, and integration (RSOI) tasks, they might be observed or attacked by the simulated opposing force. Doing all of this at the same time is hard with just one brigade present; with the SFAB rotation bringing both 1-2 SBCT and 5th SFAB together at the same time, it proved even more burdensome.

In addition, the brigade's signal company is not an entire army signal company and has less than twenty people. These twenty or fewer people were not prepared to fix over fifty different individual teams' issues. S.Sgt. Demella and Sgt. Mercado from our communications section were probably some of the hardest-working people in the battalion that first week at Fort Polk. I saw them constantly in the company areas during our time in the rotational unit bivouac area (RUBA) talking on the phone with help desks, assisting teams in acquiring satellites, and all-around trying to make the ones and zeros talk to each other. This was a huge learning experience for all our communications specialists throughout formation. In the end, every team was certified from the signal company stating they had validated all systems with the brigade. Tracking each of those communications systems and getting them to work in "the box" proved to be a daily challenge for the entire battalion, as well as the brigade.

The subsequent challenge for us was determining what our role and relationship was going to be with Ghost Brigade, 1-2 SBCT. In the RUBA, we were fulfilling two roles. The first part was that we were both just two Army units trying to survive JRTC's reception, staging, onward movement, and integration process, which is hard work by itself. Getting equipment ready to move, downloading equipment from railcars sent from across the country, and getting the laser and sensor Multiple Integrated Laser Engagement System (MILES) gear issued and installed causes plenty of headaches too. It's the normal friction people experience bringing a large amount of people and equipment together in a short amount of time. The second part was determining what the advisor-partner force relationship looked like. The relationship was more complicated sometimes for 5th SFAB members because we were unable to determine whether our counterparts from 1-23 IN were telling us something while role-playing as the "1-162nd Motorized Rifle Battalion," their scenario name, or if it was just the Tomahawk battalion talking with us. For instance, in one of our competition-to-crisis scenarios the SFAB brigade and battalion command teams were invited by the "ambassador" to a social at his "residence." Upon entering the social, we realized there were a lot of role players there, mostly JRTC hired civilians, but also there were our partner force counterparts. The hired civilians had positions like deputy defense minister, or commander of XYZ brigade from a random location, or a "US Embassy" security cooperation officer. As some of us relied on real-word experiences in places like Thailand, we started asking specific questions about organizational structure, processes and procedures, and other aspects of the embassy only someone with insider experience would know. We soon realized the role players only knew so much about their script and didn't always have the depth of knowledge we expected. On the other hand, after talking with Lt. Col. Sean Lyons I knew he understood exactly what the status of his unit was but oddly he had taken all his unit patches and rank off his uniform. The role-playing Ghost

Brigade commanders stuck to themselves and didn't really mingle with the rest of the "embassy guests." My best guess was that since they were in uniform and present at the "embassy" function, they were role playing.

Even as the overall brigade's focus at Fort Polk had been preparation for this climactic training event and our NCOs had made their value evident, the 1st Battalion officers were still on their phones. They had to break away from tactical communications platforms, JRTC planning, and tactical rehearsals to check their email or make a phone call to do Indo-Pacific work. It was a constant back and forth mental switch vacillating between the two efforts, the big impending entry into "the box" and attempting to negotiate our way into places like Indonesia, India, or Malaysia. One minute I was talking to Capt. Oleg Sheynfeld about the Philippines or Capt. Dan Lee about his Mongolia mission, and the next I was talking with Majors AJ Vogel or Scott Orr about the South Torbian Army—the fictitious army from the imaginary country of South Torbia in the JRTC scenario. Capt. Matt Thimble and Maj. Morgan Maier were in video telephone conferences and exchanging emails with the attaché office in Malaysia right up until we had to turn our phones off before leaving for the box. During the JRTC scenario, rotational unit members, like those of us from the 5th SFAB or 1-2 SBCT, were not authorized to use their smartphones, with only a few exceptions for command teams. Due to the competitive environment in which we were fighting, there were risks associated with turning on a smartphone. The OPFOR could use their electronic warfare capabilities to locate the user, thus targeting the unit or command post.

Before we turned in our phones, they negotiated with both the Army attaché office and the Malaysian Army about opportunities for Matt's team to come and train with the Malaysians. The US Army usually had bilateral training events with our Malaysian partners throughout the year, but COVID had caused significant disruption to those events. We took this as a good sign. Of course, after hearing about the opportunity to work with the Malaysians, I promptly asked Maj. Maier how his relationship was going with C Company, 1-162nd Motorized Rifle Battalion, his role-playing counterpart.

The week of reception, staging, onward movement, and integration (RSOI) time in preparation for entering "the box" puts a significant amount of pressure and stress on leaders, as they must accomplish the series of tasks previously mentioned. Because we were working dual missions, leaders were getting pulled in multiple directions. People under stress can often create conflict with the people around them. Different personalities react differently to stress. Unfortunately, we had to relearn this particular lesson. Cmd. Sgt. Maj. Overway received a phone call from one of our first sergeants that one of his assistant team leaders had collapsed on the stairs. We immediately jumped in our vehicle and drove up to the company barracks and planning areas about five minutes away. We saw the sergeant first class sitting down with his head in his hands on the steps being tended to by one of the company medics. He was clearly incoherent and not carrying himself as one would expect a senior infantry NCO should even in the stress-inducing environment of a JRTC. We talked to the company commander and first sergeant about the situation and decided to send him to Behavioral Health. Something wasn't quite right, and we wanted to make sure he received the care he needed.

Cmd. Sgt. Maj. Overway and I also decided to dig a little deeper to find out from those who worked closest with him what might have been going on. Was he having family issues at home, financial problems, or something else? Cmd. Sgt. Maj. Overway and I separately conducted some sensing sessions with the sergeants and staff sergeants from the team. During my sessions, they looked at their feet for a while until I asked specific questions about team internal dynamics. Cmd. Sgt. Maj. Overway and I learned separately that the team leader, a captain, and the assistant team leader, a sergeant first class, were not getting along and their leadership styles were clashing. The differences caused confusion within the team and frustration among the individual members. When Behavior Health told us that the sergeant first class was fine but under a lot of stress, we knew we had a more serious problem on our hands. Unfortunately, Cmd. Sgt. Maj. Overway and I had never had the opportunity to really know the innerworkings and personalities of the team previously. We didn't see this particular MAT during our time in Yakima and the brigade's exercise. We needed to do something at that moment regardless.

We moved the assistant team leader to the battalion headquarters, but the problems did not vanish. Looking back, we had placed a Band-Aid on a sucking chest wound that would come back to haunt us over the course of our deployments in foreign countries. The internal personality clashes continued for that team, but they were able to hold it together for both the JRTC rotation and their country deployment later. The sergeant first class ended up doing a fantastic job in the operations center on the battalion staff, but the team was left without an assistant team leader for a couple of months. He was a true blessing at the battalion level and thrived in his new role. One of my peers in 4th SFAB had mentioned to me following their JRTC rotation that they wished they wouldn't have waited to make changes concerning personality conflicts between leaders. We did a half step that would require future counseling and mitigation measures while in-country. The situation reinforced, once again, that people matter and relationship dynamics matter a whole lot too, especially in small, tight-knit teams.

Most business professionals suggest not to ignore conflict among their rank-and-file employees. What should be done instead is to try to clarify what the issue is and bring the parties together to talk about those issues so they can find an amicable solution. Resolution oftentimes requires some type of compromise. Collaboration among all parities involves finding a solution that satisfies the concerns and discrepancies, so they are able to work together cohesively again. Not all conflicts can be resolved to the satisfaction of the parties involved. Effective resolution of conflicts requires follow-up and constant monitoring as well. The Army was no different in this regard. We learned from our mistakes.

COVID added another layer of complexity to what we were trying to accomplish. Mitigation of some sort was a formation wide effort during our JRTC rotation. With all that we did to lessen the impact of COVID, we still had issues with it impacting operations for the whole SFAB formation. The most significant outbreaks of positive COVID test cases came from our role-playing 1-23 IN battalion partners. Our Brown Berets feared that if they tested positive for COVID near the end of the rotation, they could potentially find themselves in an additional two weeks of quarantine. They then ran the numbers on what testing positive might mean if it happened midway to the end of the rotation. The answer was that they would not get back home until after Christmas leave had already started for the unit. That was significant for us because we had planned the first departures of our Indo-Pacific mission to start during the third week of January. As fate would have it, we had our first outbreak in the 1-23 IN, resulting in half of the platoon being quarantined before we even entered the box. This, in turn, created a lot of fear and apprehension because we had been unsuccessful in containing COVID from spreading.

Another example of COVID impacts came during midway through the rotation. We found out that the forward support company (FSC) members had been sharing vaping cigarettes and not washing their hands while handling food. The lack of following the basic medical protocols reulted in all the 1-23 IN cooks from the FSC being quarantined because they all tested positive for COVID. As a fail-safe we ate MREs for the remainder of our time in rotation. We had been duly humbled by this situation and were now exhibiting some concern about working with our assigned partner forces, not knowing if they were following the COVID medical protocols. This was a poor starting point to try to build trust between our two units. But how would we do it with a reluctant partner and where there was a lack of trust between units? Somehow, we would need to persevere.

Into the Breach

A level of trust was produced through difficulty and hardship during the simulated fight. But before that could begin, our 1-2 SBCT partners departed to the training area twenty-four hours in advance of any 5th SFAB elements. Departing early allowed the Ghost Brigade to get set in position before SFAB Brown Berets arrived for the simulated training exercise. Ghost Brigade had to understand what exactly they were supposed to do to fulfill their role as a fictitious foreign partner force. I recall watching their vehicles drive past our battalion command post in the RUBA for what seemed like forever. The ostensibly endless vehicle after vehicle passed along the dirt roads, leaving low-hanging clouds of dust along the roadways. The brown powder left the grass and weeds with a light coat of dust.

The overall concept for the scenario was to have the circumstances in the fictitious country of South Torbia go from competition to crisis (with guerrillas and insurgents fighting the host country), then into some sort of conflict (or shooting war where a neighboring near-peer country invaded the host country).[39] The idea was to test the units along the entire spectrum of conflict. Both of these phases were done in the live-simulated environment where we shot blanks and used the MILES later. The third phase was the live fire. The 1st Battalion, 5th SFAB and 1-23 IN (a.k.a. 1-162 motorized infantry) went through all three of these different phases in the JRTC scenario. These new concept scenarios were intended to depict the value of the SFAB to our 1-23 IN partners who did not want to be at JRTC supporting another unit's event. They had reluctantly done so because they had no alternative. The first phase of our scenario was fought in a counterinsurgency environment or competition environment. Then we all moved into the live-fire area and finally onto fighting a peer adversary in the defense and offense.

The entire 5th SFAB had to enter the box along one single road, minus 2nd Battalion (who were first in the chute for executing the live-fire exercise in the northern training area), so our entry had to be sequenced based on the time it would take to drive to our partner force locations. I'm always the most nervous the night before driving into the box than most any other time during the rotation. I continually thought about things we may have missed or should have anticipated and didn't. I kept wondering if we should have done another rehearsal, or whether all our communication's equipment would work, and couldn't stop thinking about what would happen if the formation got attacked on the way in. I was especially nervous about driving into the box on a single road since this would leave us vulnerable to an attack. Lt. Col. Tim Ferguson and the 3rd Squadron took the lead because they had the farthest distance to travel to the eastern edges of the training area. Everyone understood that these exercises were pretend, but they were still very serious. Most were nervous like me because they really wanted to win and be successful.

We were able to tap into some internal knowledge to give us

an edge to win during this scenario. Of course, winning is a relative term at a CTC. You never actually win because the observer/controller-trainers and FORSCOM leadership would simply modify the script to continue to test a unit's fighting abilities. We knew this, but still wanted to perform our best. Maj. AJ Vogel, the 1st Battalion executive officer, had previously served with the brigade combat team, 1st Brigade, 10th Mountain Division that was stationed at Fort Polk. Due to their proximity, 1-10 BCT unit members frequently had to serve in a variety of roles to support rotations at JRTC, including as guest O/C-Ts. His previous experiences at JRTC allowed him to learn a lot of the tactics, techniques, and procedures (TTPs) that 1-509th Parachute Infantry Battalion, nicknamed "Geronimo," as the opposing force (OPFOR) in our exercise was known, used to wreak havoc on the rotational unit. AJ, of course, shared what he had learned with us. AJ mentioned where Geronimo hid to ambush the forces, as well as where and how they moved across the terrain. Additionally, our assistant team leader from MAT 5131, Sergeant First Class Daniel Dougherty had served in Geronimo, as well. He used to be one of the very OPFOR who would harass rotational units, keep them on their toes, and make them stay up late at night. Sfc. Dougherty told us they would attack early in the morning after keeping a unit up all night, or the following night when the unit was tired and most vulnerable. When I asked him about his thoughts about going into the rotation, he laughed and just said, "Geronimo does this fight ten times a year and knows the terrain better than anyone. It's just the way it is." Not exactly very reassuring . . .

All our advisor teams moved into position without incident, which was such a relief. Naturally, the first thing we did was get our multiple communication platforms up. Commanders always want to be able to talk with their subordinate units to maintain situational awareness and make sure they can reach their boss.

Asking about our communications status across the formation would be something Mark Goodwin, our battalion communications officer, knew I would ask about every time I walked into our tactical operations center (TOC) tent. Out came the cables, antennae, and generators to get everything operational, similar to the way we had practiced in Yakima back in September. We collocated our TOC next to our partners from 1-23 IN in anticipating of collaborating, planning, and working with them to best achieve our mission. Unfortunately, during the entire first part of this rotation, competition, or the counterinsurgency phase, the 1-23 IN staff didn't collaborate with us and would not even allow us into their TOC tent. I never found out if this was due to the planned script scenario, part of the overall rotation plan, or not tied to JRTC at all and it was just the culture of 1-23 IN.

One explanation was that JRTC was trying to balance two different brigades' training objectives, first the 5th SFAB and second the 1-2 SBCT's. We started to understand what this meant better when the 1/5 SFAB staff officers walked the thirty or so feet from our tent to theirs and try to talk with their 1-23 IN counterparts. Our CATs and MATs and their infantry companies and platoons were fighting insurgents and North Torbian infiltrators. I recall Capt. Josh Henry, our fire support officer and battalion planner, attempted to talk with his counterpart about coordinating AH-64 Apache attack helicopters for one of our CATs and 1-23 IN's infantry companies in preparation for one particular attack. His counterpart said he didn't have time and was planning for their live fire. The irritated look on Josh's face indicated he was a little frustrated with how his relationship was going with his counterpart. It became clear to us that 1-2 SBCT's primary training objective was executing their large battalion-level live-fire exercise. Due to JRTC's size and the land available in Louisiana, the simulated scenario training area was physically separated by a two-hour drive south from the live-fire complex up north. Our sense was that 1-23 IN was planning for that movement and the subsequent live fire. Understandably, the live fire was dangerous, and people could actually get killed. It was intended to test a battalion's ability to synchronize all lethal direct and indirect fires against the enemy. While we worked through the competition portion of the crisis, our counterparts in 1-23 IN were solely focused on the live fire. We were partners in name only because we were working on different problems and had contrasting priorities. The undeveloped relationship caused challenges for us to achieve our primary mission to advise, support, liaise, and assess our partners. We couldn't complete our mission if we didn't understand fully what the 1-23 IN were doing.

Gaining battlefield understanding is critical for commanders to make decisions and allocate resources. One way the military creates understanding is to generate reports. Brig. Gen. Taylor and the brigade headquarters staff developed a series of reports that were to be sent up daily. The number of reports became cumbersome for us. The reports were identified by different color codes. For example, red reports designated something about the enemy, blue reports were for the US [SFAB] friendly forces, and green reports discussed anything relevant about our partner force, in our case 1-23 IN, known in our exercise as the 1-162 Motorized Infantry Battalion of South Torbia. There were also yellow reports to describe anything civil or unknown in nature. A drive-by shooting or robbery might trigger a yellow report. Furthermore, the reports were numbered with additional numerical differentiation. For instance, the Green 3 was an engagement report between a US leader and a partner force leader to capture what they talked about and any agreement or significant outcomes. The Green 5 was an organizational assessment formatted so that the team could provide an overall review of the green force's capabilities along the lines of the different warfighting functions (maneuver, mission command, intelligence, fires, protection, and sustainment). There were so many various reports that the 1st Battalion began to call them the rainbow reports. Brig. Gen. Taylor used the number of reports received by teams to measure the effectiveness of our understanding of the simulated battlefield. Those of us in 1/5th SFAB (blue force) and the 1-23 IN (green force) at the battalion level struggled to understand and visualize the enemy situations.

Unfortunately, due to our staff size, the communications systems available, and the number and types of computers at the battalion level, we could not process multiple reports from thirteen different subordinate units in a twenty-four-hour period. The battalion TOC is supposed to receive, distribute, and analyze information, submit recommendations to the commander, integrate resources, and synchronize resources. There was way too much information for anyone to truly understand or process it. We did the best we could, but I always felt we did not do the greatest job in this regard because we did not have the resources to complete it in a timely fashion. We couldn't put any analysis into the reports and instead just put them into one file and sent them away. Maybe it was time to find a better way, but we wouldn't end up hashing out a compromise until later.

As we worked with 1-23 IN at echelon or every level from platoon, company, and battalion, our team leaders and company commanders had to figure out how to work with the leaders with whom they partnered. Because of the experience and rank difference at the platoon leader (one to two years in the Army) compared to an SFAB team leader (six to eight years in the Army and former company commander), levels of advising and coaching were manageable. Our majors paired up with captain company commanders, whom they had six to eight more years of experience than. There was a good opportunity for professional mentorship. I recall meeting up with Maj. Chris Wallgren and 1st

Sgt. Workman at one point. They described to me how they were coaching their counterpart company commanders to properly execute troop leading procedures, a step-by-step process the Army uses to plan a mission. All junior officers learn this process at their basic training courses but, as with many things, it's easy to learn in the schoolhouse, but harder to execute in a live environment. Maj. Wallgren and 1st Sgt. Workman gently reminded the company commander what he should be checking on and what he should be planning for and anticipating. Due to their experience, they foresaw friction points and potential shortcomings. Much of what they were teaching was time management in a crisis situation and remaining focused on only those tasks that were the most critical to accomplish.

On the other hand, at the battalion level, I was supposed to partner with someone I was only senior to by two years or less. The close equality in experience contrasted greatly with what my major-led company commanders and captain team leaders encountered. It was a little uncomfortable for me since we were both testy commanders trying to succeed in FORSCOM's simulated, but realistic, battlefield. Therefore, I could only be a third-party observer of how Lt. Col. Lyons operated with his staff and his subordinate commanders. I learned early that I could recommend about one or two big things a day working with my JBLM house neighbor. He was his own commander, and I wasn't going to teach a whole lot to someone who had eighteen years of Army experience under his belt. Instead, I started with suggestions based on what my staff was telling me and what I observed myself. I would recommend things like requesting additional aircraft, inserting rehearsals for upcoming missions, and commander injects into the staff planning process to keep his own battalion staff on track. It wasn't rocket science but by 1-23 IN succeeding in their mission, we would in effect succeed in ours. Making sure we could use our communications systems to quickly gather and disseminate information, understand the enemy and terrain, and build trust with our partners would get us there.

Sometimes building trust with a counterpart means just spending time with them. To that end, during the first phase of the rotation Cmd. Sgt. Maj. Overway and I accompanied Lt. Col. Lyons when he was visiting one of his infantry platoons. His platoon worked with our MAT 5121. Capt. Dustin Freeman and Sfc. Herman, MAT 5121's team leader and assistant team leader (sometimes simply called the team sergeant), worked with Lt. Col. Lyons's platoon located in a remote village away from everyone else. The unit was deliberately isolated to stress our communications and logistics systems. At the village there were role-playing civilians, local role-playing military and police, and a simulated mayor milling around a few large Conex boxes painted and modified to look like buildings with signs hanging on them to indicate what they represented, such as the market, town hall, and police station. Dustin worked with the platoon leader to figure out how to secure the village from the insurgent groups in the area. He advised and mentored the young lieutenant to work with the local forces and integrate them and his own platoon into a defense. There were layers of scenario script for each of the characters and role players to create a rich learning environment. It was good to see our two groups working together. I think it helped Lt. Col. Lyons see this positive relationship and how our SFAB MAT could help one of his platoons. He also realized that Capt. Freeman was able to use his communication systems to request logistics support on Lt. Col. Lyons's platoon leader's behalf. It was a step in the right direction in building our rapport and demonstrating some "value-added." As our site visit started to wrap up, I suddenly heard the distinct whistle of artillery simulators. Those sounds are never a good sign. The insurgents were starting to attack the village with simulated indirect fire. Hence, Lt. Col. Lyons's group and ours decided to leave quickly. We didn't want to be part of that unpleasant experience and us being there would genuinely get in the way of the valuable training those leaders were about to experience together. The brief episode became a sort of joke for me, Lt. Col. Lyons, Cmd. Sgt. Maj. Overway, and Cmd. Sgt. Maj. Nicholson that we had cowardly fled in the face of the enemy.

After two days of observing what was happening, it became apparent to me that each of the individual MATs, partnered with the infantry platoons, were running through what the Army calls situation training exercise (STX) lanes. As JRTC tried to simulate how to train both an SFAB and BCT, it pulled part of one of their old counterinsurgency scenarios used to train units for Iraq and Afghanistan out of the books, and that's what we did for about four days. It was not bad training, but it was apparent this part of the rotation had been used before by FORSCOM. At the conclusion of the competition phase of the training scenario our battalions moved up to the live-fire location. The 1-23 IN was still hard to read and I believed we were starting to connect with our counterparts, but I felt we had not built a strong rapport with them yet. Our perception was that they still perceived us as more a nuisance than anything else. We were still viewed as the new, untested Army unit that had sucked up a lot of talented officers and NCOs from the rest of the force. However, that all changed once we went into the live-fire scenario. For our relationship, the live-fire portion was a turning point.

Transitioning between the simulated scenario environments to the live-fire scenario takes about a day because the Army training units must relocate and drive multiple military convoys along the Louisiana backcountry roads. Most of the day I was crammed into the back of an up-armored high-mobility multipurpose wheeled vehicle (HMMWV) with all my body armor and equipment on. The seats were designed for someone at least four inches shorter than me and not wearing any military equipment. Any chance I had to get out and stretch my legs and back I took advantage of it. Traffic flow on these small backcountry roads was harrowing for all involved, and adding to that displeasure, we were required to take our weapons off all of the vehicles we were transporting. I guess the local parish authorities in Louisiana didn't like the Army roaming around with large machine guns pointed in all directions.

We began to build credibility and "value-added" with the 1-23 IN when we arrived at the designated assembly area for the live fire. Upon arriving I saw many of 1-23 IN's support vehicles lined up like they were in a motor pool back in JBLM and infantry Stryker vehicles parked as if they were at a range. *Something isn't right,* I thought. In a tactical environment, units spread out their vehicles and camouflage their people to prevent enemy observation. After my vehicle parked, Cmd. Sgt. Maj. Overway and I walked over to the nearest group of 1-23 IN Strykers to find their SFAB counterparts. It happened to be CAT 5120, Maj. Wallgren and 1st Sgt. Workman. Their SFAB vehicles were tucked into the tree line about thirty to forty meters away from their counterparts, spread out but close enough for the mounted weapons to provide all-around security. I asked 1st Sgt. Workman what was going on. He told me he had explained to the 1-23 IN company commander to get his vehicles into a tactical formation, but he didn't listen. "Sir," Workman said, "we're going to get hit with artillery here real soon." I agreed and our MATs and CATs were reporting the same thing to the 1st Battalion TOC. It was clear 1-23 IN had decided to turn the vast fields into a bivouac area instead of a tactical assembly area. Hearing the whistling sound of artillery simulators is the worst thing you can hear at a CTC. It makes your skin crawl and puts a knot immediately into your stomach. Usually the results are treating simulated casualties, moving, and distracting from the mission you're trying to plan. We recommended 1-23 IN adjust their perimeter, but unfortunately, Lt. Col. Lyons and his leadership dismissed our recommendation and continued to focus on issuing the live-fire order to their leaders. As we predicted, the whistling artillery simulators started dropping all over the place late in the night. After a night of minimal sleep, the 1-23 IN adjusted their perimeter again when the sun rose. It was a case of "I told you so," but we felt it was a step in the right direction with our relationship.

For this particular live fire, in reality 1-23 IN Tomahawks could execute it with or without SFAB Brown Berets hanging around. Consequently, to force the Tomahawks to include the SFAB in their plan, we were given control of all the air assets, including attack helicopters, intelligence, surveillance, and reconnaissance systems, and attack F-16s. Using these capabilities in the live fire makes it more realistic and frankly more exciting. Having the SFAB control these enabling air assets also best simulated how the United States might support a partner or allied force in the Indo-Pacific during a conflict. Like any unit at a CTC, the Tomahawks struggled with planning and synchronizing everything in a time-constrained environment with JRTC O/C-Ts all over the place controlling, or altering, the scenario. After the assembly area fiasco and being hit with simulated artillery fire, the 1-23 IN started realizing they could use our help after they executed their first blank run for the live-fire exercise. During the blank run, as I watched my CATs and MATs move about the live-fire complex on my map screen and listened to the radio, it was clear to me the whole affair was not synchronized. The blank run felt like I was hearing the orchestra or symphony during the warm-ups before the concert. All the parts and talent were there, but sections and individuals were doing their own thing. It was noise, not music. What we needed to do was help make sure 1-23 IN units and assets were moving and firing at the right times. The most important thing we got 1-23 IN to do was conduct a detailed rehearsal of their attack on a terrain model. For most military folks this is a no-brainer. However, it was the linchpin that was needed to synchronize all the moving pieces. When you are in the fight you cannot always see all of the moving pieces. Therefore, observers can help determine what is missing. The same thing happens with coaches watching a football or basketball game. They look at the whole picture, whereas the athletes sometimes get tunnel vision. The same happened with 1-23 IN Tomahawks. They had tunnel vision and didn't see the need for the rehearsal. We were able to help get the Tomahawks back on track with simple coaching and advising from the platoon, to company, to battalion level.

This relational turning point physically manifested itself at the battalion level, with me and the SFAB battalion staff being allowed access into the Tomahawk TOC tent, something we previously hadn't any access to. During the live fire, Sfc. Eric Zacherson, our fire support NCO, sat in the 1-23 IN TOC with a radio to communicate directly with the AH-64 Apache attack helicopters to provide close air support to Lt. Col. Lyons's companies and platoon as they executed the live fire. The smile on Sfc. Zacherson's face when I saw him following the live fire said it all. He was happy to provide precision support inside the TOC and was even a little chattier than usual. I also saw Captains Josh MacKenzie, Josh Henry, and Jeff Lockwood hunched over the same maps their counterparts were using inside the stuffy tent. By then we all had a little body odor, but it didn't matter because we were working side by side. Collaborating in this way allowed us to start working closely with the 1-23 IN battalion staff and anticipate the next fight back down south in the simulated JRTC scenario environment, which was occurring concurrently as the live fire. Simultaneously fighting and planning future operations is something all units struggle with. Lt. Col. Lyons realized the SFAB staff and company commanders could serve as an extension to his staff to think through his unit's problems. We couldn't do all the work for them, but we could ask the right questions and call our brigade headquarters to see what 1-2 SBCT headquarters was considering. It was at this point that 1/5 SFAB and 1-23 IN started to work together as a team. We still had much to learn, but I was happy with the breakthrough.

After successfully executing the live fire, both battalions drove back south and ended up in a gravel parking lot-like holding area for almost twenty-four hours. Normally the gravel lot is used as a short safety pause to ensure units transition and don't have live bullets going into the simulated environment. However, we were held there longer because COVID had struck in the Tomahawk battalion and some of those in the Ghost Brigade. At this point, many of us thought that the whole rotation was in jeopardy due to the rising COVID cases. Thankfully all the 1/5 SFAB Brown Berets had kept themselves safe and didn't have to quarantine. The Tomahawks however were losing whole platoons. In fact, it was during the next phase of the operation that we decided Capt. Oleg Sheynfeld and Sfc. Peno from MAT 5132 should disengage with their assigned partners with 1-23 IN's B Company platoon and instead work with the battalion's scout platoon because the B Company infantry platoon was reduced to just a handful of healthy soldiers. We knew we couldn't adhere to the rigid decisions made weeks earlier and needed to adapt to the changing conditions, so we could meet our training requirements. The short pause and COVID concerns took a little of the enthusiasm and momentum we had built toward the end of the live fire away. It also hit our 1-23 IN partners as well. As Cmd. Sgt. Maj. Overway, 1st Sgt. Keen, and 1st Sgt. Workman and I were standing around one of our vehicles eating when one of them nodded and made a comment about some of the Tomahawk soldiers walking back and forth from the tree line to the long line of portable toilets. The soldiers slightly dragged their feet as they walked, helmets crooked on their heads, and their uniforms showing the wear of over a week of continuous use in the field. They commented that based on their experience and observations, the 1-23 IN soldiers were getting physically and mentally tired. It would take a lot of energy on our part to push or pull them through the final phase of the training rotation. As fate would have it, these seasoned SFAB NCOs were right.

By, With, Through . . . and Sometimes For

We were about to enter the final phase of the JRTC rotation, full scale fighting on the defense and offense. We had gained a better understanding of our counterparts in 1-23 IN through the counterinsurgency and competition phase of the fighting and started to build a much better relationship with them during the live fire. However, everyone was feeling the stress and strain of the rotation, and the Brown Berets were no different. We were all tired, concerned about COVID, and anxious about the next phase of the fight. However, this was our certification rotation and we wanted to demonstrate not only to our counterparts but to FORSCOM and the larger US Army that the SFAB concept would work in partnered large-scale combat operations. We were still motivated, but we could see our partners starting to wane. It wasn't their CTC rotation and they still saw themselves as our training aides and not quite our partners. We wanted to finish strong but also knew our biggest challenges likely still lay ahead of us. We were called upon to do even more for our partners.

The Special Forces often use the motto By, With, and Through when describing working with partner forces during a fight to achieve desired effects against an enemy force. The Special Forces advancing with the Northern Alliance in Afghanistan during the initial invasion phase of Operation Enduring Freedom presents an excellent example of working with and through a partner force to accomplish a goal. The SF used the air power available to them, intelligence, and logistics to arm the Northern Alliance, which eventually defeated the Taliban. The SF used a foreign partner with the majority of the manpower to fight and defeat a common enemy. The conventional US Army adopted the By, With, and Through operational approach across the Middle East.[40] We used Afghan National Security Forces to fight against the Taliban and Al Qaeda. I didn't realize it, but I had used the concept previously during my own deployments to Afghanistan and Iraq.

While I was in Iraq from 2018–2019 as a squadron (battalion) commander, Lieutenant General Paul LaCamera took command of the combined joint task force in charge of Operation Inherent Resolve. He understood that we needed to do more than just By, With, and Through with our Iraqi and Kurdish partners if we wanted to defeat ISIS. He expanded the motto to read By, With, Through, and Sometimes For during his initial engagements with his subordinate commanders in Iraq and Syria. A National Geographic special on Colonel Pat Work's brigade fighting alongside their Iraqi and Kurdish counterparts demonstrates a little of the "for" aspect that then Lt. Gen. LaCamera mentioned.[41,42] I don't know if he took that addition from somewhere else, but when he said the phrase, it was the first time I had heard it. Sometimes we needed to do the backside planning, synchronizing, and intelligence work for our Iraqi and Kurdish counterparts to make them successful in defeating a common enemy. We talked about this expanded concept back at our home station in Washington when discussing how to implement the SFAB's advise, support, liaise, assess (ASLA) concept in the Indo-Pacific. In the final phase of our JRTC rotation in the swamps of Louisiana we had the opportunity to apply that adage it in practical terms. We wanted to "win" against the OPFOR and sometimes our Brown Berets had to do some things *for* our 1-23 IN counterparts in order to make that happen. I can specifically recall this occurring twice during the last phase of the rotation.

Part of transitioning to defense in the scenario for the 5th SFAB and 1-2 SBCT was to determine how to array the friendly forces against our attacking enemy. Brig. Gen. Taylor tried to walk the 1-2 SBCT commander through a variety of options and possibilities prior to making a final decision. Based on my conversations with Brig. Gen. Taylor, he was trying to focus on the array of forces with enough flexibility to meet the enemy should they take one of the two main axes of attack and requested division- or corps-level assets to find and strike the enemy before they were able to engage us. Maj. Scott Orr, our operations officer and Capt. Pete Smith, our battalion logistics officer, were thinking about crossing points, synchronizing digging assets, and caching ammunition and Class IV (engineering materials). The two types of Class IV we needed were materials like pickets, barbed wire, and concertina wire to help construct obstacles, and plywood, sandbags, and extra shovels and pickaxes to use in creating protective cover for equipment and troops. Usually in US doctrine, a defending unit should be able to fight off a unit three times its size; this is called the 3:1 ratio. The Army had a similar calculation for determining attack ratios.

Because of the ratio difference, the defending unit must stockpile ammunition and request barrier material, medical supplies, and fuel, to name a few needed resources. The most challenging part of the defense is anticipating the enemy's avenue of advance and specific routes they will use to attack you. There was a swampy crossing point in Fort Polk that 1st Platoon, C Company, 1-23 IN, and their advisor team, MAT 5131 had selected for such a route.

Businesses undergo a similar process when planning. They begin with defining the problem, then move into data collection and analysis, add any recommendations, and finally implement the plan. It is during the definition of the problem phase that they perform a feasibility assessment that includes a situational analysis, collect any supporting logic, and formulate an estimation of cost in terms of resources required. Part of the plan is to set your objectives or goals and determine what constraints you might face or could require modification. While defining your assumptions and collecting any pertinent data, you also need to analyze any alternatives or other options, in this instance, the calculations for attacking, etc. Simulations help teams to optimize their performance, both on and off the battlefield.

As the commander, I couldn't move about the battlefield as easily or as quickly as the O/C-Ts, but I still wanted to get a sense of how some of my team leaders and assistant team leaders were doing. I needed to fill in some knowledge and personality gaps from our Yakima training, so I asked Lieutenant Colonel Russ Wagner, my O/C-T, to use his well-established network of O/C-Ts to provide me and Cmd. Sgt. Maj. Overway any feedback. We had missed personality clashes and some team internal dynamics that had manifested themselves in the RUBA, and I didn't want to make that mistake again. I also wanted a candid assessment of my SFAB teams so that I understood their strengths and weaknesses and any training gaps I might have failed to anticipate over the previous six months.

A bit later Lt. Col. Wagner came to us and provided some observations of Capt. Matt Thimble and Sfc. Dougherty from MAT 5131. The team members, including Capt. Thimble and Sfc. Dougherty, were personally continuing to find and emplace obstacle material well into the night before the OPFOR attack. In the defense, emplacing obstacles is critical to delay or stop an enemy advance so you can defeat or disrupt their attack. At the same time the Brown Berets scrambled to help make their position stronger and more defensible, the rest of his partner platoon rotated through rest, local patrols, and guard watch to maintain security. Apparently, Capt. Thimble scrounged and located additional concertina wire leftover from some previous rotation and placed it on the bridge crossing in their sector. All the Brown Berets were actively working with members of the infantry platoon. They didn't just come in, make some recommendations, then leave. The Brown Berets were getting behind their partner's machine guns to verify their sight picture and that the Command Launch Unit (CLU) associated with the simulated Javelin missile functioned properly. Although we didn't get to see MAT 5121 in action with our own eyes, both Cmd. Sgt. Maj. Overway and I were quite proud that they had fully embraced the By, With, Through, and Sometimes For mentality. The MAT had bonded with their infantry platoon and earned their trust. Lt. Col. Wagner said the O/C-Ts were impressed by the entire team's commitment to establishing strong defensive positions, conducting rehearsals, and sighting the platoon's key weapons systems. The O/C-Ts further mentioned that the actions of MAT 5131 were directly responsible for stopping the OPFOR's main attack. Their comments were quite a compliment, especially coming from O/C-Ts who see ten or more rotations a year.

Once the OPFOR had culminated in their attack against our defenses, it was now our turn to go on the attack. We regrouped and set our sights on breaking through the enemy's defenses. During the attack in the southern part of the training area, the 1-2 SBCT conducted a combined arms breach through a low-water crossing point, a complicated offensive operation designed to open pathways through an enemy's obstacles then fight the enemy on the opposite side. There is an art and science to making sure all the specialized equipment is prepped, leaders are briefed, and the operation is well-rehearsed. The concept was to move A Company, 1-23 IN through dense terrain and secure the far side of the estimated breach point. Once complete, their B Company and engineers from the 1-2 SBCT engineer company would actually breach the obstacles, reduce them to permit people and vehicles to pass, and allow their C Company to pass through and continue the battalion's attack. While simple in concept, the enemy (OPFOR), the terrain, and internal synchronization could all impact the result in this contested environment.

While the initial phases of the attack went well, A Company and the Brown Berets that accompanied them failed to secure all the positions on the far side of the crossing point. As I heard reports come in over the radio, I knew the situation was not promising. The 1/5 SFAB CATs and MATs fed all that detailed information to me at my command vehicle, forward positioned with the units and my tactical operations center, located several kilometers to the rear of the fighting. Our robust communications package served the Brown Berets well, providing critical information and helping us understand what was actually going on in real time. I shuffled back and forth between my command HMMWV and Lt. Col. Lyons's command Stryker vehicle, giving him detailed updates, recommendations, and helping to bring clarity during the chaos. At one point, Cmd. Sgt. Maj. Overway controlled AH-64 helicopters over our vehicle's radio to press the enemy and buy our partners time. Meanwhile I tried to assess the combat power remaining of 1-23 IN's companies and platoons and understand the status of 1-2 SBCT's engineers and artillery units. Unfortunately, at that point the attack began to stall because the engineer breaching assets were not synchronized with the infantry advancing along a single route to the breach point. Because of this mistake they were left exposed and were continually hit by simulated indirect fire and enemy air attacks. The distinct sound of enemy helicopters overhead was nerve-racking. I was also confused because I did not know whether Lt. Col. Lyons or the engineer battalion commander was in charge of this mess. Luckily, we had some SFAB leaders positioned at critical points, specifically our B Company.

Maj. Chris Wallgren, 1st Sgt. Workman, and I talked over the radio to understand the situation and determine how to help. As

Maj. Wallgren and I spoke, I realized B company CAT and MAT leaders had just taken charge of the whole situation and were trying to gain accountability of the Tomahawk infantrymen and identify which breaching assets were still functional. Brown Beret sergeants and staff sergeants had taken charge of 1-23 IN infantrymen, placed them behind cover, returned fire, and bounded forward with them to continue the attack. They ended up pushing platoons across the bridge crossing point, moving them to cover, and physically moving the mine-clearing line charge into position to open up a lane through the enemy's mine-wire obstacle. Essentially, the Brown Berets took control of their partner's company in order to make them successful. Talking with the O/C-Ts later, who had a great vantage point, I found out that Maj. Wallgren and 1st Sgt. Workman's personal leadership and direction were the only reasons the brigade could complete the combined arms breach successfully. Those Brown Berets showed how valuable the "For" is when working with a partner force struggling at a decisive point to meet its mission. The 1-23 IN weren't able to lead through the attack, so the Brown Berets did it for them.

C Company, 1-23 IN, and Maj. Morgan Maier's CATs and MATs were in process of achieving their objectives when the follow-on attack stalled out and lost momentum. The sun was just coming up after a long night of hard work when we received the change of mission message over the radio, signaling the end of the exercise. There was a general sigh of relief from all involved parties because they had managed to survive yet another CTC rotation. Just like the end of any exercise, we needed to account for all the personnel and equipment used in the fight. This can be a confusing time for some because of the aftermath of a series of adrenaline rushes and the hurried nature during the simulated combat. But we had to ensure we had accounted for everyone and everything we had come into the box with. With no time to waste, we moved to the large assembly areas and waited for further instructions. People, vehicles, equipment, companies, platoons, CATs, and MATs started to slowly appear in the large grassy area in the middle of the Louisiana pines. We also needed to wish everyone our sincerest Happy Thanksgiving!

On Thanksgiving Day 2020, Ghost Brigade and 5th SFAB members, (we were known as the Vanguard Brigade), shared a Thanksgiving meal underneath some pine trees or in the open area. Most of the Brown Berets ate with their own teammates and talked about the mission. They soon drifted back to their vehicles staged in long columns ready to drive back to the RUBA the following day. As Cmd. Sgt. Maj. Overway and I mingled with our Brown Berets and wandered between their vehicles, we could see SFAB team equipment scattered all over the ground. Young NCOs in their brown T-shirts were cleaning weapons, coiling communications cables, and accounting for their equipment parts. I was proud to see them doing exactly what they needed to do following a mission, recover their equipment. Normally the recovery process is driven by the battalion or brigade headquarters after a CTC, typically by the commander or XO. I came to find out 1st Sergeants Lane, Keen, Workman, and Bochmann had all determined the priorities of work after we finished the last attack and got their Brown Berets moving in the right direction. In the SFAB I was happy to see the whole process was driven by the NCOs.

Thanksgiving night we had a light rain and the following morning the SFAB leaders moved back to the containment area to begin a series of professional after-action reports, during which we discussed what went well during the rotation, what we could have done better, and what we were going to do as a brigade in the future to be a better unit. After-action reports are essential in the US Army because they help make leaders and the entire organization much better; they are a cornerstone of our training process. Unfortunately, 1-2 SBCT was not included in this discussion because they were not the training audience. I find this a bit remiss because everyone who participated in the training exercises could have benefited from this process to help them become better soldiers and units.

Our completed JRTC rotation tested a training concept in which FORSCOM certified an SFAB and trained an Army BCT at the same time. Combining the certification and training of two significant units at a CTC had never been done before. Our Brown Berets on the ground were the individuals problem-solving and gritting it out to make the concept happen. The way the Army saw it, this was a two-for-one. This approach is similar to how a grocery store like Kroger tests concepts of the shopping experience in small stores before expanding. They also execute a two-phase approach where they roll out a new product and evaluate buyers' opinions about the products. Based on our performance at the rotation, FORSCOM planned to use this model again to train other Army BCTs and certify SFABs. It generally served their purpose, but 1-2 SBCT seemed to be somewhat disengaged because they felt like a training aid instead of a valuable asset for learning. In retrospect, we needed to include them more in the process so they could see how to reap the rewards of increased training efficiency and benefits of becoming a better unit after this rotation. Businesses do this by engaging via open communication between all levels of stakeholders inside and outside of their organization, known as stakeholder buy-in. The benefits of doing things this way is that the higher ups can visualize new ideas and generate new opinions that can in turn shape the organizational structure by driving long-term growth and profitability. The Army, in many ways, is not that different. I think if 1-2 SBCT had been more involved in LTP, had been evaluated by O/C-Ts during the rotation, and had participated in the after-action report process, it would have changed their mindset. Regardless of 1-2 SBCT's opinions on this training, it was my belief that they did gain some valuable tools that they could execute afterward.

During the rotation we had learned our strengths and weaknesses, shortcomings in our training preparation, and lessons in relationship building. All valuable insights. However, as we discussed these important points in detail with our OC/C-Ts, I found my thoughts drifting to the Indo-Pacific. The Indo-Pacific became the real priority of the 1st Battalion Brown Berets as soon as the change of mission call had come over the radio. As soon as we could turn phones back on and boot computers back up, the officers had their first opportunity to see what information they had missed over the fifteen days of being in the box and in their communications blackout window. In many cases, we were still eagerly awaiting responses from DATs and foreign militaries to see which, if any, of our SFAB advisor teams had the approval to depart in January as planned. It was now the end of November, which did not leave us a lot of time to recover and prepare to deploy during our departure window in January.

Our planning estimate for the timing of 5th SFAB's inaugural deployment into the Indo-Pacific determined that teams would need to be ready to depart as early as the end of January. The January planning factor meant the 5th SFAB headquarters prioritized 1st Battalion to move all our people and equipment back to JBLM to recover it and pack the equipment into containers for transport across the Pacific Ocean via ship. We were happy to move to the front of the line for much of the recovery at Fort Polk and even happier to get back to our families after missing Thanksgiving. However, even the best of plans can go awry, and the one thing we did not plan on confronting was COVID's continued impact on the world. We would find out later that we did not need to rush because there were huge entry issues with the pandemic looming large across the world in January of 2021.

The Hardest Places

Finishing the 5th SFAB's JRTC ended our dual work. We no longer had to think about the looming FORSCOM-directed training event and could focus on USARPAC and INDOPACOM's missions. However, even after completing JRTC, we still had many unknowns to work through to get SFAB teams into any Indo-Pacific countries. Concrete departure dates were still not set, some teams didn't have any agreements with their assigned country's partner force, and COVID kept many travel aspects temporarily irresolvable. Before JRTC we had established assignments and organizational processes to squeeze out as much uncertainty as possible. With a few of the countries we experienced the emotional extreme peaks and valleys of progress. Grit, I think, had pulled us through.

Earlier, we attempted to bring order to the imposing problem when looking at the large map of the Indo-Pacific by assigning parts of the region company by company just before departing for Yakima in the fall of 2020. Assigning specific areas helped with coordination, decentralization, and general ease of supervision. We wanted to quickly raise the level of internal support for our engagements, if necessary. For instance, if a captain team leader could not get through to a defense attaché office staff officer, usually a foreign area officer major, then our experienced company commanders, also majors, could get involved. If that didn't work, I could talk with the Army attaché or the defense attaché, who usually had an equivalent rank or one slightly senior to mine. If that didn't work, then we asked Brig. Gen. Taylor for some help. One company needed more help than we anticipated, which surprised me and Brig. Gen. Taylor.

We assigned Maj. Morgan Maier's C Company Southeast Asia, including Thailand, Indonesia, Brunei, Malaysia, Vietnam, Burma, and Japan. Later their assigned engineer team would add Fiji to the list. With most of these countries, we believed there were long-standing, good military-to-military relationships that provided some momentum for SFAB teams to get into the country. We had already worked with both the Thai and Indonesian armies in the last few months. We assigned C Company to these areas because C Company had still been receiving new personnel right up until the start of the JRTC rotation in November and was slightly behind the other two companies in terms of unit building, equipment reception, and training.[43] Therefore we assumed assigning them the "easy" region in terms of rapport building and coordination requirements made sense.

C Company had a lot to do. They were tasked with integrating new people, training, and then retraining on SFAB-specific tasks, as well as receiving new equipment for their mission. I recall meandering up to the third floor of our battalion headquarters to stretch my legs and talk to the Brown Berets at some point before we left for JRTC and popping into Maj. Maier's office. I asked him how things were going, and he spouted back in his monotonous and sarcastic voice that everything was fine—no challenges, just his company still had empty positions he needed to fill and the people he did have were scattered to the four winds attending training. Lots of work to accomplish with not enough people. Oh, and the USARPAC and embassy staff officers were ignoring his emails and probably listed him as a blocked sender. Everything was running smooth. I laughed and proceeded to talk about how his glass of problems was in actuality half full and what I could do to help. In all honesty, we had expected C Company to get easy entry into their assigned countries because we thought they had less convincing to do to achieve this goal. However, we were mistaken in that assumption. C Company experienced some of the most difficult obstacles for entry into their assigned countries than nearly any of our other teams. At the top of the list was Malaysia. We put a lot of time, thought, and effort into the Malaysian mission and didn't get it off the ground. It was a failure that caused us significant work as we attempted to pivot the team intended for Malaysia to other missions and opportunities.

The US Army had been in Malaysia on routine engagements with the Malaysian Army in recent years. These exercises included the upcoming KERIS STRIKE and BERSAMA WARRIOR series in 2021, which the 5th SFAB expected to support in some capacity.[44,45] Capt. Matt Thimble, Maj. Morgan Maier, and I were convinced that Matt's team would eventually go to Malaysia to work and train with the Malaysian Army. The Malaysian Army was clearly open to working with the US Army and other services and had some common bonds already established because of these relationships. The British had ruled or had significant control of Malaysia from 1824 to 1963. The British-Malaysian model for fighting a counterinsurgency fight was frequently referenced in US Army writing during the Iraq and Afghan wars. We believed that this was a natural fit.

Most of our briefs with the defense attaché office and offices of defense cooperation in the embassies were neutral, at least in the beginning. We thought we could turn somewhat of a lukewarm reception to our favor. We endeavored to explain our new organization and what we were capable of. Maj. Maier and Capt. Thimble maintained an open and running dialogue with the embassy throughout the fall of 2020. Over time, and with a concerted effort, we were able to convince the Malaysian Office of Defense Cooperation (ODC) office that we had some common interests and by Brown Berets working with the Malaysian Army we could achieve some of their Integrated Country Strategy goals.[46] We don't know what the tipping point was, but I'm convinced it was simply our persistence and continued reference to historical bilateral exercises between our two armies. We kept "assuming the yes" would eventually come, and MAT 5131 would go to Malaysia. Our hard work and dedication paid off about the time we were in Louisiana and the Malaysian ODC finally told us that they would support an SFAB advisor team coming to Kuala Lumpur. Both we and the Malaysian ODC office expected the Malaysian Army would agree to the endeavor. It was only a formality given the favorable prior engagements between the two armies. We were elated that this venture looked promising. I felt a little relieved and emotionally felt we were on the verge of a win by the agreement.

We held out hope that because of our ability to demonstrate how we operated in Thailand the previous summer, even with COVID looming, we would get the green light to proceed. During one of those late-night video telephone conferences, we discussed in detail the medical protocols followed before departure to Thailand, procedures taken while working with the Royal Thai Army, and training accomplished during our short time there. I felt at this point that a contract was finalized, the pens were on the table, and all parties were on the verge of signing. As fate would have it, the defense attaché office never quite got an affirmative response from the Malaysian Army and then in December of 2020 everything was canceled due to COVID gaining momentum across the globe. For the Malaysian Army that meant canceling all their major exercises, including KERIS STRIKE and BERSAMA WARRIOR. We were back to our emotional low. We attempted a Hail Mary pass by proposing a virtual staff-to-staff exercise. Major Ian MacGregor from 2nd Battalion, 5th SFAB (CAT 5120) had done a similar exercise with the Indonesian Army in September 2020. Maj. MacGregor's team members went on an off-cycle workday at JBLM to align their day with the 1st Division Kostrad, located in Indonesia. The two-week event served as part of stop-gap measure for the Garuda Shield exercise that year since most of the in-person military-to-military engagements between the US and Indonesia had been canceled. It seemed like a good model Capt. Thimble could follow with the Malaysians. After discussing this with the Malaysian defense attaché office team, we nervously waited for a response as they pitched the idea to the Malaysian Army. I can't verify it, but I'm sure even the stoic Maj. Maier hit the refresh button on his email frequently late at night in Washington State hoping for a response from across the Pacific Ocean. To our dismay, a response finally came in the negative. This came before our unit's Christmas leave break. It felt like getting a stocking filled with coal. Now what?

The COVID crisis had brought so much uncertainty to our team and our mission. It was an emotional roller coaster as Capt. Thimble and Sfc. Doughtery's MAT tried to determine which country might give us a chance and when that might be possible. For this particular team, as December transitioned to January, they remained in limbo. I felt their frustration when on the halls of the battalion's third floor. The NCOs from the team would tell me they didn't know which country's culture or history to study as part of their preparation. Learning brief pleasantry phrases like "hello," "please," or "thank you" was out of the question because Southeast Asian languages are so different. They couldn't hide the look of disappointment from their faces. Normally wandering the hallways and talking with the Brown Berets gave me energy and revitalized my efforts. However, talking with MAT 5131 did the opposite. I would go back to my office and slump down in my chair and stare at a map of the Indo-Pacific. My eyes would wander from country to country on the map and mentally review all the correspondence regarding that country. Options, opportunities, or openings? Had we missed something? Was there somewhere we could send this team to meet the USARPAC and INDOPACOM commander's intent and fulfill the obligation Cmd. Sgt. Maj. Overway and I felt to provide an opportunity for all our Brown Berets to deploy and work with a foreign partner force? What doors could we open? Staring at the ceiling and pacing around my office didn't help. I looked back at the map. My eyes roamed from Indonesia, to Singapore, up the Malay Peninsula, then settled back on Thailand.

We could send this unassigned team to Thailand. Shifting efforts to send Matt's team into Thailand made sense to us because we were already planning to send Capt. Brenton Clark and Sfc. Emmanuel Moore from MAT 5133 and Maj. Morgan Maier and 1st Sgt. Bochmann's CAT 5130 there. The RTA was extremely pleased with our recent partnership with them in August 2020 and were happy with the RTA composite company's participation with MAT 5113 at JRTC. When our battalion headquarters and the rest of the SFAB teams left in August 2020, the RTA hoped we would send the same number of teams back to Thailand, if not more. Sending the same number from our August 2020 mission was untenable due to the other priority missions throughout INDOPACOM—but maybe we could send a third.

In speaking with the foreign area officer who was working with us from the Joint US Military Advisory Group (JUSMAGTHAI) and defense attaché office, the addition of another team was doable.[47] However, the COVID situation still presented all sorts of issues for the Thailand mission, as well as others around the world. Col. Wayne Turnbull, the defense attaché and JUSMAGTHAI chief, was focused on getting an airborne jumpmaster predeployment site-survey team from the 82nd Airborne Division into Thailand in preparation for the large exercise during the summer of 2021. The large exercise was to include a large contingent of paratroopers dropping into Thailand. It was critical due to safety requirements for 82nd Airborne Division jumpmasters to survey the intended drop zones for the exercise's parachute jump. Col. Turnbull was hesitant to ask the RTA and Royal Thai Government for any more exceptions to country entry on behalf of the US military, so he didn't want to ask permission for any of the SFAB teams. We assumed that because there was a huge number of US military already coming over as part of this exercise that our SFAB teams could somehow get in-country too.

Eventually after some repeated requests, Col. Turnbull agreed to ask for permission for just one twelve-person team, Capt. Brenton Clark and Sfc. Moore's MAT 5133. When I talked with him he said, "Well, maybe I could bring them into country if I tell the RTA that they are coming to work for me in the JUSTMAGTHAI." I cringed when I heard him say that. I recalled our introduction the previous summer when he had showed me around the JUSMAGTHAI compound like a used car salesman trying to woo an unsuspecting buyer; it had made me feel like there were ulterior motives beneath the surface. Something didn't seem right at this point, either, and I felt he was using his influence to build a small fiefdom in Thailand by increasing his staffing capacity while demonstrating personal significance with the RTA. I discussed this dilemma with Brig. Gen. Taylor. If we said yes, we may lose some operational control of our team, which was outside Maj. Gen. Jackson's, the SFAC commander's, intent. SFAB teams were to remain separate and distinct from embassy work. If we said no, then we would need to go back to the drawing board and have three teams without missions. Brig. Gen. Taylor decided to call Col. Turnbull to get a sense of the situation. After their discussion, Brig. Gen. Taylor came away with the same feelings I had that something just didn't seem right. Still, we felt that we could agree up front to Col. Turnbull's conditions but also knew that once the RTA learned an SFAB team was in-country, they would work to get the Brown Berets to a tactical RTA unit—exactly where they needed to be. Therefore, we decided to move ahead with planning for the team to go to Thailand. This meant we needed to prepare visas and the newly required COVID paperwork that the Royal Thai Government now required to be presented to their COVID Response Task Force. All of this paperwork had to be approved before we were able to enter their country. COVID had again added another layer of bureaucracy to the entire process. What was most striking to me was the fact that we had to work so hard and had so many misgivings working with fellow US military officers. In retrospect I realized that our unit didn't have the requisite foreign country experiences, understanding of how embassies and attaché offices work, the inter-military politics of the attaché world, nor the considerable reputation to fall back on like our Special Forces brethren. We had much to learn.

Since we'd had such difficulties with Malaysia and Thailand, Capt. Thimble and Sfc. Dougherty's team felt that Indonesia might be a viable option. After discussing the possibilities with other 1st Battalion leadership, I agreed. We would take a shot there. Capt. LeShaun Smith and his MAT 5132 team had worked on Brunei and Indonesia as conceivable missions. We eliminated Brunei from the list due to COVID travel restrictions, the exercise planning issues we faced, and the capacity of the Brunei defense forces to absorb another nation trying to conduct bilateral training with them. In Indonesia, Colonel Ian Francis, the office of defense cooperation chief, and Major Matt Gross, his deputy, were great supporters of the SFAB. Their enthusiasm emanated in part from Gen. Andika, the Indonesian Army chief of staff, who had been extremely happy with the October 2020 JRTC rotation in which 2nd Battalion, 5th SFAB provided an SFAB team to partner with an Indonesian infantry company just like our MAT 5113 did with the RTA. We didn't think adding a second SFAB team to the list would be a problem. Prospects seemed encouraging, or at least so we thought.

In our estimation, we had strong support from the US military folks in the Indonesia Embassy, a willing partner force (Indonesian military), and the bureaucratic backing of the USARPAC desk officers to send both MAT 5132 and MAT 5131 to Indonesia. We thought our problems were solved.

We were wrong.

Even with all the military support behind our proposal, we found just getting one team into the country ended up being a challenge in itself. The next lesson we learned as we attempted to achieve INDOPACOM objectives in foreign countries was that the Department of State gets a vote on our activities, and it had veto power. The acting US ambassador to Indonesia, the charge de affairs, and her inner circle had different thoughts entirely about US military partnerships in the country. Unfortunately for 5th SFAB, Ambassador Sung Y. Kim, a career US diplomat with experience involving military operations in places like South Korea and the Philippines, was called back to Washington DC by the newly elected Biden administration to serve as the acting assistant secretary of state for East Asian and Pacific Affairs in Foggy Bottom, Washington, DC. The Indonesian charge de affairs became very risk averse with regard to allowing nonpermanent-party military into Indonesia for a variety of reasons, some of which included COVID rates in Indonesia, unrelated deaths in the Indonesian Embassy staff, and the medical evacuations of US military personnel from other countries. Right around the time we were working on getting our MAT into Indonesia, a nonpermanent US military person required an emergency medical evacuation from a nearby country. Based on the limited information we received about the incident, the evacuation experienced some delays and bureaucratic hurdles due to poor medical planning. The result was that the charge de affairs in Indonesia lost trust in the military to conduct proper medical planning and became reluctant to allow nonpermanent military personnel into Indonesia, potentially even those preparing for large-scale military-to-military exercises. It caused us to relook at our medical plans and provide Col. Francis details on our plans that we would not have otherwise done, so he could help alleviate the Indonesian charge de affair's concerns.

One late evening in February 2021, Col. Ian Francis called me. I had hoped for good news since Col. Francis had been such an advocate and tried every avenue to work the internal politics of the US Embassy in Indonesia. Over previous emails and phone calls we had brainstormed ideas together to figure out how to navigate resistance and the naysayers in the embassy.

"Hey Ian, how's it going?" I said happily when we made our connection. By this time, I had been promoted to colonel and could call him by his first name rather than "sir," as dictated by military protocol.

"Hi Dave, how are you," he replied in a tone that wasn't as chipper as his normal demeanor. I felt unwanted news was coming so I braced myself. "It's not going to happen," he said.

He told me that it was unlikely that more than one SFAB team would be able to come to Indonesia and that neither Capt. Matt Thimble's MAT 5131 nor Maj. Morgan Maier's CAT 5130 would be able to make it during our employment window (January–June). My heart sank and I let out a long sigh as I sat on the couch in my JBLM sunporch. "Ok, Ian, I understand," I finally replied. By now, we clearly understood that the State Department controlled what military forces came into countries outside a declared theater of active armed conflict. This was very different from the Army's previous experiences in CENTCOM and Iraq and Afghanistan. It was disheartening to hear for everyone. The search for missions continued. Trying to meet the INDOPACOM objectives with a new Army unit was much harder and more frustrating than I had ever anticipated. Attempting to explain to Amy after such a phone call the challenges we were facing was a little therapeutic. However, as I talked it out, it also highlighted our dilemma of having an assigned military mission but ironically not being able to meet it due to a lack of support inside the US government with a relatively unknown and unproven unit.

There were other reasons we worked so hard to find SFAB teams missions across the Indo-Pacific. Of course, our number-one job was to get SFAB teams into the places that USARPAC and INDOPACOM needed them most. We sought missions based on their strategic impact and guidance. By January 2021 we had secured missions for fourteen of the eighteen SFAB teams assigned to 1st Battalion for our deployment window, all of which were in some stage of final planning. The locations included Mongolia, India, the Maldives, Bangladesh (which got canceled later), the Philippines, Indonesia, and Thailand. The second reason was internally focused, command related, and was more personal because it meant fulfilling the obligations made to every Brown Beret in the formation. Our volunteers came to the 5th SFAB with the understanding that each person would receive some sort of advanced training in their specialty and that they would have the opportunity to deploy to a foreign country and work with allies or partner forces. The Army and the unit controlled the training and schooling commitment. Achieving the advanced training commitment wasn't easy but our senior NCOs like Cmd. Sgt. Maj. Overway understood the Army schooling system that made it possible. Securing the overseas deployments on such a large scale was uncharted territory for all of us. Leaders worked hard to fulfill foreign country experience to maintain the trust with our Brown Berets who had taken a risk joining our speculative unit. Sadly, we were learning fast that deploying teams into foreign countries was dependent upon many other factors besides mission and training.

Our only goal was simple—get into Thailand and train with the RTA. We later learned through other contacts that the RTA senior leadership had not imposed any restrictions on the number of SFAB teams for partnership training. In fact, they wanted as many as possible and as much training as we could expend. The RTA was happy to accommodate another SFAB MAT. Our RTA contacts were flabbergasted as to why there were any barriers to entry on the number of Brown Berets. This information confirmed what we already suspected—Col. Turnbull had fabricated the restrictions for some reason. With this newfound information, Maj. Maier sprung back into action. He reconnected with the FAO staff officer at JUSMAGTHAI in March 2021. The Royal Thai Army then formally requested the second team through JUSMAGTHAI. At that point, Col. Turnbull couldn't say no. This had been a win for us, yet there was a bit of tension in the weeks leading up to that decision. We finally confirmed a mission for Capt. Matt Thimble and Sfc. Doughtery's MAT 5131. They would go to Thailand and work with the RTA. By the time we found out, it was too late to also send Maj. Morgan's CAT 5130. The whole situation still surprised us.

The effort to get permission for our small US Army teams to enter a foreign country was overwhelming and something that the entire 5th SFAB did not expect. It was an ongoing negotiation and learning process on a short timeline. Businesses negotiate contracts for weeks and months before they can come to fruition, especially when it involves an overseas venture. Phil Knight's early experiences in Japan to negotiate with factories to produce the now famous Nike shoes must have been nerve-racking and emotional. His book *Shoe Dog* talks about his nervousness in trying to get those factories to make his shoes specific to his designs, as well as working out the shipping costs and delivery dates. We experienced some of the same frustrations and feelings Phil Knight did. However, we had also distributed and franchised much of the struggle.

The Brown Berets in 1st Battalion, 5th SFAB found themselves doing very similar things to the Nike entrepreneur. Not every company ran into the problems C Company did, which surprisingly required more assistance. Most of the time the Brown Berets handled the challenges themselves and only required periodic engagements by me or Brig. Gen. Taylor. Instead of factory owners or managers, team leaders like Capt. Oleg Sheynfeld and Captain Alex Lara negotiated with the Philippine Defense Attaché Office and Joint United States Military Assistance Group—Philippines (JUSMAGPHIL) on arrival dates and local life support contracting.

They also worked with JBLM's Installation Transportation Division and eventually freight companies to determine shipping dates for equipment and transportation costs from the port of entry to the training destination, coordination and negotiations many of them had never done before but they were determined to achieve their mission. The team leaders and assistant team leaders were empowered and comfortable with learning their way through these procedures. The Army agencies on the other side of the negotiating table were usually not. The Army agencies were accustomed to working with senior leaders and moving hundreds of troops on predictable timelines. The SFAB enterprise didn't fit this mold, having small, agile teams independently coordinating missions. It wasn't all new, but because the SFAB was a new "start-up," everything was new for the Army agencies involved and the partner forces.

In many cases these negotiations with freight companies, defense attaché offices, and partner forces continued right up until the teams boarded their flights and even continued while in-country. There were false starts and delays due to country-entry restrictions and the pandemic. Eventually, all the Brown Berets assigned to the 1st Battalion, including our artillery, engineer, and logistics-enabler teams, made it across the IDL and into the Indo-Pacific. That was only possible because we had decentralized the work, empowered leaders, and shared information. With JRTC and Christmas in our proverbial rearview mirror, we were ready for the Brown Berets to achieve USARPAC and INDOPACOM objectives. January 2021 started a new year and was a landmark in the 5th SFAB and SFAC's story in the Indo-Pacific.

THE TRAINING CYCLE | 213

Author David Rowland pounds a tent stake while his trusting partner, First Sergeant Rich Lane, holds it as they set up their operations center at Yakima Training Center, Washington." Photo courtesy of the author.

1/5 SFAB field grade officers pose after a planning session at the Joint Readiness Training Center, Louisiana. From left to right: Trevor Rowlands (LAC 5620), Colin O'Toole (kneeling E-CAT 5510), Chris Wallgren (CAT 5120), Author David Rowland, Morgan Maier (CAT 5130), Scott Orr (1/5 operations officer, BAT 510), Dan Ludwig (CAT 5110). Not pictured AJ Vogel (1/5 executive officer, BAT 510). Photo courtesy of the author.

1/5 SFAB command teams pause for a photo at the Joint Readiness Training Center, Louisiana. Front row from left to right: Lee Sikon, Rich Lane, author, CJ Overway, Dan Ludwig, Travis Keen. Back row from left to right: Chris Wallgren, Chad Workman, Trevor Rowlands, Jovia Sutton, Morgan Maier, Duane Bochman. Photo courtesy of the author.

PART III

INTO THE INDO-PACIFIC

CHAPTER 7

Green Light!

JANUARY 2021 began 1st Battalion's six-month utilization window for operations, activities, and exercises in the Indo-Pacific. It was time for the Brown Berets to start meeting their counterparts throughout the region and building relationships on behalf of the USARPAC and INDOPACOM commanders. We had our "green light." What lay ahead included visiting Pacific tropical islands, driving through snowstorms, and carefully navigating the international political landscape. We didn't anticipate and train for all the small ankle-biter problems and foreign country domestic challenges—nor could we have. But we had cultivated an entrepreneurial mindset in our officers and NCOs to tackle such hurdles without constant supervision while using their best judgment. We were excited but knew all the agreements weren't yet in place and plenty of coordination was still necessary. Even picking January as our departure month was very unscientific and simply an educated guess.

Brig. Gen. Taylor had broached the topic of when I felt the teams would be ready for deployment into the Indo-Pacific during a phone call one day in the fall of 2020. I incorrectly assumed at that point that foreign militaries and US military embassy staff would welcome the Brown Berets with open arms. So, I made some huge assumptions and told him I believed we could be ready by the end of January of 2021 since it seemed long enough after JRTC that our honed combat and ASLA skills would still be fresh. January was also after the holiday season but still enough time we could receive, recover, and pack our equipment from our JRTC rotation. He still pushed me for an exact date. I quickly checked my Outlook calendar and scrolled through the months for a firm time we might commit. Directly after Christmas leave was not a good time because the teams needed time to get themselves together. Two weeks after that was Martin Luther King weekend and most likely Brown Berets would like to spend one last long weekend with their families prior to deployment. I then settled on the Tuesday after the MLK holiday, January 19, 2021. I relayed this date to Brig. Gen. Taylor, who said he would inform USARPAC. He also stated that the end date for our time in the Indo-Pacific was going to be June 30, 2021. June 30 became an equally important date for every 1st Battalion Brown Beret to return home. After completing the next round of training, Lt. Col. Anthony Gore and the 2nd battalion, 5th SFAB, would be in charge of the 5th SFAB's missions in the Indo-Pacific. They would start their employment rotation window in June.

After that conversation, and USARPAC's confirmation, January 19 became the planning date that drove the remainder of the conversations with defense attaché offices, offices of defense cooperation, partner forces, FORSCOM, and JBLM Installation Transportation Division. During this whole process, we learned that only a few of the teams would be leaving in January. This separation of our teams added to the emotional highs, lows, and general frustrations that come with any deployment. But even though we were on separate schedules, ultimately all of 5th SFAB would get the satisfaction of accomplishing an important strategic mission.

Teams were assigned to different countries, but not everyone could go at once, as negotiations continued for the remaining parties well past January for country entry, and they navigated the disparate and inconsistent nation-specific COVID protocols. Ultimately, January was the month we received our green light to depart Washington State and head into the Indo-Pacific. It was time to go execute our assigned missions, develop relationships, and achieve national security objectives. We were nervous, excited, and anticipative to finally be moving forward!

Getting Out the Door: Self-Motivation

The first team to leave JBLM and cross the international date line wasn't a MAT led by an infantry officer, and they weren't initially heading to work with a partner force. Instead, Logistics Advisor Team (LAT) 5612, led by Captain Alex Lara and Sergeant First Class Terrance Parrish, spearheaded 5th SFAB into the Indo-Pacific. LAT 5612 headed to South Korea to complete training before going south to the Philippines. The brigade headquarters assigned LAT 5612 to the 1st Battalion Force Package to supplement our capabilities beyond our organically assigned MATs. Since the US Army has a large footprint in South Korea dating back to the Korean War, it also stores equipment and is prepared for large-scale combat to start at just about any moment on the Korean Peninsula. The LAT knew understanding the strategic logistics requirements would help them strengthen the US-Philippines relationship via South Korea.

I had begun my own Army service in South Korea as a brand-new 2nd Lieutenant. I vividly recall jumping out of bed when the alert sirens went off right outside my barracks window and marshaling at our company area just about 100 meters away to prepare for an attack. My old unit was no longer in South Korea, but the "be ready to fight tonight" mentality was still emphasized in the units stationed there, as well as those larger Army BCTs that rotated through the country. The most significant and most crucial component of maintaining that mentality was the logistics aspect.

LAT 5612 wanted to understand what it meant to marshal large numbers of service men and women, get the combat equipment issued, and move them to fighting position prior to going to the Philippines. Maintaining equipment for immediate use requires planning, detailed scheduling, and space. While the LAT was still waiting on responses from the Philippine Army about what training they were going to do together, they knew, historically speaking, that the US Army had previously maintained large bases and depots in the Philippines. The US wanted to rekindle the strong US-Philippine military relationship and explore the potential of having depots or bases there again. The team wanted to be ready to answer any questions from the Philippine Army, should they ask about the requirements to marshal large numbers of troops or store significant equipment over a long duration. At the time, President Duerte of the Philippines was considering what to do about the Visiting Status of Forces Agreement (VFA) between the United States and the Philippines.[48] In our view, having the South Korean background information presented us with the opportunity to contribute to a renewed US-Philippine relationship at the strategic level. Capt. Lara and Sfc. Parrish identified their understanding of strategic logistics as a gap in their team's knowledge. When Capt. Lara first broached me with the idea of going to South Korea, I was a little reluctant. Why couldn't he go to a logistics hub or port in the United States? "Sir, nothing like what exists in South Korea exists in one place in the United States," he told me. Then Capt. Lara logically explained how the Korean peninsula uniquely demonstrated how to both store and maintain stock equipment and simultaneously receive additional personnel and equipment for a wartime environment. Many places in the United States have one or the other, but not both. It seemed like Capt. Lara and LAT 5612 needed to learn a little bit more before heading to the Southeast Asian Archipelago. I was convinced they should go and at the same time proud of them. They had done their mission analysis, identified a gap in their knowledge, and actively pursued a way to overcome it.

Thus, our logistics team led the way into the Indo-Pacific region, conducted a two-week quarantine at Camp Humphreys in South Korea, and then proceeded to Busan and Waegwan, major logistics hubs. LAT 5612's trip to South Korea was simple because they weren't going to train with the South Korean Army. The 8th US Army in command of US forces in South Korea considered their trip a temporary duty, which is administratively very simple and did not require visas and special approval from the South Korean government. At Busan and Waegwan, Brown Berets learned about theater-level logistics. The team watched Army field support brigade personnel issue equipment to units rotating onto the Korean Peninsula from the United States. Eyes were wide open as they viewed the rows and rows of vehicles and equipment in marshaling yards and warehouses. The Busan and Waegwan experts talked to Capt. Lara and his team about port operations, reception staging and onward integration (RSOI) operations, and care of supply in storage (COSIS) on the Peninsula. Young SFAB NCOs conversed with seasoned civilian maintainers about scheduling, ordering parts, and the skills necessary to stage equipment over a long-time horizon. It was eye-opening for the entire team, and the Army field support brigade, especially a Mr. King at the Busan Storage Center, ended up being an excellent host for the Brown Berets.

The logistics team delayed their departure from South Korea while they and MAT 5123 waited for Philippine approval of their certificate of entry. This resulted in them staying another week in South Korea. Entry into the Philippines was all a matter of the bureaucrat process and the current COVID conditions, neither of which we could control.

Many of the 1st Battalion teams experienced some sort of

waiting or delay process because of the nature of the operating environment. For many, it was a test of resiliency with sometimes little work to do. Most teams had an internal training plan for the anticipated two weeks of quarantine that had been foisted upon us at arrival into the country. It was actually a similar situation to what A Company and others had encountered in Thailand in August of 2020. The team leadership generally picked two training or planning topics per day, one for the morning and one for the afternoon, six days per week. Brown Berets then had the rest of the time to conduct physical training, exercise, and prepare for the virtual classes they taught as part of the rotation.

Air Force Tale of Woe: Persistence

While Capt. Lara and LAT 5612 were starting their mission in South Korea that January, back in Washington State we were getting ready for the first significant movement of the battalion. Maj. Ludwig was preparing a company advisor team, maneuver advisor team, field artillery advisor team, engineer advisor team and a logistics advisor team (CAT 5110, MAT 5112, FA-AT 5421, ECAT 5510, and LAT 5611) to fly on a C-17 to one of the least anticipated Indo-Pacific countries that the 5th SFAB ever conceived they might go—Mongolia.[49] During our endeavor to get the teams there, both Majors Ludwig and Orr demonstrated decisiveness and persistence as we embarked to work with our geographically significant partners in north Asia. It was a mission I never envisaged would come to fruition.

Some time in the fall of 2020 during one of our routine battalion planning meetings for our Indo-Pacific deployment, Maj. Dan Ludwig said, "I'm going to get a team to Mongolia," and the rest of the group, including myself, laughed. He took it as a challenge, and we all gave him the *Good luck* look that actually meant, *It'll never happen.* However, Dan had the last laugh on all of us. He stayed up late making phone calls to Hawaii and eventually networked his way to an officer in Ulaanbaatar, US Army Lieutenant Colonel Phil Luu, a super proactive defense attaché to Mongolia who saw working with SFAB teams as a unique opportunity. He and his office ended up doing whatever it took for the SFAB to gain access to train with the Mongolian Armed Forces. Typically, headquarters folks in Hawaii view Mongolia as an economy-of-force country, meaning the US Army and the rest of the DOD send just enough forces to participate in exercises to maintain good relations with the Mongolians. The defense attaché office in Mongolia didn't get the attention that his counterparts received in places like Indonesia, Japan, or Thailand, which routinely see large-scale exercises. Lt. Col. Luu easily convinced Ambassador Michael Klecheski of the strategic opportunity the SFAB offered to the US-Mongolian relationship and pitched the idea to the chief of staff of the Mongolian Armed Forces (MAF), Major General Ganzorig. Lt. Col. Luu's staff then followed up with the necessary paperwork to bring the SFAB teams into the country under COVID conditions.

Geographically, the 5th SFAB saw Mongolia as a great opportunity given the comments in the Interim National Defense Strategy. Mongolia was a developing democracy, shared borders with both Russia and China, and seemed like a good place we could reinvigorate and modernize our partnership.[50] What we did not know was that the Mongolians were extremely active on the world stage. They had often exercised their Third Neighbor Policy,[51] which meant that they had engaged in relationship building with countries other than China and Russia. For example, Mongolian Armed Forces units had deployed to many peacekeeping operations, including in South Sudan, Iraq, Afghanistan, and the Democratic Republic of Congo. Many of their officers and NCOs had military experiences outside Mongolia and had much to offer international partners. We could help the United States capitalize on Mongolia's Third Neighbor Policy by developing a relationship with the MAF. By doing so, the Mongolians might have more options when it came to diplomatic or economic negotiations rather than solely relying on Beijing or Moscow.

The geography of Mongolia, while a strategic opportunity, was also a logistic and diplomatic hurdle. The US Army could not contract a freight company to move US military equipment into Mongolia without going over or through Russia or the People's Republic of China (PRC). Given this challenge, the only opportunity 5th SFAB had to get the equipment into the country was to request an Air Force C-17 Globemaster aircraft.

Using a C-17, I naively thought, would be simple. One branch of the US military was going to help another branch. I, and many others in 5th SFAB, learned that there is a long process that must happen to actually bring this type of deal to fruition. The request must go through transportation channels, get validated by USARPAC and INDOPACOM, then get routed through the Air Force to see if they could source a C-17 to meet our time window. Additionally, we needed to secure funding to pay for the C-17 and those aren't cheap—another learning point. Additionally, due to our flight route, the control of the Air Force's aircraft shifts around based on whether they are located in the continental United States (CONUS) or outside the continental United States (OCONUS), which required the Air Force to coordinate on our behalf. Finally, we learned how the Air Force prioritizes missions, and unfortunately, we didn't master this part of the bureaucracy and were rated almost last in priority. At the end of the day, 1/5 SFAB rented a C-17 to transport us from Washington State to Mongolia. It was almost like renting a car, to put it in the simplest terms, but someone else was driving and another third party decided our route.

There were two things that impacted our flight and all future flights to Mongolia. First, the Air Force had charted the flight path to cross the Pacific Ocean to overfly the PRC airspace because it was the most expedient way to get there along normal flight routes. Second, this route therefore required diplomatic clearances and the PRC was not enthusiastic about granting that. The Air Force did not want to take off without diplomatic clearance, so we waited. It wasn't until the last minute that the PRC granted us the privilege to overfly their airspace and we were off to Mongolia.

Prior to being granted our proper clearances from the PRC, Majors Dan Ludwig and Scott Orr had helped plot some alternative scenarios. One possibility was to launch the C-17 and allow it to fly from JBLM to Alaska for refueling and then on to Japan. We would then wait in Japan for the PRC clearances to come to fruition. There was an innate risk that this would not work. However, we took the position of "assume the yes," hoping that the diplomatic clearances would eventually come through. After gathering the details of the flight options and status of diplomatic clearances, I talked this plan over with Brig. Gen. Taylor. When we finished our conversation debating the risks and rewards, we decided that it was best to have the C-17 cargo and personnel over the international date line. Arranging things this way meant that the C-17 transportation was now an INDOPACOM and USARPAC problem, which relieved the burden of waiting in Washington and requiring control from the Air Force's CONUS based Air Mobility Command. If we followed through with this plan, the 5th SFAB would be responsible for all costs associated with keeping the C-17, its crew, and our Brown Berets in Japan if the PRC did not grant the diplomatic clearances we requested to overfly their airspace, which, in addition to being problematic from a budgetary standpoint, would not do our reputation any favors. We wondered if that's what Gen. LaCamera, the USARPAC commander, privately really wanted. Most of the staff officers in the Air Force and USARPAC had said we should wait in Washington State. But in the end, we decided the reward was worth the risk to get our Brown Berets out of the proverbial starting blocks.

Even though the C-17 was delayed for twenty-four hours in Alaska, the aircraft, equipment, and personnel finally made it to Mongolia in January 2021. They only had to wait in Japan for twenty-four hours for the final diplomatic clearances to come through. In fact, the US government officially issued a demarche—a kind of diplomatic protest—against the PRC for delaying our flight request. At the time I didn't know what a demarche was, but once I found out, I had it printed and proudly presented in our mostly empty, but growing, trophy and awards display in our battalion conference room. The teams arrived in subarctic temperatures and were quickly whisked away into COVID quarantine, or so-called COVID jail by some 5th SFAB members. Everyone experienced some sort of quarantine during the deployment period. We had persisted in getting to yes, had taken a gamble by launching the aircraft from JBLM, but had come out on top. I was glad to have officers like Majors Ludwig and Orr who were willing to staff us to success. Once they exited quarantine, they had plenty of work to do with the MAF. Just getting Brown Berets to such a seemingly impossible place was a win in our book.

The Subcontinent: Innovation

Concurrent with sending our logistics team to South Korea and addressing the Mongolia C-17 issues, Capt. Mathew Brown, Sfc. Javar, and MAT 5113 were heading to a different country with their team. This time they were heading to work with another proud and professional organization, the Indian Army. Their team was part of a more extensive exercise called YUDA ABHYAS and were added to the exercise during the final exercise planning conference.

Once again, they'd be working alongside the Ghost Brigade. Brig. Gen. Taylor was adamant that the SFAB should participate in the exercise and establish contacts with the Indian Army, which he and others saw as essential to developing relationships in the Indo-Pacific region. The exercise, held at the Mahajan Field Firing Ranges in Rajasthan, India, is an annual partnership exercise focused on strengthening the Indian and US armies. The Brown Berets would need to adapt to the situation they found themselves in and innovate to demonstrate to the Indian Army and the other US Army units that they were value-added as part of the exercise.

This team experienced a series of delays aboard the C-17s allotted for the exercise as they carried two small elements of MAT 5113 on two different aircraft as well as the members of 1-2 SBCT. These old partners from 5th SFAB's JRTC rotation were the largest contingent of the entire exercise. Our SFAB team had been added to this exercise during the final planning and did not have a designated role written into the agreed-to activities. This was a hindrance of sorts. However, we had the right people in the right positions to help clarify things and get us back on track. I started my series of weekly point-to-point phone calls with each of my team leaders and company commanders throughout the entire deployment. Capt. Mat Brown struggled with integrating into the exercise without being seen as just another "platoon" in the eyes of both the Ghost Brigade and the Indian Army unit, 11th battalion, Jammu and Kashmir Rifles (JAKRIF). In order to make any headway we had lots of dialogue with our Indian counterparts and eventually were able to identify the right people Capt. Brown needed to speak to.

The turning point with the Indian Army's perception of the SFAB was the interaction with our professional NCOs. Before MAT 5113 departed for India Sfc. Javar briefed the team on the India Integrated Country Strategy, a key document for the

Embassy to list priorities and essential goals for the mission. A key component of that was a deliberate effort to strengthen "people to people relationships." Our NCOs fully embraced that effort and from day one and actively sought out the Indian Soldiers and officers to build those relationships, even before the official start of the exercise. Before the Brown Berets had a clearly defined role in the exercise that did what they did best, make friends. S.Sgt. Brandon Gallop organized an informal basketball game between the Brown Berets and their Indian counterparts. The informal basketball games expanded into opportunities to explain what SFAB teams were and how they could complement the Indian Army. Their efforts to build foundational, personal, relationships created the maneuver space to dynamically adjust our role in the exercise. The basketball games led to briefing Indian Army senior leaders about the SFAB and demonstrated their expertise in their chosen profession. One of the first opportunities began with Sfc. Javar's NCOs turning the simple weapons firing range into a larger training and exchange opportunity. After conducting a stress shoot event while exchanging primary battle rifles, S.Sgt. Tylor Williams, the team senior operations advisor, gave a detailed class on the operation of the PVS-14s night vision goggles and PEQ-15 aiming laser before the night event. The Indian Army officers, NCOs, and soldiers were very interested in the US equipment and the Brown Berets were happy to satisfy their curiosity.

The NCOs also understood their audience. They incorporated the needed humility and made the effort to treat every person they interacted with dignity and respect. They were great ambassadors for America in every interaction during the exercise. Demonstrating and teaching simple classes started to distinguish the Brown Berets as a capable and professional group of individuals. This led to invitations to teach additional classes to larger groups of the Indian Army.

S.Sgt. Gallup, the military police advisor, conducted two blocks of instructions to a combined Indian and US Army audience on advanced situational awareness and tracking and another class on tactical questioning. Due to his in-depth knowledge and the schooling the SFAB had arranged for him, S.Sgt. Gallup could easily teach these classes to add additional value to the exchange between the two armies. Also, S.Sgt. Marcus Parker, the fire support advisor, conducted close-quarter's battle rehearsals with the Indian Army and provided a block of instruction on room intervention techniques, which is the Battle Drill 6 equivalent for the US Army where trainees learn to enter and clear a room while minimizing casualties and collateral damage. This provided a way for the US Ghost Brigade to master their proficiency before joining the Indian Army in combined training. As a result, the Indian Army knew what to expect when working with their US counterparts. Finally, Sgt. Tau Vaaia, the team's intelligence advisor, facilitated a class and discussion on sensitive site exploitation and tactical questioning. S.Sgt. Gallup and Sgt. Vaaia facilitated the discussions to build on the classes in advanced situational awareness and tracking from earlier in the exercise. The Indian and US brigade leadership also sat through those blocks of instruction. Following the presentations, Col. Boardwell and Cmd. Sgt. Maj. Langs, the 1st Brigade, 2nd Infantry Division leadership, gave Sgt. Vaaia a challenge coin award for an excellent presentation that highlighted the strength and intelligence of the US Army's NCO Corps. These NCOs adapted to their conditions and demonstrated they were important members of the entire exercise.

While Exercise YUDH ABHYAS was focused on building interoperability between the US and Indian armies, cultural exchanges were also an important part. The Indian Army was an excellent host and took great pride in the facilities, food, and availability of souvenirs to make sure their guests were happy.

One interesting event was the evening Indian film. While not all the Brown Berets, nor the rest of the US contingent, were particular film afficionados, Capt. Brown and Sfc. Javar knew the viewing was an important part of the cultural exchange. Thus ten or eleven of the twelve Brown Berets were present for the lengthy three-hour event. Each night, usually after 9:00 p.m., an Indian major selected a film to watch. The Brown Berets sat through films like *Uri: The Surgical Strike* and *Ship of Theseus*. Sometimes the films were entertaining and sometimes not. In either case, it didn't matter because by consistently participating, the Brown Berets showed their appreciation and gratitude for their host's efforts and were rewarded with increased interaction, trust, and openness with their counterparts.

The twelve-person team ultimately had an outsized effect on the entire exercise. Due to the team's professionalism, the Indian Army's public affairs section decided to use Sgt. Vaaia to be part of a highlighted interview and dialogue with an Indian Army captain. Sgt. Vaaia was a great representative for both the SFAB and the US Army. Later in the spring, S.Sgt. Williams of MAT 5113 was featured in the April 2021 issue of *ARMY Magazine*. The favorable publicity was an excellent win for the SFAB enterprise.

After the exercise was finished and most of the team returned to the United States, they continued to punch above their weight class. US Army and Indian Army planners invited Capt. Brown and Sgt. Vaaia to attend the Executive Steering Group meeting that set the stage for US Army-Indian Army relations for the next two years. Usually, the Army sends much more senior people to these events, usually lieutenant colonels and colonels. The conference is very detail-oriented, and dialogue goes back and forth about what each army would like to get out of the relationship. Our team members were there because of their maturity and ability to converse about SFAB and Army opportunities. They didn't get to participate in some of the senior sidebar discussions that generally happen with these sorts of conferences. Still, their presence was a step in the right direction for our small but capable organization. They represented the Army well and beat the C-17s carrying the rest of the team and their equipment back to Washington State by traveling on commercial aircraft.

The teams that left for South Korean training, the initial move into Mongolia, and the 5113 supporting YUDA ABHYAS were the only parts of our formation that left anywhere close to on time in January. Every other team in the formation experienced false starts and delays. It was a challenging time of uncertainty for those Brown Berets and their families. I know many spouses asked their soldiers, "When are you leaving?" That's a question every Army spouse wants to know. The second is always "When are you coming back?" Both of those questions were difficult to answer, and sometimes the response was just "I don't know." I found myself saying that on multiple occasions to Amy. The families shared some of the same emotional exhaustion that the entire battalion experienced.

Where to Park the Headquarters: Singapore Attempt—Long-Term Focus

Prior to our first SFAB teams departing Washington State in January 2021, we needed to address one difficult question: where to conduct mission command, or command and control, for all these teams going to various locations throughout the Indo-Pacific. We needed somewhere to park the Mission Command Post and battalion staff. Our number-one preference was to go to a place like Singapore, where the Navy already has a co-use footprint, and there are good military-to-military relationships already established. This would also put the command post in the "Hotel" time zone,

UTC+8, which included the countries of Mongolia, Singapore, China, Taiwan, and the Philippines. Korea and Japan would be one hour ahead, and Thailand and Indonesia would be an hour behind. Additionally, as an essential Asian logistics hub, there were flights to just about anywhere and cargo ships heading to almost every destination in the Indo-Pacific. Singapore presented us with a lot of advantages.

The second option we considered was Thailand. We had already experienced the good rapport between the US and Thais and knew they were very welcoming in general. Part of the challenge would be keeping our mission separate and distinct from Col. Turnbull since he had previously stated that he wanted any SFAB forces in Thailand to work for him. Based on previous interactions and phone calls, the brigade concerned about that perspective. The other consideration was what type of impact could the battalion headquarters have by working with the RTA at the division or higher level. With multiple senior leaders at the US general officer level coming in and out of Thailand, we thought that we would likely not be able to work with many senior RTA officers. So we put Thailand at the bottom of our short list.

Businesses consider many factors when trying to determine where to locate. They must think about the type of location (industrial, commercial, etc.) and whether or not those locations fit their budgets. They must also consider the brand and how the location would support that brand development—just like how an upscale restaurant may not want to be in a college quad or a rural area because their target audience needs to be diners with larger budgets to pay for their fare. At the 5th SFAB we had some similar issues to face as we endeavored to find the right place to locate our mission command element. The missing ingredient was that we had not done this before. We were lucky to find some resident knowledge at the national level and other knowledgeable people that we could engage with and the USARPAC staff, who could help critique our ideas as they evolved.

However, in the end we ended up placing the headquarters in the most unlikely location—Mongolia. Due to the work of Lt. Col. Phil Luu and the openness of the Mongolian Armed Forces, we determined Mongolia was the best place to place our battalion headquarters. We thought we could accomplish a lot more with the Mongolian Army, and they were willing to host us. Other factors that helped us to cement this decision was that Thailand and Singapore continued to have COVID travel restrictions throughout the winter and spring of 2021. The uncertainty of this situation was weighing heavily on the battalion. As such, Mongolia appeared to be the land of opportunity for us. It was the next best place for us to coordinate actions throughout the Indo-Pacific.

We never gave up on Singapore, however, and believed that the Singapore location was the real long-term solution to our headquarters placement. We remained focused on setting up a temporary facility in Singapore and hopeful about getting there once conditions afforded us that ability either later in the spring or early in the summer of 2021. Our initial attempt was to get a four-person advanced party in before the rest of the battalion headquarters would arrive. In the end, we were only partially effective on this modest venture. We planned to send Captain Lee Sikon, the Headquarters and Headquarters Company commander, in an attempt to establish our foothold at the Sembawang Naval Base,[52] where the United States Navy Region Center Singapore (NRCS) occupies spaces used to coordinate support activities throughout the Pacific.[53] We wanted to eventually put our battalion headquarters there.

I exchanged frequent emails and had multiple phone calls with Col. Chris DiCicco, the Army attaché in Singapore, trying to negotiate our four-person team into the small city-state. We discussed our intended purpose and potentially how we could work with the Singapore Army if needed. I again found it strange how we needed to describe to other military officers the reason we needed to conduct mission command of our subordinate elements within the same region rather than remaining in Washington State. Part of our discussions also involved the DOD civilians running NRCS and finding physical spaces that had electricity, internet connectivity, and air conditioning—an essential element working in the tropical environment. Eventually, Col. DiCicco agreed to take our case to the Singapore Ministry of Defence (the British spelling of *defense* is *defence*).

One day in February, Capt. Sikon knocked at my door and had good news. He had heard from the DOD civilian that our mission was approved. I was delighted! The only catch was that it was for only one person due to COVID travel restrictions. Capt. Sikon asked if we should accept or continue to try for one other person or wait for all four slots. "Take it," I said. "We need to get a Brown Beret to Singapore as soon as possible." Capt. Sikon left forty-eight hours later. I followed up with a phone call to Brig. Gen. Taylor to let him know what we were doing.

Eventually, our senior intelligence NCO, Sfc. Bryant Murphy joined Capt. Sikon in early April. Both would remain in Singapore until June and continued to find ways to bring the entire battalion headquarters to Singapore. Unfortunately, that never happened on our deployment. Our communication NCO, S.Sgt. Kim, and logistics NCO, Sfc. Omar Moore never made it to Singapore due to the strict COVID travel restrictions. After months of having their bags packed in anticipation of heading to the heat of Singapore, we instead brought them to Mongolia in May. Both were delighted to finally deploy with the rest of the battalion overseas and actively contribute to the SFAB mission in a foreign country.

Meanwhile Capt. Sikon and Sfc. Murphy worked in Singapore.

During one of our frequent VTCs, I asked them if they had frequented any of the food-hawker *centres* famous throughout the small city-state. "No," both of them said. "We just go from the naval compound and back to our quarters." I smacked my forehead and proceeded to explain to them how Singapore is known for its fantastic food and the intersection of so many cultures. Exploring the varieties of food was one of my favorite memories during my visit to Singapore as part of Exercise TIGER BALM (the longest-running bilateral exercise between the Singapore Army and the US Army) back in July of 2013. Unfortunately, we had sent two of our Brown Berets who were much more comfortable eating chicken nuggets, plain salads, and macaroni and cheese than anything else. They were the complete opposites of foodies or gastronomes. While I eventually convinced them to visit one of hawker centres, they didn't frequent them. They were hard workers trying to establish a footprint for 5th SFAB, and they remained focused on their mission.

Capt. Sikon learned how the United States military negotiates long-term use of a foreign government's military facilities. He initially tried to see if the battalion headquarters could support that year's Exercise TIGER BALM, but that option failed. Capt. Sikon went back and forth between the Singaporean Defence attaché, USARPAC desk officers, and the INDOPACOM J5 (policy and plans), attempting to convince everyone it was a good idea for INDOPACOM to put a SFAB battalion headquarters in Singapore. It was another couple of rounds of explaining to various staff officers what the SFAB was, how it was organized, and what the SFAB was designed to do. There was a distinct disconnect between what we were thinking in terms of weeks and months to make the approval happen whereas the higher-level staffs thought in terms of months and years.

To set the conditions for other battalion headquarters to follow us, Capt. Sikon conducted a complete site survey, an extensive and detailed checklist that verifies all the life support and work requirements to operate at a designated location. He also had the opportunity to brief the US Navy installation commander, who was in charge of the entire NRCS facility, to explain what the SFAB was trying to do. We may not have been able to move the battalion headquarters from Mongolia to Singapore during our Indo-Pacific deployment, but we secured the facilities for the next battalion and initiated the approval process with INDOPACOM to establish a mission command node in Singapore. We knew Singapore was the ideal location for the next five to ten years for the 5th SFAB—but someone else would need to complete the process.

The Paradise Mission: Branding

Back in the fall of 2020, Brig. Gen. Taylor had told me that he wanted the 1st battalion to get a team to the Maldives. This surprising request came when we reviewed Indo-Pacific strategic documents and pushed our CONOP paperwork through the Joint Staff approval process. I naively told him that the Maldives wasn't on the list, and I didn't understand where this request was coming from. Then, after a few conversations and a quick search on the internet looking at worldwide shipping and trade routes, I could easily see why the Maldives is an important strategic location. Any ship traffic that must pass from the Pacific Ocean into the Middle East and Europe must sail past this small collection of islands. This mission would require some flexibility and would ultimately become one of our best branding opportunities with senior USARPAC leaders.

The Maldives is also a classic worldwide vacation destination for those looking for sandy beaches and clear blue waters. Getting there as a tourist is relatively easy, just swipe the credit card with a travel company and make sure your passport is handy, and off you can go. That isn't the case if you're trying to work with the Maldives National Defence Force (MNDF) and you also want to bring articles of war like body armor, helmets, pistols, and automatic rifles to this paradise destination location.

The Maldives fell into the region for A Company. Maj. Dan Ludwig and 1st Sgt. Keen assigned the Maldives mission to MAT 5111, Capt. Matt Orders, and Sfc. Chris Avila. They had been in the battalion for a long time and had performed the Thailand mission earlier in the summer of 2020. Since we anticipated this being a short mission, the team was given another mission in Bangladesh supporting Exercise TIGER LIGHTNING later in the summer. I empowered and trusted Matt and his team to do all the research and develop the relationships necessary to perform his ill-defined mission. There was little information for the team to start from, as there hadn't been a US Army conventional force in the Maldives for several years. From overhearing conversations later in the winter, I know that the team got some friendly teasing from their peers because of the Maldives' picturesque location.

While researching the Maldives, Capt. Orders informed us that the defense attaché office that represents the US military is located in Sri Lanka. I found this a bit strange. It's a bizarre way to work the US-MNDF relationship, from my perspective. Consequently, the security cooperation officer doesn't have the opportunity to meet with the MNDF leadership on a regular basis. Interactions were instead arranged and scripted according to travel considerations and necessity. Lt. Col. Travis Cox, an Army officer, served as the security cooperation officer for the Maldives and was open to allowing the SFAB train with the small force. He also cautioned us to understand that they get a lot of requests from militaries to work with the MNDF, so they sometimes get overwhelmed. Lt. Col. Cox also reminded us that India sees the Maldives as their "back door" and provides a lot of support to the country. However, he said he was willing to give our new unit a chance and I consider Lt. Col. Cox an early adopter of the SFAB concept who saw employment opportunities with the unit.

The MNDF eventually agreed to a short training window for five weeks starting in February 2021, as long as the training ended before Ramadan that year. The timeline worked well for 5111 because they were prepared to transition to Bangladesh later in the spring to support USARPAC's Exercise TIGER LIGHTNING. When checking on MAT 5111's progress, I was happy to hear from Capt. Orders and Sfc. Avila that they had figured out how to ship their equipment across the Pacific and Indian Oceans with minimal assistance from the battalion or brigade headquarters. I was quite impressed. They did all the research, paperwork, and contracting necessary by themselves. The team ended up sending their equipment with two "pallet riders" on a C-17 that stopped multiple times along its route to get this equipment across the Indo-Pacific. Strategic airlift movements and coordinating with a defense attaché office and embassy not even located on the same island as their partners was normally done by Army division- and Corps-level staffs. But once more, a 5th SFAB captain and several awesome NCOs made it happen.

The team left Washington State at the beginning of February. Matt sent me a few pictures of his quarantine location. The pictures showed stunning ocean views from their rooms, lounge chairs surrounded by tiki huts, and luscious vegetation contrasting with beautiful white sand. I can tell you no one else in the entire battalion felt terrible for his team in COVID quarantine. They later made up for it by conducting excellent training with the MNDF and executing an exceptional interaction with some visiting VIPs.

It had been a long time since the United States Army and the MNDF had trained together, so Capt. Matt Orders and Sfc. Avila went about setting a new standard for the relationship. The training focused on shooting, medical, and small-unit tactics. Between reviewing the frequent videos MAT 5111 sent the battalion headquarters and the weekly touch-point phone calls I had with Matt, it was evident the team did some excellent training. It helped to see the MNDF soldiers were very attentive students to the Brown Berets. The team did all the agreed-to training plus some combative night training done after duty hours and not part of the official program. Sfc. Avila did a lot of combative type training for physical fitness, and the MNDF soldiers wanted to learn about it, so he started teaching them basic techniques. It's pretty impressive to note what trained and motivated NCOs can do once they are given the opportunity. It also showed the MNDF that the team was flexible with their schedule and was sincerely interested in making them better as a professional force.

Getting MNDF excited about the fundamental training the Brown Berets were doing with them required relationship building. Sometimes even the most fun military training can become bland and repetitive. First, the team wanted to do something for the community. So Capt. Orders asked the MNDF Central Area commander if they could do some sort of community service project to show their appreciation to the MNDF and local populace for welcoming their small group of Americans. The commander coordinated a large event through the local island council that consisted of school, police, and other civil entities. The Brown Berets picked up trash and did some landscaping to help clean and beautify the area. Local children stared, laughed, and smiled as the NCOs kidded with them as the did their work. Nobody teaches this type of stuff in any US Army school that I'm aware of.

The Brown Berets reenforced the military-to-military partnership and relationship during several off-duty events. The authentic smiles on the faces of Staff Sergeants Kurtis Sobocinski, John Vilca, and Joshua Berteaux and their MNDF counterparts while scuba diving, fishing, and playing volleyball indicated they had a good time together. Sharing meals was especially important, as the team participated in traditional Maldivian music and dancing. I'm not sure if you'll ever hear the Brown Berets brag about their dancing skills to their significant others, but it's clear they put their hearts and souls into attempting to mimic their hosts. I believe the MNDF officers and soldiers enjoyed sharing their country and culture with the SFAB Brown Berets, and the 5111 team members definitely appreciated seeing something new and different from Washington State.

The team worked hard to understand the MNDF on and off duty so they could deliver a more tailored product during their time together. Besides building personal relationships, their curiosity was indulged in the form of individual open-source research and MNDF doctrine. Later, this curiosity and investment in their partner force manifested into the highest praise when the MNDF's Marine Corps commander stated he thought discussions of future 5th SFAB engagement were the most interesting things he had heard all day at the October 2021 Executive Steering Group (ESG) meeting. This meeting involved 5th SFAB, USARPAC, and other US military entities and was a significant compliment. The commander was enthusiastic about signing up for more SFAB partnership due to MAT 5111's genuine curiosity to understand their partners's motivations.

On the US side, the investment in the relationships and training culminated in a VIP visit by the deputy commander of USARPAC, Major General Daniel McDaniel from Australia, and Cmd. Sgt. Maj. Scott Brzak, the USARPAC command sergeant major, when they visited the Maldives for the closing ceremonies of the SFAB-MNDF training. With the MNDF in the lead, they demonstrated to both the US and MNDF senior leaders the training they had conducted over the previous weeks. This was quite a milestone. The senior leaders became SFAB believers and supported the idea of more SFAB missions.

Cmd. Sgt. Maj. Rob Craven, the 5th SFAB command sergeant

major, accompanied Maj. Gen. McDaniel and Cmd. Sgt. Maj. Brzak during the visit. He called me in Mongolia as they left the training area. "Sir," Cmd. Sgt. Maj. Craven said, "your guys hit a home run. You have no idea what that team just did for the 5th SFAB and rest of the SFAC enterprise. It was awesome."

I said, "CSM, you just saw what all of our SFAB teams are doing in nine other countries. That's the real message."

Brig. Gen. Taylor told me later that Maj. Gen. McDaniels and Cmd. Sgt. Maj. Brzak talked about their Maldives SFAB experience with multiple other senior US leaders in Hawaii and the Pentagon. Here was a small twelve-person team in the middle of the Indian Ocean building brand recognition. It was only possible because the MNDF valued the relationships built by Capt. Orders and Sfc. Avila's team.

The Maldives was a great mission because of the spectacular military interactions and because it was in a great location. As I would tell team leaders during my point-to-point conversations later during the deployment window, "Experiences may vary by teams in 5th SFAB." That was certainly the case as one of our other MATs struggled to work with our allies in South Korea.

The Hermit Kingdom: Patience

Capt. Orders and Sfc. Avila had made superb progress with the VIPs from Hawaii in the Maldives on behalf of the SFAB. Meanwhile, back in Washington State the battalion was making strides toward partnering with our allies from the Republic of Korea (ROK). It is important to note that South Korea is an integral strategic partner in the northeast Indo-Pacific. We were under the assumption that this would be an easy and simple mission to arrange since there are thousands of US troops on the ROK Peninsula with a four-star general in charge of them. However, just like all the other partner and ally countries the SFAB was trying to work with, this one had its own set of challenges to overcome. The SFAB team bound for Korea needed to be both persistent and patient to achieve mission success.

Many on the 5th SFAB and USARPAC staffs wondered why we needed to send Brown Berets to a place where the United States military already had excellent military-to-military relationships, myself included. There was an ongoing debate within the enterprise on where SFAB teams would provide the most value. Should they go to places where we had weak or limited US Army engagements with allies and partners or instead go to areas to strengthen existing stalwart relationships? Within the battalion, captains, sergeants, and staff sergeants had those same discussions. We discussed the benefits and disadvantages of various courses of action and the countries we should go to. Eventually the USARPAC commander weighed in on the discussion and told Brig. Gen. Taylor to send a SFAB team to South Korea to work with the ROK Army. That ended our debate, but the discussions for where to send future SFAB operations were continuous. It was also up to us to turn his guidance into a reality against an institution resistant to change.

On our part we chose MAT 5122, led by Capt. Greg Lentz and Sfc. James Kennedy, for the Korean mission. The 8th US Army is in charge of all US Army forces assigned or rotated through the Republic of Korea. While in South Korea, MAT 5122 would fall under their command authority. The rough plan we devised with the 8th US Army Operations officer, G3, a colonel, was for the team to train with ROK Army (ROK-A) units preparing to attend an upcoming National Training Center (NTC) rotation with one of the US Army's armored brigades. They would accompany the ROK-A units at NTC similar to what we had done with the Thais and Indonesians at JRTC. This would be the first time that a SFAB team accompanied an INDOPACOM allied force to the NTC. To us, the mission seemed straightforward.

As the dedicated sergeants and staff sergeants from 5122

finalized their plans and coordination for departure, staff officers on the USARPAC and 8th Army staffs questioned whether or not the SFAB had the appropriate funding and statutory authorities to work with the ROK Army on the Korean Peninsula. That seemed like an irrelevant question for many of us since the US Army and many other US military services had thousands of troops on the Peninsula. Nevertheless, it became yet another unforeseen bureaucratic sticking point due to the way command authorities interfaced between the 8th Army, US Forces Korea, USARPAC, and INDOPACOM. Luckily, a select few influential staff officers on the USARPAC and 8th Army staffs wanted our mission to succeed and started helping us get to yes. As the 1st battalion had done many times throughout our mission window, we called for Brig. Gen. Taylor to assist us. Luckily, he had a network of colonels he could ask to determine who was saying no and who could say yes. The debate culminated in a late-night phone call between Brig. Gen. Taylor and an 8th Army operational lawyer. The lawyer agreed with our interpretation of the orders and mandates. Team 5122 could train with the ROK-A only if the training was tied specifically to preparation for the upcoming NTC rotation. We didn't know it at the time but later learned the agreement to this particular interpretation eventually ended the team's mission sooner than expected.

One unique aspect of 5122's particular mission was that the team members planned and resourced for three weeks of dedicated range training from Washington State. Planning their events remotely meant they did virtual terrain walks of the US run ranges they used in Korea, requested specific training aides for the situational training exercises (STXs) they ran for the ROK-A units, and coordinated for the life support requirements for both parties. Normally Army units struggle to get command approval for training, arrange the necessary resources, and finalize training events at their home station when they do everything face-to-face and while walking the physical terrain. As someone who has planned and resourced situational training exercise training for several infantry units on five different US Army installations, I was extremely impressed that the team was able to pull it off. It wasn't until they finished their required quarantine requirements that the Brown Berets saw the training facilities with their own eyes to finalize their scheme. They also had to figure out how ship their equipment and navigate the country-entry requirements.

Team 5122's partner forces were the Capital Corps and I Corps commandos. The ROK Army designed one company from the Capital Corps and two companies from the I Corps to attend the NTC rotation later in the summer of 2021. Thus, the team prepared situational training exercise training to help replicate the stress and challenges they would face at Fort Irwin, California. They also tried to determine how the commandos could complement a US armored BCT going through the rotation and what their role might be to liaise between the units. Integrating the commandos into a NTC rotation was not well developed yet.

Scenario writers and brigade commanders did not know how to utilize the foreign units during CTC rotations normally because they did not understand their strengths, weaknesses, or unique capabilities. As a result, foreign units who participated in these momentous training events found themselves relegated to secondary roles like securing rear areas or providing security for support units. Some countries who sent units to the CTCs did not find the experience as valuable as they were expecting. The SFAB's charge was to change these misunderstandings and create benefits for all parties, like we had with the Thai and Indonesian Armies at Fort Polk.

To meet the training requirements, Capt. Lentz and his team developed a plan that included medical, reconnaissance, and offensive operations to prepare the commandos for their rotation.

They decided to do the medical portion first since it was not resource intensive and provided an easy way to illustrate "value-added" to our South Korean counterparts.

Medical training was quite popular in every country that the Brown Berets found themselves. Many other countries are not as well equipped as the US is to intently train on individual medical proficiency. Even so, combat casualty care at the point of injury is critical to a soldier's survival on the battlefield after sustaining injuries. The lack of medical training for frontline combat soldiers came down to foreign units not having the time, resources, or knowledge to develop a program that could certify and adequately train their soldiers. Luckily for them, we did. US Army studies learned through field experience demonstrated that injured soldiers treated at the point of injury with basic medical skills followed by evacuation to a higher-level medical facility have a much higher probability of survival. Therefore, the US Army emphasized medical training, including in the 5th SFAB, where we incorporated a medical aspect into every training event. The certification program in 2020 and 2021 was called Tactical Combat Casualty Care (TCCC). Additionally, Brown Berets attending the Combat Advisor Training Course at Fort Benning underwent one week of supplementary medical-specific training out of the nine-week course.

The first-responder trauma training that the ROK Army commandos requested, and the Brown Berets provided, included practicing simple techniques to stop bleeding, prevent shock, and what to do to prepare a patient for evacuation. These fun exercises helped to build rapport and confidence between both groups and served as a baseline for what they would experience in the real-life situational training exercise scenarios in the following weeks. Individual ROK soldiers were extremely excited to participate in the medical training, and the ROK chain of command appreciated seeing their soldiers' confidence in their skills increase.

MAT 5122 was unsure what their partners would be asked to do at NTC nor what the Commandos capabilities were, so putting together relevant training required creativity and adaptability. Hence the Brown Berets developed a broad plan focused on the basic fundamental battle drills and individual soldier skills. The company of the Capital Corps started first. Brown Berets walked alongside their ROK counterparts as they practiced reacting to fire, taking cover, and treating then evacuating mock casualties. The Brown Berets fostered after-action reviews and helped the commandos determine how they wanted to improve their skills in preparation for NTC. As they conducted the training, the team members realized the commandos were a very capable and disciplined organization. Besides gaining valuable insight into US Army training methodology, the commandos asked questions about how an armored brigade combat team was organized, what the terrain was like at Fort Irwin and the National Training Center, and what the Brown Berets thought their tasks and purposes would be once they arrived at NTC. These were all questions a professional force would ask before any big training event. After living, eating, and training side by side with the Capitol Corps commandos, the team also learned they viewed attending NTC as more an opportunity to strengthen the US-ROK alliance and leadership development opportunity than a culminating training event like most US BCTs do. In reality, the ROK commandos were engaged in wartime operations against their North Korean counterparts on a daily basis. They had an existential threat right along their border on which they focused their time, resources, and manpower.

After the Capital Corps commandos rotated out and the I Corps commandos rotated in, the MAT 5122 Brown Berets realized they needed to increase the throughput of the training and slightly modify it based on the commando's potential missions at NTC if they were going to succeed. So they decided to draw on the broader experiences found internal to the team. Staff Sergeant Jesus Echevarria, the team's intelligence advisor, was a former infantryman and graduate of the US Army's Armored Reconnaissance Course. Between S.Sgt. Echevarria and Capt. Lentz, they put together additional training that covered some of the basic fundamentals of US reconnaissance planning using maps of the National Training Center. The additional training gave the commandos insight into how a BCT might plan and utilize their formation and familiarized them with Fort Irwin's challenging terrain.

The culminating training event at the military operations in urban terrain site at the Rodriguez Training Complex in South Korea was a platoon attack in an urban environment. The site consisted of multiple buildings designed to simulate a small town or part of a larger city found anywhere along the Korean Peninsula. The facility allowed the Brown Berets to progress training with the I Corps from simple single-room and single-story building clearing to maneuvering between multiple multi-story buildings and clearing them. Commando platoon leaders were issued some basic imagery of their objective and a rough estimate of the enemy situation and expected to conduct an attack a few hours later. ROK Commando leadership and the Brown Berets were able to evaluate the platoon leadership on their planning and execution of the attack. Once the attack began, time moved quickly due to the intense nature of the exercise. Commandos reacted to enemy fire, coordinated with simulated air support over the radio, and treated their casualties. The Brown Berets found this was the most well received and fun training day they experienced with each of the commando units. It was a great opportunity to interact with their ROK counterparts during the high-energy event.

Throughout the training Brown Berets would return to their areas at night and start writing. They wrote assessments of the commandos—strengths, weaknesses, and capabilities. These assessments were then provided to the armored brigade staff that the commandos were expected to partner with at NTC as well as the scenario writers at Fort Irwin. Providing a comprehensive assessment of the ROK commandos allowed both groups to better understand how to integrate the commandos into the training and develop scenarios that allowed them to train on their own key and essential tasks. Doing so set the conditions for the commandos to be used in a manner that met the South Korean general officer's expectations at NTC and got them "into the fight."

Throughout the training, the relationship between the Brown Berets of MAT 5122 and the commandos became closer. The Brown Berets also experienced the slight difference between the Capital Corps and I Corps units. Outside of the situational training exercise training events themselves, the Brown Berets ate how and what their ROK counterparts ate—which is much different from American food—and slept in the same barracks. In one instance, one of the Capital Corps commando sergeant majors brought in a wide variety of pork products that they enjoyed. Apparently, the products were translated as smashed pig head, intestines, and some other parts of the pig prepared in a way none of the Brown Berets had heard of before. Luckily when these supposed delicacies came out, it was the end of the duty day, and they could wash it down with some Korean beer. The Capital Corps commandos also introduced the Brown Berets to *jokgu*, which the commandos claimed was invented by the Korean military and is essentially a form of foot volleyball. Needless to say, the Americans were terrible at the sport and the ROK commandos got a great laugh at their expense. No one decided that it was worth keeping score. Following the night of smashed pig head and jokgu, the relationship between the two groups transformed from what might have been perceived as a formal and scripted exchange to one of true partnership capable of exchanging candid feedback and willingness to make mistakes for the sake of learning.

In contrast to the Capital Corps commandos, the I Corps commandos were extremely competitive. One of the company commanders jumped at the first chance to do physical training together before even starting the situational training exercise training. The two groups met in the early morning darkness and began a run that led to a nearby field, where they spent the next two hours competing against each other in a variety of feats of strength and races. It was a grueling morning for everyone, but the Brown Berets kept up and proved themselves worthy. A little over a week later at the situational training exercise training area, the same commando company met the Brown Berets at the base gym. As a sign of respect, they insisted they and the Brown Berets remove their shirts for a group photo. Sfc. Kennedy, the keeper of standards and discipline, reluctantly agreed to the request, although looking at his facial expression on his face in the picture, it's evident he did it ever so begrudgingly.

As MAT 5122 and the I Corps commandos concluded their second of three weeks of training, the US Army did something totally unexpected. Forces Command (FORSCOM) canceled the upcoming NTC rotation that included the ROK-A commandos with less than three months' notice. Canceling a NTC rotation was something unheard of in recent Army history and came as a shock to the 5th SFAB, USARPAC, and the 8th Army. I remember calling Brig. Gen. Taylor about the cancelation to verify the accuracy of the information. He also didn't think it was true until doing his own research and calling his points of contact at NTC and FORSCOM. What made the announcement worse was that it wasn't precommunicated to anyone involved in the rotation before coming out as a public release, causing some embarrassment to the Brown Berets working alongside the commandos, as well as senior leaders in the US 8th Army.

After a series of negotiations between the ROK Army, 8th Army, and FORSCOM, NTC decided the commandos could participate in a later rotation at the end of the summer. Unfortunately, this meant that Capt. Lentz's team would not see the fruits of their labor since the battalion's Indo-Pacific mission window ended in June before the NTC rotation started. This also raised the question of what 5122 would do until the end of the 1/5 SFAB mission window in June. Could they stay and continue working with the commandos or another ROK Army unit?

At the tactical level, Capt. Lentz discussed potential partnership training opportunities with commando leadership at the company, battalion, and brigade echelons. They all wished to continue training with the SFAB team. The desire to continue the partnership encouraged those of us from 5th SFAB because it validated our investment in the commando-Brown Berets relationship and the training Capt. Lentz and his team had put together for NTC. Capt. Lentz, as a junior officer among many colonels and generals, inserted himself into the senior-level discussions within the 8th Army to inform them of the training opportunities MAT 5122 could accomplish with the commandos with the remaining time they had. Unfortunately, decision delays with senior ROK general officers on future training between the SFAB and the commandos caught the attention of the USARPAC and 8th Army staff officers that had been previously hesitant to permit the whole SFAB training concept on the ROK Peninsula. These staff officers quickly moved into action and voiced their concerns.

The general consensus from the US chain of command was that since FORSCOM had delayed the NTC rotation, the SFAB mission was complete and MAT 5122 remaining in-country would exceed the mission authorization tied to NTC. The debate on our mission authorization continued for almost two weeks. Meanwhile, the Brown Berets sat in limbo, unable to train with their partner force but also not quite sure if they were heading back to Washington State yet. Fortunately, the team was filled with ingenuity and was patient. They used this idle time to conduct internal training on tactical combat tasks they had not completed before deploying and tasks they needed additional repetitions on to become more proficient. Finally on May 2nd, 2021 Capt. Lentz was told their mission was complete. The Brown Berets wasted no time packing their equipment and moving it to the logistics holding area for return to the United States.

While the team's mission did not end as planned, it did demonstrate their patience for gaining entry into a country with a large US military presence and waiting for those in authority to make decisions when circumstances change. More importantly, MAT 5122 demonstrated to the ROK Army and the senior US Army officers in the 8th Army that SFAB Brown Berets can contribute to the ROK-US relationship. Many of the senior US Army officers changed from lukewarm supporters of the SFAB concept to strong advocates. Thus, our investment in the Korea mission was a success.

The Philippines, Pearl of the Orient: Adaptability

COVID had delayed Capt. Oleg Sheynfeld and Sfc. Nate Peno's MAT 5123 and Capt. Alex Lara and Sfc. Terrance Parrish's LAT 5612 by a month after their arrival in-country. COVID was not the only hinderance. There was also a slew of bureaucratic requirements including reduced staffing at the US Embassy, the Ministry of Foreign Affairs, and a backlog of visa requirements at the Philippine Embassy in Washington DC. All of these added to the delays. Despite these hurdles, these teams were resolute in expanding their value to the embassy staff, JUSMAGPHL, and the Philippine Army. By the time their mission had come to a close in the Philippines in June 2021, the Filipino units were requesting more SFAB partnerships and the defense attaché office shuffled Capt. Sheynfeld to various meetings with senior Philippine Army commanders to give them SFAB capability briefs. These meetings were a far cry from the first phone calls and emails initiated in the fall of 2020. The Brown Berets from MAT 5123 and LAT 5612 were persistent and adaptable as they helped reinvigorate the US-Philippine strategic partnership on behalf of USARPAC and INDOPACOM.

Defense attaché offices and our host nation partners typically correlated the arrival of the SFAB teams with an existing USARPAC or INDOPACOM exercise. Our engagements in the Philippines were no different. The exercise which MAT 5123 and LAT 5612 were associated with was called BALIKATAN. Capt. Sheynfeld and Capt. Lara were told by the 5th SFAB staff and Embassy and JUSMAG staff that they were to finalize the details of their agreed-to activities with the Philippine Army once they arrived in-country. The fact the US Embassy staff in Manila and the JUSMAGPHIL conceded to such a nebulous plan was highly unusual. Usually, the agreed-to activities were finalized over a two-to-three-year time horizon. Captains Sheynfeld and Lara completed their negotiations for their agreed-to activities in less than two months.

The teams arrived in Manila in early March 2020 and began their fifteen-day quarantine. As the Brown Berets vacillated between boredom, planning for their engagements with their counterparts, and exercising, they began to pick up on rumors that the BALIKATAN exercise might get canceled and the Philippine government might institute additional COVID lockdowns. USARPAC staff officers attempted to develop options for senior leaders to salvage the exercise in some capacity to maintain the US-Philippine military relationship. Adding to this dilemma was the precarious and evolutionary dialogue between President Duerte and the US regarding the Visiting Forces Agreement (VFA) and COVID vaccines.[54] Since it was a COVID climate, vaccines were being requested as leverage to allow this exercise to proceed, among other things. The Brown Berets were smack dab in the middle of this geopolitical turbulence and beholden to those senior diplomats and military officials who were the decision-makers in these situations. How would things get resolved?

The teams remained in Manila following their mandatory two weeks of quarantine and began working with the HQPA G8 staff, which was the staffing section that approves agreed-to activities. Capt. Sheynfeld and his team put together a proposed training calendar for the HQPA G8 staff for consideration. Simultaneously, Captains Sheynfeld and Lara talked with their points of contact in the Philippine Army's 1st Brigade Combat Team (1st BCT), their designated counterpart unit, and received unofficial confirmation that 1st BCT was willing to host and work with these unproven SFAB units at Fort Magsaysay. However, the Philippine Army officers said all their directives needed to come from HQPA before they could proceed with detailed arrangements. This was a lengthy bureaucratic process, which eventually involved multiple HQPA staff elements. Luckily, Capt. Sheynfeld befriended Philippine Army Maj. Capugeon Cabugeon from the G8 staff and won over some hesitant US Army JUSMAGPHIL officers who helped the Brown Berets better understand the overall Philippine Army situation. The wait was nerve-racking.

Finally, after about two weeks of debate, the BALIKATAN exercise was officially "modified." This meant that everything was canceled except the US Marine-sponsored virtual staff exercise portion and whatever the SFAB teams would do. This was the crack in the opening door the Brown Berets decided to rush through. Upon official HQPA notification, the teams negotiated their way from Manila to Fort Magsaysay past a series of COVID checkpoints along the route. Pulling up to each of the checkpoints caused everyone in the vehicles to hold their breath and pray that they would get past. It was a tense drive through the tropical hills and lush greenery. Everyone breathed a sigh of relief and relaxed their tense muscles as they pulled into their hotel near Fort

Magsaysay. They had made it to their Philippine counterpart's location. It was another small victory. Now it was time to meet their 1st BCT hosts.

The Philippine Army's 1st BCT is their premier conventional army unit, modeled off a US BCT, though not fully built out in terms of personnel and equipment. Still, the Philippine Army frequently tried to get the 1st BCT involved with US forces to develop its combat capability since it was frequently called upon to help address the country's insurgency issues on the island of Mindanao. MAT 5123 prepared to work with the brigade headquarters and its assigned infantry battalions while Capt. Lara's LAT 5612 was scheduled to work with their logistics staff and support battalion. Unfortunately, the Philippine Army thought BALIKATAN was going to get canceled completely and began sending 1st BCT units to the insurgency hotspots. The Brown Berets needed to figure something out at Fort Magsaysay because they weren't authorized to accompany the Philippine Army on combat operations against an active insurgency.

They first reverted back to salesman mode. Capt. Sheynfeld and Capt. Lara started by educating officers from the 1st BCT and other Philippine Army units at Fort Magsaysay what the SFAB was and what it did. Next, they revised the training plan with the Filipino officers and determined what they could accomplish together. Once they received final approval from HQPA, they decided to begin with a series of small engagements on a variety of topics then progress to more complicated training like a platoon-level situational training exercise. I believe this was the Philippine Army testing to see if the SFAB teams could deliver on what they were selling before committing more people and resources to the partnership. As Brown Berets waited for the final approval, they decided to do something to demonstrate they were altruistic in their attempt to build on the US-Filipino relationship.

SFAB team members found themselves far away from their own

families over the Easter celebration in 2021, but still captured the spirit of the holiday. As they traveled the short distance between their hotel and Fort Magsaysay to pitch ideas to their counterparts, they noticed a very impoverished neighborhood nearby their hotel. Fort Magsaysay and the adjacent communities are in a relatively remote location just west of the Sierra Madre Mountain range on the island of Luzon. Many families with children lived there. In a gesture of selflessness and goodwill, the Brown Berets decided to purchase a bunch of meals from the hotel with their personal money and give the food to the families who lived nearby. They walked the narrow alleyways along dirt paths and handed out the boxed meals to children and parents who lived in small shacks topped with tin roofs. The families were especially appreciative, and I have never been prouder of them for taking the initiative to do this. This was not something that anyone ever gets trained to do but is born out of a value-based culture.

Fortuitously, in the wake of the Easter holiday the OG 5 and OG 8 departments at HQPA approved the team's planned engagements with the 1st BCT and some of the other units on Fort Magsaysay and were eager to commence training and engagements. They began with a series of logistics and intelligence sharing classes taught by our team NCOs to both Philippine Army officers and NCOs. These first engagements were critical for the SFAB Brown Berets because they set the tone—and their reputation was on the line. Before each class Capt. Sheynfeld and Sfc. Peno rehearsed the instructors over and over again to make sure they knew the material and perfected a presentation model they thought appropriate for their audience. Like so many classes, they started off slowly as the Philippine Army officers and NCOs assessed their American counterparts. Soon, as the SFAB NCOs demonstrated their competency in the topics, they asked questions and were more interactive. SFAB NCOs executed these initial classes flawlessly and were soon asked to expand the class types and audiences on Fort Magsaysay.

After MAT 5123 and LAT 5612 proved their bona fides, the 1st BCT was ready to commit more people and resources to the SFAB training engagements. The 1st BCT assembled a composite infantry platoon for the training. The Brown Berets identified training locations, developed scenarios, and found training aids. Filipino soldiers and NCOs went through close-quarter combat training and basic platoon maneuvers many of the Brown Berets had experienced at Fort Benning, Georgia (home of the infantry) or at their previous assignments. To make the training realistic, the Brown Berets created several engagements and organized a live and thinking opposing force. While commonly used for US Army situational training exercises, an opposing force is an unusual component for many foreign military's trainings. The Brown Berets also incorporated casualty treatment, sensitive site exploitation, and calling for fire to increase the complexity as the 1st BCT members progressed. This training was an audacious task to pull off in such a short time frame, but the quality of the event proved to the 1st BCT leadership and other Philippine Army units on Fort Magsaysay that the SFAB teams could deliver on their promises. The Brown Berets also demonstrated respect for the Philippine Army by adapting their training to reenforce Philippine Army-specific tactics and doctrine. The situational training exercise also identified shortcomings for follow-on training opportunities with the Philippine Army.

Our teams were making progress developing relationships with their Philippine Army counterparts, but it didn't stop there as they immersed themselves in the Filipino culture. Capt. Sheynfeld befriended the local district police chief as part of his official duties. The district police chief decided to invite his new American friends to his home. It was more than just a small gathering and invitation to dinner but turned out to be a feast composed of a massive spread of traditional Filipino food and drinks on the police chief's farm accompanied by local villagers. In a surreal moment, the Brown Berets stuffed themselves with platefuls of various dishes and poorly sang karaoke in the middle of flooded farm fields. The event was a far cry from the cool and wet climate of Washington State. When I later talked with the Brown Berets about this particular moment, their mouths started to salivate as they talked about the wonderful Filipino food they had eaten that day.

On another occasion, the hotel manager from the hotel where the Brown Berets were staying invited them to his home. He urged them to come over under the auspices of challenging them to a friendly basketball game, something the team members surely thought they would dominate in against their unsuspecting hosts. The group was surprised and humbled to find out that they were, in fact, invited to another large Filipino dinner attended by the hotel manager's family and his neighboring farmers. To their astonishment, the farmers invited the Brown Berets to test their water-buffalo riding skills on their work animals. The local farmers stared in awe and curiosity as their American guest climbed aboard the beasts and beamed with enjoyment through the whole experience. It was another case of embracing the local archipelago culture.

While the Brown Berets enjoyed experiencing the Filipino culture and were successful in developing partnerships with the units on Fort Magsaysay, not everything went to plan. MAT 5123 and LAT 5612 never received their military equipment they had shipped from Washington State after going through the excruciatingly detailed process of coordinating for shipment across the Pacific Ocean. Missing some of their specialized and work-related equipment caused them to adapt their training and do much of it without essential items. They weren't able to demonstrate the value of their organic capabilities like the Unmanned Aerial Surveillance systems or robust communications packages. Unfortunately, their containers were stuck in Singapore with the shipping company and never made it to the Philippines before the team departed in June. The lack of equipment caused the teams to be extraordinarily resourceful and learn how to conduct training with the minimal equipment they carried. Other times they acquired equipment from Philippine Army supplies or purchased them in the local economy. *Adaptability* became the motto for the day for the teams. Determining which equipment to carry with them on commercial aircraft versus what to put in their containers was a painful and frustrating lesson for all to learn.

However, training with the Philippine Army continued. The SFAB teams modified their training and worked with Fort Magsaysay units on urban combat tactics, intelligence, communications, fires, maintenance, logistics, the military decision-making process, and medical techniques. In an endeavor to get the word out about their training exercises during this environment of COVID complications, they performed some virtual training over VTCs with training schools and units throughout the Philippines. It was pretty amazing that they successfully sought out opportunities to engage with our partner forces and demonstrated incredible flexibility with regard to what was being taught.

One highlight was the medical training. Sgt. Tyler Matherson and S.Sgt. Eui Yoo taught a weeklong Tactical Combat Casualty Care (TCCC) class for the Filipino NCOs at Fort Magsaysay. They modeled it exactly on the TCCC course taught in US units as part of their medical readiness program. The Philippine Army participants received hands-on medical training not normally associated with infantry units. The TCCC course was so popular that when it finished, Sgt. Matherson and S.Sgt. Yoo were asked to participate in a discussion on developing a similar TCCC program for the entire Philippine Army. These young NCOs sat in rooms with Philippine Army senior officers and medical professionals and discussed how to implement the program across the entire force.

Having such a national-level impact was not uncommon. In a similar way, S.Sgt. Monique Richards, MAT 5123's logistics advisor, taught the Philippine Army classes on property accountability, forecasting logistic estimates, and how to properly store and secure weapons and ammunition. Recognizing some of the Philippine Army's challenges, she organized a series of VTCs focused on the institutional logistic capability issues that included senior Philippine logisticians, senior logisticians from 5th SFAB located in Washington State, and logistics planners from USARPAC headquarters located in Hawaii. She identified problems and their solutions, and if she didn't know the solution but knew who might, she organized all parties to brainstorm some answers.

Using an existing network to develop the US-Philippines partnership was used more than once. Capt. Alex Lara leveraged his US Army Logistics Career Course (LCCC) alumni network to expand the number of units his logistics team worked with. As such, the transportation and armaments battalions' commanders located at Camp Bonifacio near Manilla, also both LCCC graduates, invited LAT 5612 to their battalions to conducted partnership training.

Capt. Lara's team demonstrated their skill and adaptability working in Manilla with one of the Philippine Army's armament companies that was in charge of their newly acquired Improved Target Acquisition Systems and tube-launched, optically tracked, wire-guided (TOW) anti-tank missiles they had received from the United States in 2020. Unfortunately, the armament company did not have the technical knowledge nor skills to account for all the parts and didn't understand how to setup the missile system. For a variety of reasons, the Tactical Aviation and Ground Munitions (TAGM) training team's entry into the Philippine's had been delayed for almost a year. The Philippine Army told the Brown Berets their dilemma and inability to capitalize on this new, advanced weapons system. Sfc. Lucas Simmonds, the

LAT's maintenance advisor, leveraged the US Army logistics enterprise to help inventory the systems and prepare them for training and a live-fire demonstration. He called back to the United States, acquired manuals, and helped walk the armament company through the entire system. The Philippine Army was extremely grateful that they could move forward with this newly acquired weapon system. The team had helped solve a significant unforeseen problem for the Philippine Army by building trust with their partners and proving themselves dependable and reliable.

The team culture that the SFAB exhibited in the Philippines was something that we hoped to leverage and replicate across the other teams in other countries. They were adaptable and had become such a cohesive unit that Capt. Sheynfeld and Capt. Lara coordinated transfer of heaps of pertinent information with their SFAB replacements from 2nd Battalion, 5th SFAB soon after their arrival in-country. This was truly handing over the baton. They showed them the easy way to go about getting entry requirements approved, how to ship equipment, contracting, funding, and other cultural sensitivities that go hand in hand when working with the Philippine Army or embassy staff. They were building the foundation for a long-term strategic partnership with their newfound friends in the Philippines.

The Land of Tigers and National Heritage Sites: Structured Experimentation

Over the past decade, the United States Army has increased the number of large-scale exercises with the archipelago known as Indonesia. Many Indonesian officers previously attended US Army schools, including their Army chief of staff at the 5th SFAB's inaugural mission, General Andika Perkasa.[55] MAT 5132, led by Capt. LeShaun Smith, demonstrated persistence and adaptability, both entrepreneurial characteristics, as they traveled to three different division headquarters, four brigade headquarters, and trained with nine infantry battalions across the island of Java with one stop on the island of Sulawesi.

Capt. LeShaun Smith and Sfc. Michael Bidwell were the team leader and assistant team leader assigned the Indonesian mission. Unfortunately, Sfc. Bidwell could not make it because of a delay associated with his passport and visa requests. Sfc. Bidwell's visa had been entrenched with the Defender Pacific Exercise visas but was destined to remain in bureaucratic purgatory between the military's passport office on Fort Belvoir and the Indonesian Embassy in DC. This was primarily due to COVID impacts and the rapidly changing policy on exercises and travel. Navigating the visa and country-entry requests with foreign governments was a major learning point for every team, including MAT 5132.

Capt. LeShaun Smith was an engineer officer that I had hired on the recommendation from my friend Lt. Col. Rhett Blackmon. SFAB MATs were normally led by infantry officers. I spent a lot of time searching for talent regardless of branch or specialty and wanted to hire the person with the appropriate talent and skills necessary to thrive in the security force assistance environment. Capt. Smith was a bit older than some and had previously served as an enlisted Army medic. After his term of duty was up and he completed his college education, he worked as a high school teacher. I felt he had the right stuff to round out our team and brought some skilled diversity to the team.

While our sister battalion, 2nd Battalion, 5th SFAB, sent a team to Indonesia to train with the Indonesian National Military and accompanied them to JRTC at Fort Polk in October of 2020, that success did not translate into an immediate advantage for the 1st battalion's inaugural deployment to the country.[56] We found that our biggest hurdles were on the US side, not the

Indonesian side, of the country-entry process. Dogged persistence, patience, and grit finally got our maneuver team into the country.

As stated before, during normal relations and circumstances outside of armed conflict, the State Department oversees all US activities in a foreign country. During that time, there was one person in charge, the US ambassador. Ambassadors are the direct representative of the president of the United States and have significant authority over all actions that happen inside the country, including the US military.

Team 5132 was busy packing and assembling visa packets to get into Indonesia when we found out that the sitting ambassador had been called back to DC by the Biden Administration to serve as the president's assistant secretary of East Asian Affairs in the State Department. The return was for an undetermined amount of time. Ambassador Sung Kim was a very seasoned senior foreign service officer who had previously served in the Philippines and had historically had a good relationship with the US military. His departure from Indonesia would significantly slow our progress getting the team into the country since the ambassador's temporary replacement, the charge de affairs, was more risk averse.

In Indonesia, 5th SFAB was incredibly fortunate to have Col. Ian Francis as the Army attaché. He was an early adopter and staunch supporter of the SFAB concept. Col. Leo Liebreich, the defense attaché, and Majors Matt Gross and Brian Vega from the office of defense cooperation were also stanch supporters of SFAB efforts to partner and work with the Indonesian National Military. Col. Francis and the attaché office worked extremely hard to get our team through all the bureaucratic hurdles hindering our team's entry to the country. He was also persistent, though, with much more diplomacy and patience than any of the Brown Berets, as they were eager to get to work with the Indonesian National Military.

Gen. Perkasa had given his full support to the request from the SFAB to train side by side with the Indonesian National Military. There had been some upheaval in the South China Sea, and he hoped to modernize the army to meet the challenges he foresaw. The Indonesian Embassy in Washington DC had been ready to issue the team's visas for nearly eight weeks. However, when the Indonesian Foreign Ministry in Jakarta discussed this issue with the US Embassy in Jakarta, the Indonesians informed the Brown Berets that the US Embassy staff were reluctant to allow any Department of Defense personnel into their country. We needed some help to move our visa request along. Brig. Gen. Taylor endeavored to intercede but was met with resistance. He engaged both Maj. Gen. Braga and USARPAC's political adviser to speak on behalf of the SFAB with the US Embassy country team in Indonesia.[57] These senior people had been incredibly supportive of the SFAB missions during our inaugural deployment into the Indo-Pacific. Through a series of phone conversations and emails, they were able to educate the embassy team on what the SFAB was, what it did, and how it would help to support the Indonesian National Military Army mission. We hoped it would be enough.

After an additional four weeks of interactive requests and negotiations, the country team finally agreed to allow the SFAB team in-country. Colonel Ian Francis called me on Friday, March 5, 2021, to give me the highlights of his conversation with the political adviser and the country team and told me MAT 5132 could proceed with travel from Washington State to Indonesia. The Brown Berets had been flexible, versatile, and patient while waiting the process out and immediately booked flights with a fervor. Col. Francis and I wanted the team to leave within the seventy-two-hour window so they could capitalize on this opportunity. We did not want to give anyone the chance to reconsider.

Delays happen, but nobody could ever blame a delay on the SFAB NCOs. They were first-class at coordinating and arranging equipment lists for country entry, paperwork for containers, and any final administrative paperwork to fly over or enter a foreign country. They had learned that research, detailed planning, and determination can make just about anything happen. In fact, Staff Sergeant Travis Bales of MAT 5132 eventually developed the Indonesian country entrance standard operating procedure adopted by the 25th Infantry Division. Their fortitude and resilience were the cornerstone of the SFAB brand within the organizational chain of command (FORSCOM), the operational chain of command (USARPAC), and the defense attaché offices we worked with. We had to produce results and deliver on promises in the early days, just like any fledgling start-up.

Since getting the green light, we had planned out about 70–80 percent of what the Indonesian National Military wanted us to do with their army over the coming four months. We were unaware that USARPAC might have some ideas of their own. The team learned about USARPAC's plans while they endured two weeks of COVID quarantine.

During wartime, USARPAC headquarters provides resources, trains, and sustains forces in the Indo-Pacific. It also provides intratheater sustainment and logistics for forces forward deployed. However, the headquarters hasn't supported a major war since Vietnam. In most cases it is focused on engagement strategies with partners and allies.[58] In Indonesia this meant the USARPAC staff was focused on the GARUDA SHIELD exercises that were slated to take place in August of 2021. These exercises encompassed three islands and helped to develop the capabilities of the Joint Pacific Multinational Readiness Complex. Thousands of US armed forces personnel had been preparing for this large upcoming exercise.

Large formations from both the 82nd Airborne Division from Fort Bragg, North Carolina and the 25th Infantry Division from Schofield Barracks, Hawaii were scheduled to participate in GARUDA SHIELD. Again, the US Embassy country team in Jakarta was hesitant to allow entry of the exercise site-survey teams. These teams were necessary because they developed support and logistic plans required to bring in large formations to conduct the bilateral training with the Indonesian National Military. They address life support requirements (food, living quarters, latrines, showers), transportation, and training areas, to name a few. For the airborne units, they specifically need to survey the airborne drop zones to certify that it is safe for US Army paratroopers to jump into during the exercise. Some of the US Army leadership in the chain of command wanted to change the SFAB team's mission from partnering with the Indonesian National Military and transform it into an exercise advanced team that would execute some site-survey tasks.

While this was a good idea from a resourcing perspective, if the mission changed, it would also change the funding and authorities that the team was using. Most importantly, the team wouldn't be doing what General Perkasa of the Indonesian National Military desired, including building trust and relationships across the Indonesian Army. For the funding and authorities, the topic remained a blurred and disputed area for the SFAB enterprise and SFAC. The 5th SFAB led the way on deploying teams into a large number of countries using appropriate funding and authorities outside armed conflict and exercises. These inquiries sparked a lively debate about our mission. I disagreed with my boss, Brig. Gen. Taylor, on this particular issue. They had asked our team to be their Advanced Operational Node (ADVON), and I was passionately against that because I felt it took away from the SFAB's primary mission. How to proceed on this controversial issue was internally debated and I should have kept it that way. Unfortunately, I had put someone on the Cc line of an email regarding ADVON support versus SFAB-Indonesian National Military partnership training that I should not have. Lucky for me, Brig. Gen. Taylor was a patient and forgiving boss. He and

I had a phone call while I was in Mongolia, and he reminded me about email protocols and what constituted internal "family" business and what did not. I didn't make the mistake again and we developed options on how to balance our two requirements. As a result of this discussion, we cut away two qualified Brown Berets for two weeks during the team's mission start to accompany a staff member from the Indonesia Embassy Army attaché office to various training exercise sites throughout the country.

Sending these two Brown Berets, Staff Sergeants Travis Bales and Joseph Gesumaria, to do the site-survey mission worked out very well for our team in the end. Brig. Gen. Taylor was right. We were able to keep multiple customers happy and demonstrate value to the Indo-Pacific community of interest, as well as the "big Army" and its large tactical formations, the 82nd Airborne and 25th Infantry Divisions. The team was small but had operational and strategic impacts for the entire enterprise. Colonel Neal Mayo, brigade commander from the 25th Infantry Division, was coming to Indonesia for the Defender Pacific Exercise later that summer. He had written me a letter thanking me for the details that our two-person Brown Beret team had provided to him during his staff member's visit for the site team survey. Although I had been reluctant to cut these two men away from our partnered training and agreed-to activities, they had been sent anyway and had obviously made a big impact with regard to the overall USARPAC mission. That was great news for all of us. It also demonstrated our flexibility and provided key information that could be used for future events.

Indonesian National Military Gen. Andika Perkasa, the Army chief of staff, had personally welcomed Capt. LeShaun Smith and Team 5132 to Indonesia immediately after they exited quarantine. He promptly laid out his vision for the SFAB-Indonesian National Military partnership. Nobody knew that this meeting was being filmed and posted on Instagram. The video quickly became viral and made them social media favorites.

Gen. Perkasa was a graduate of US Army schools and he wanted to expose his tactical brigades and battalions to our US Army NCOs. What resulted from this venture was a three-and-a-half-month grueling trek to visit and train seven different units across the nation. So, in essence, every nine to fourteen days the team picked up and moved to link up with another unit for training. They traveled long Indonesian roads in a minibus followed by an Indonesian National Military cargo truck carrying their equipment. All but one of these units had never been visited by foreign forces or worked with the US Army previously. It was a new experience for everyone!

Their first stop was with the Indonesian National Military's 17th Airborne Brigade commanded by Colonel Marwan. The colonel and other leaders told them that they had participated in a virtual staff exercise with the 2nd battalion in the fall of 2020 and were excited to finally work with US soldiers in person. They had taken scads of pictures and created PowerPoint presentations and eagerly showed them to the Brown Berets and told them how much they had particularly enjoyed the classes on intelligence preparation of the battlefield and mission analysis, which were all part of the Army's military decision-making process (MDMP). Some of the Indonesian staff officers flocked to Capt. LeShaun Smith and the 5132 team members to discuss the variances between US MDMP planning and the Indonesian Army method of planning. It was a good initial introduction to an enthusiastic audience.

After a day of introduction and site orientation, it was time to get to work. On the first training day with the battalion, the Brown Berets walked into a conference room filled with seventy-five junior enlisted soldiers, two staff officers, and the battalion commander. They also had a Philippine Army system and a translator. Only a handful of the Indonesians understood English, and the Brown Berets realized the translator struggled to rephrase military terminology from English to Indonesian. The Brown Berets stumbled through the classes but weren't sure if the training was paying off. They realized the best interactions they were having with the battalion was during physical training when the Brown Berets paired up with small groups of Indonesian National Military soldiers for different exercises. Demonstrations of US Army tactics proved very popular as well since many of the Indonesian soldiers, while not understanding what was spoken or translated, could clearly grasps the concepts when seeing it acted out. The prepared classroom instruction with PowerPoint presentations was clearly not going to work with all their partners. The Brown Berets needed to change their entire approach.

After MAT 5132 had rotated through the first two Indonesian National Military units, they realized they could have a more significant impact with their partner force and build stronger bonds with them by modifying their training plan. Staff Sergeant Steven Politano, the operations NCO, and Staff Sergeant Gabriel Yalung, the communications NCO, developed a new method of interacting with these units. Instead of keeping the mix of fifty- to seventy-person groups together, they divided them into nine- to twelve-man teams or squads and donned their body armor, helmets, and weapons to pair up with their counterparts. Each squad had a Brown Beret sponsor that accompanied them throughout their training events. The sponsor aided in creation of better group dynamics and stronger bonds with the Indonesian National Military soldiers. Overall, they found this was a good ratio. For training, they created three primary stations for groups to rotate through. One focused on military operations in urban terrain, with special emphasis on a four-person team conducting single- and multiple-room clearing. The second station was medical training, which was very popular, and involved selected basic medical skills pulled from the US Army's Tactical Combat Casualty Care system. At the third station, groups trained on basic small-unit tactics such as a squad attack, a simple attack involving a base of fire with another maneuvering element. While the squads and Brown Berets trained on these three primary areas, Capt. Smith and S.Sgt. Gabriel Yalung worked with the Indonesian National Military battalion leadership using the Remote Advise Assist Virtual Accompany Kits and mission command techniques. These kits consisted of modified Samsung phones that created an internal tactical network and allowed Capt. Smith to track the squad movements and communicate with them. The kits demonstrated how the SFAB and Indonesian National Military could interoperate during combat operations and work together. Changing the training methodology and plan required some negotiations between the Brown Berets and Indonesian National Military because it deviated from the agreed-to activities. However, it better met the needs of their customer, the Indonesian soldiers, and everyone was happy. The Indonesian National Military quickly posted some pictures and short clips on Indonesian social media of the groups training together. Given the hundreds of thousands of views and comments, it was clear what the Brown Berets were doing was popular.

The NCOs who developed this training methodology had broad latitude to revamp the training according to the situation on the ground as it developed. These members of the SFAB acted as an autonomously empowered team that allowed them to be creative and flexible in their course design. This, in turn, allowed them to thrive and develop keen leadership and problem-solving skills. This kind of trust was not typical except in the Army's special ops units. In our case, the Army had built a conventional force where

NCOs from various fields could come and thrive in an environment where they could develop as leaders and problem-solvers in an ambiguous environment.

One of the advantages of the smaller groups and squads was the opportunities for competitions. Competition brings about esprit de corps, even in small groups. Squads competed with each other in many of the other SFAB planned training events like shooting, land navigation, or medical lane training. It also allowed sports competition during physical training and some sillier games that built even more camaraderie. For instance, there was a game the Indonesian National Military liked to play where groups of soldiers and their Brown Berets formed a type of conga-line of eight to ten people with a balloon attached to the rear of the last person. The goal was for the person in front to pop the balloon of another team. It was a funny contest to watch as caterpillar-looking groups of American and Indonesian soldiers snaked back and forth attempting to outmaneuver each other. The Indonesians really got a kick out of watching their American counterparts embrace the game. Pats on the back, smiles, and lots of high fives between team members followed once the match was over. The team also shared American games. Luckily one of the Brown Berets had decided to throw an American football into their gear. They attempted to teach their Indonesian counterparts ultimate football, which in reality looks like chaos on the field as the Indonesian National Military players were never quite sure what they were supposed to do. There was laughter again on both sides.

After visiting four different units, the Brown Berets had fallen into a certain pattern for their daily interfaces with the Indonesian National Military soldiers. For the most part they consisted of unit physical training, combat skills training, cultural performances or engagements, and numerous Indonesian meals (both formal and informal in nature). Their Indonesian National Military counterparts were nothing if not enthusiastic. As the Brown Berets rotated through different units, the morning physical training also varied. Sometimes physical training included foot marching around the local villages, a few times they bicycled through the city while dodging scooter and pedestrians, and others they played soccer on fields surrounded by tropical jungles and rice paddies. It was definitely a surreal experience for each Brown Beret.

They also shared their meals together and refreshed themselves during the hot days training, especially lunch. The first couple of days of authentic Indonesian food was a shock to many a Brown Beret digestive system after the Western-style hotel food they'd eaten during quarantine. It took a while for the teams to get accustomed to the differences of food and how their digestive systems might process that food. Eventually they learned to love it, so much so that Sgt. Blair Butler, the intelligence NCO, thought it was worthy of sharing and as such took to the Indonesian National Military's social media to speak about the wonderful food. Additionally, by the time they departed Indonesia, Sgt. Butler had picked up a significant amount of Bahasa, the Indonesian official language.

At every unit they worked with the Indonesians would try to get the Brown Berets to eat Durian fruit. Durian fruit is local to Indonesia and is also found in other countries in the region. It also smells horrible. Some say it smells like rotting garbage when cut open, others the strong stench of gasoline. The Indonesians loved it and were always amused to see the look on the Brown Berets faces as they popped pieces into their mouths, dutifully chewed, and forced the food down their throats.

The Brown Berets also had opportunities to explore some of the cultural aspects of Indonesia. A few of them explored one of the most well-known cultural sites, the Bromo Volcano, a national heritage site. The trip to the Bromo Volcano included bouncing along in Range Rovers and holding on for dear life on the back of motorcycles across sand dunes, mostly in the pitch dark. Their reward for this harrowing travel was a fantastic sunrise experience at the top of the volcano. At another Indonesian National Military location they visited the Borobudur Temple, the world's largest Buddhist temple and met with the Javanese sultan along the northeast coast of Java. In Salatiga, they met with the mayor and bicycled through town with its elected officials and the local Indonesian National Military unit in a public display of friendship between the United States and Indonesia. The Brown Berets certainly had some unique perspective-broadening experiences.

Among the Brown Berets, Staff Sergeant Michael Welch, military police advisor, and Staff Sergeant Jun Choh were some of the Indonesian National Military's favorite trainers. The Indonesians were particularly impressed with S.Sgt. Jun Choh. He was an infantry NCO whose family had immigrated from South Korea to Washington State when he was young. Having a fellow Asian serving in the US Army resonated with the Indonesian soldiers on how multicultural the United States is. He quickly became an Indonesian social media favorite and was featured in many of their interviews.

By the time the team had transitioned to the western portion of the island of Java, they had been to five different Indonesian units. The initial phase of their work had been a breakneck nine weeks and the Brown Berets were admittedly worn out. They were attempting to meet the high expectations of Indonesian National Military Gen. Perkasa. Another part was brought on from the changes in environment, specifically coming from the Pacific Northwest into the jungle-type environment located at the equator. Ramadan had ended and this gave the Brown Berets a much-needed four-day respite while many Indonesians enjoyed the holiday. The Brown Berets made the most of this by performing equipment maintenance and taking care of some administrative and logistical planning for their final mission. Their swansong mission in Indonesia was north of Java on the large island of Kalimantan, and required additional coordination to fly their combat equipment and weapons to their destination.

Throughout their cross-country travel, the Brown Berets were able to assist the US Embassy as well. Besides teaching numerous medical first responder classes, Sergeant Zachary Mendola, the team's medic, conducted over fifteen local hospital site surveys. This provided the Embassy's Protection Detachment significant, detailed information on hospitals for which they had no prior information. While a small task during each of their stops, it helped the US Embassy team tremendously to understand medical capabilities across the expansive country.

The inaugural mission for the Brown Berets of MAT 5132 with the Indonesian National Military was the most celebrated on social media of all of our missions. Social media posts highlighted the significant impact and capabilities that our small team had on a partner force and the US Army enterprise at large. The team was instrumental in providing information from this interaction and training those participants for the Defender Pacific exercises that took place later that summer. The information assisted those units in learning how to construct training exercises with the Indonesian National Military in advance of getting on the ground there. MAT 5132 had planted the seeds of goodwill between the US Army and the Indonesian Army that will serve us well for years to come. Capt. LeShaun Smith and his team had experimented with how to develop this relationship while training with their newfound friends. It was remarkable what they were able to accomplish.

Back to the Original Early Adopters: Self-Motivation

The SFAB's ties to the Royal Thai Army were deeper and stronger than any other national army in the Indo-Pacific. This was due to a number of factors, including us hosting the Stryker training in Washington State, our collaborative training with them in Thailand in August of 2020, and accompanying them to Hawaii with a JRTC rotation. The RTA had concluded that the 5th SFAB was a very capable foreign partner and that they could work cohesively with us. We felt the same. Surprisingly, the teams going to Thailand required a lot of self-motivation due to many unforeseen obstacles placed in their path. Overcoming the endless series of hurdles was exhausting, but the Brown Berets from MATs 5131 and 5133 were determined to make it to Thailand and work with their partners.

Both teams had not participated in the previous training with the RTA, but luckily those that did worked only one floor below in the 1st Battalion Headquarters building. They relied heavily on the earlier experiences of their peers to understand RTA personalities, training methodologies, and temperaments. MAT 5131 was led by Captain Matt Thimble and Sergeant First Class Daniel Dougherty and MAT 5133 was led by Captain Brenton Clark and Sergeant First Class Emmanuel Moore (not to be confused with Sfc. Omar Moore, our battalion S4 NCO), both very capable teams. Captains Thimble and Clark each understood the internal dynamics of the JUSMAGTHA and what Brig. Gen. Taylor and I had experienced earlier in negotiating and deciding on their mission to Thailand. They also knew their goal was to get out of Bangkok and go to whatever tactical partner units the RTA general staff decided on. Even after securing permission to go to Thailand, the teams still experienced delays getting to their final destinations.

COVID lingered and languished across the globe, which caused fluctuations in medical protocols. In addition to that, the military junta had returned to Myanmar (also known as Burma) and was wreaking havoc on the border with refugees attempting to cross into Thailand. Both aspects caused the senior RTA staff members to pay attention to two small SFAB teams coming into the country. Finally, COVID had created additional bureaucratic entry steps for the certificate of entry process, which neither the Royal Thai Government, the RTA, nor JUSMAGTHA fully understood.

Captains Clark and Thimble were persistent. They, along with their company commander, Maj. Morgan Maier, made phone calls and sent emails to just about everyone they could find that was involved in the country-entry process. They mapped out the requirements, timelines, and visa requirements as part of their research. After what seemed like an eternity of back-and-forth, we executed a last-ditch effort and called in a favor from one of our contacts inside the RTA headquarters. Luckily for us, this person managed to break some of the bureaucratic delays and helped the critical paperwork get approved. Capt. Brenton Clark and Sfc. Moore's MAT 5133 finally arrived in Bangkok in late March. Capt. Thimble and Sfc. Dougherty's 5131 arrived in late April 2021. Both teams went immediately into quarantine upon arrival.

As the SFAB teams went about finalizing their plans and coordinating with the RTA General Staff while in quarantine, I sent a note to my old friend Major General Pena, who commanded the RTA 11th Infantry Division and the two subordinate regiments our teams would eventually work with. I admired him as a leader and felt he was a valuable partner for the SFAB and the US Army. I would happily serve under his command. He was delighted to hear that SFAB teams had returned to Thailand to work with the RTA. Maj. Gen. Pena didn't know if the Brown Berets would work with his unit, but I believe he talked to the RTA General Staff about it since soon after we were told the teams would likely work with the 11th Infantry Division. I don't think it was a coincidence.

While both teams had made it to Thailand, they still faced obstacles. First, they still needed to finalize specific agreed-to activities with the RTA. Having those approved allowed them to conduct detailed planning with their partner units in the 11th

Infantry Division and settle their life support contracts. Second, due to increased COVID cases, the Royal Thai Government limited movement between provinces and delayed the teams' movement outside of Bangkok for another two weeks past their quarantine time. The SFAB leaders maintained a positive attitude and decided to use the delay to learn more about the Thai culture and history by exploring the parts of Bangkok that were still open. Excursions included visiting local food markets to get used to the food, seeing some of the ancient Buddhist temples, and simply wandering the streets of Bangkok to get a feel for the people. Meanwhile, at their hotel they cross-trained and taught each other classes on logistics and artillery operations and conducted additional hands-on medical training. Time wasn't wasted.

After weeks of waiting, the RTA General Staff finally approved the SFAB team's agreed-to activities. As expected, the MATs were to work with the 111th Regimental Combat Team and the 112th Stryker Regimental Combat Team (SRCT) from Maj. Gen. Pena's 11th Infantry Division—something we thought was a forgone conclusion but needed to run through the RTA's bureaucratic process. As the Brown Berets prepared to send select individuals to a final planning conference and conduct a site survey, they were delayed by a Thai national holiday, Songkran. I vividly recall hearing about this further delay during my point-to-point phone call discussion with Captains Clark and Thimble. Luckily, they couldn't see my head droop or hear my sigh when they passed the news. *Dang, I thought. What the hell else is going to stand in our way to work with Thais. Can this simple mission get any harder? Seriously!* I kept my frustrations to myself and reassured the team leaders and talked about turning the setback into an opportunity. All in all, the teams spent just under two months between quarantine, waiting on decisions, COVID, and the holiday in Bangkok.

Once they got out to the May final planning conference in Chachoengsao with the 11th Infantry Division, Brown Berets presented a menu of options to the RTA planners for partnered activities. The options ran the gamut of the warfighting functions (mission command, movement and maneuver, intelligence, fires, sustainment, and protection). The RTA was pleased with the flexibility in the schedule and the compromises the Brown Berets were willing to make. One significant change was moving the physical training sessions from the mornings, which is normally when US Army units exercise, to the afternoons, which was the Thai way of doing things. Extreme perspiration and fatigue were the result for many of the Brown Berets. Working out during the cool, damp mornings of the Pacific Northwest had been traded for the tropical heat and sun at four o'clock in the afternoon. But it was worth the sacrifice to work with the proud officers, NCOs, and soldiers of the 11th Infantry Division.

At long last, training finally began on June 1, 2021. Capt. Thimble and MAT 5131 worked with the 112th on Stryker tactics, techniques, and procedures in Ko Chan, Chong Buri District. Separately, Sfc. Moore and MAT 5133 worked with the 111th Regimental Combat Team in Chachoensao on air assault techniques and honing their light infantry tactics.[59] SFAB NCOs worked with Thai Army soldiers on small-unit tactics on such battle drills as squad attack as well as how to employ their new Stryker vehicles in simulated fights. They reviewed many of the tactics taught the previous summer by MATs 5111 and 5113. The training they conducted was in preparation for the 40th COBRA GOLD exercises between the US and Thailand scheduled for August of 2021. It is one of the largest multinational exercises in Asia. Participants for this exercise come from Indonesia, Japan, Malaysia, Singapore, South Korea, and of course the United States.[60, 61] The Thai Army had the benefit of working with the SFAB beforehand, and as such, was better integrated and more interoperable for the future training event.

As the Brown Berets went about working with their RTA

counterparts, Maj. Gen. Pena announced he would inspect the training to make sure it was going to plan. When word of this inspection reached the 112th SRCT commander, Lt. Col. Amphon, he and Lt. Folk, one of the RTA company commanders, immediately pulled in Capt. Thimble and Sfc. Dougherty to plan the engagement. The Thais wanted to incorporate the SFAB into the whole process, a demonstration of trust in the Brown Berets. When Maj. Gen. Pena arrived, Brown Berets and 112th staff members presented the products resulting from a full round of the US Army's military decision-making process. The combined group walked through detailed course of action sketches and planning timelines. The whole ordeal would have made any command and general staff college instructor from Fort Leavenworth, Kansas proud. Of course, this particular version had a little Thai twist to it.

Next the 112th displayed how they were learning to employ their Stryker vehicles. A platoon of Strykers—four vehicles, their crews, and dismount soldiers—conducted a react-to-contact drill against a simulated enemy. The Strykers were attacked by small arms fire that disabled one of their vehicles. The Thai platoon leadership expertly deployed his formation, established a base of fire, and maneuvered against the enemy. The whole time Maj. Gen. Pena's eyes critically watched as Thai soldiers maneuvered across the landscape with SFAB Brown Berets close at hand. Once it finished, the smile on his face indicated the 112th and Brown Berets had passed his test. During both the decision-making-process discussion and after the Stryker react-to-contact drill, Maj. Gen. Pena asked questions regarding training progress and performance. Everyone was pleased with the partnership training.

One significant advantage for the Brown Berets training with the RTA is that the RTA bases were about a ninety-minutes-drive from the typical tourist spots. They had the opportunity to experience authentic Thailand versus the one they had encountered in Bangkok. Team members ate at the nearby restaurants, shopped in the village market, and even got haircuts at the local barber shop. The haircuts were certainly a learning experience. Sfc. Dougherty, the senior NCO on MAT 5131 and enforcer of discipline and standards, realized they had not considered haircuts as part of their life support contracts, something the US Army is typically known for. So, he worked through the interpreters to find a barbershop near their hotel in the village of Bo Thong. Based on their facial expressions and body language, the barbers had probably never had a Western-looking patron ever walk into their shop. Sfc. Dougherty plopped down in the chair first and attempted to describe the type of cut he wanted through hand gestures and the interpreters. Unfortunately, when the whole ordeal was over, he came out looking like a brand-new Army private fresh from basic training—not exactly what he had envisioned when he sat down. Fortunately, Capt. Thimble was next and proceeded to take a more systematic approach to explain to the Thai barbers what he had in mind. He negotiated a much better result.

During one off-duty event, the Brown Berets visited a local nature preserve and had the opportunity to feed the wild monkeys. It was definitely a tourist destination, but nonetheless a unique adventure for all the visiting Brown Berets. Local vendors sold bananas and peanuts that allowed tourists to hand feed the monkeys. The Thai officers and NCOs escorting them laughed at their counterparts as they squirmed in uncomfortable situations with the human-like creatures. Just like eating meals together, small excursions like this one help build rapport between the two groups.

Eventually the SFAB teams' time in Thailand came to an end. We had, however, fulfilled our commitment to the RTA, and especially the 11th Infantry Division, from the previous year when we had promised to return. Luckily Capt. Thimble, Sfc. Dougherty, and Sfc. Moore were in close contact with their replacements from 2nd Battalion, 5th SFAB. The 2nd Battalion teams were in a much better position to work with the RTA after all the work the Brown Berets of 5131 and 5133 put into overcoming country-entry requirements and establishing agreed-to activities. Both MATs displayed incredible determination, endurance, and optimism while negotiating to get into Thailand. They were told no by countless people but were self-motivated to get it done. Many had told them that no US forces would train in Thailand due to COVID. They had shipped equipment that never arrived. Yet, they never gave up. Their resolve was extraordinary and a testament to their commitment to the SFAB vision and mission. It was also the first occasion that 5th SFAB Brown Berets returned to a country and unit in which they had previously worked. We hoped that it contributed to the overall strategic partnership the US was trying to build with the Royal Thai Army and Royal Thai Government.

The One That Got Away—Stuck in Paradise: Comfortable with Failure

The SFAB had been building relationships and training with the Thai Army, Mongolians, Indonesians, and others. The recognition we received from this training and interaction had been so positive. We were thankful for these opportunities to showcase our talents and value. The team that headed to Fiji proved to be the team that showed the SFAB enterprise and the US Army that sometimes its okay to fail. But it was still a tough pill to swallow for everyone.

Capt. Matt Orders had visited Fiji the previous spring in 2020 and had high hopes that the SFAB would be working with the Republic of Fiji Military Forces (RFMF) soon. During his visit, the RFMF and US Embassy had been accommodating and supportive of developing a SFAB-RFMF relationship. The serving ambassador wished to continue a good relationship with us and the RFMF.

The defense attaché and the Army attaché were also interested in us coming to Fiji to work with the RFMF. Everything indicated a mission to Fiji would be possible and relatively simple. However, the process of seeing this to fruition was not so easy.

Typically, little military attention is paid to Fiji beyond the annual exercise CARTWHEEL. The exercises' intent is to create collaborative infantry training events, conduct civic action with the local schools, and offer humanitarian programs in and around Vanua Levu.[62] The duties of the SFAB were to strengthen the RFMF by offering realistic training to increase their capacity as regional leaders and collaborators toward a free and open Indo-Pacific. Military-to-military training strengthens our bonds and builds relationships so that all parties can become interoperable with our allies in the event that they need to respond to some emergency. It reinforces the US commitment to promoting safety to our partners in the Pacific.

The attaché offices had been speaking to the RFMF about our training plans for Fiji as our planned deployment window opened in January 2021. The RFMF was totally committed previously, but they now appeared to be backtracking due to COVID. Originally, we planned to send a twelve-person maneuver team headed by Capt. Greg Lentz to the island to work with the light infantry regiment and infantry school that Matt Orders had previously visited. Call after call reinforced the feeling that the RFMF was hesitant to bring even a small twelve-person team to the island. For some reason, they were concerned about the numbers of people rather than what the Brown Berets would actually do. They asked if we would consider breaking up the team and only send four to six Brown Berets to Fiji. They were very interested in preparing some soldiers to attend the US Army Ranger School. Breaking the team up was not something we wanted to do. Doing so dissipated the team and left some without a mission. This was bad for morale and went against guidance from Maj. Gen. Jackson, the SFAC commander.

However, being an adaptable formation and wanting to meet the needs of our customer and partner, we decided to change our array of forces—we would shift our teams allocated to one country and move them to another. Due to the preparation work and cultural training we had done, this was no small task. We hadn't expected to push so hard for a SFAB team in Fiji, until we received additional guidance from USARPAC that Fiji was a strategic point where they wanted another army-to-army touch point. I decided to see if a smaller four-person engineer advising team (E-AT) led by Captain Chuck Spencer and Sergeant First Class Stephen Botelho would work better. These "enabler" teams were usually in higher demand than our maneuver teams because of their composition and, honestly, their name. While our maneuver teams were infantry in name only comprised of mostly noninfantry occupational-skill-specific Brown Berets, embassy country teams, attaché offices, and partner forces were always suspicious of the term *maneuver* because of the offensive, i.e., aggressive connotation. I expected these outside entities to be much more interested in our logistics and engineer teams.

We eventually shifted teams to accommodate the RFMF and had fully expected the engineer team to be in Indonesia or Thailand. Those countries proved to be more difficult to enter given the geopolitical and COVID conditions. Thus, everything had come to a planning and preparation standstill for Capt. Spencer and his Brown Berets until mother nature stepped in. Tropical cyclone season had begun for Fiji, and they had already experienced a few storms that year. Sending our team in at that point seemed like a reasonable solution. It was not—at least not initially. The final turning point came when I had a twenty-minute conversation with the defense attaché, a Navy commander, in Fiji and explained to him the variety of missions our engineer Brown Berets could perform. Importantly, that included humanitarian assistance and disaster-relief tasks. He agreed and said he was meeting in a few days with the Fijian defense chief. The meeting was the first meeting in over three months, as COVID had delayed engagements. After that conversation, Capt. Spencer and his team put together a few training proposals for the defense attaché, so he had them readily available as part of the meeting. I also had Capt. Spencer talk through the recommendations with the Army attaché, so he understood some of the details in case there were questions.

One morning I saw a note from the Fijian defense attaché in my inbox. I nervously moved my mouse over the email to open it. Was it going to be good news or disappointing news that would cause us to go back to the drawing board with our engineer team? I clicked and the message was encouraging. The Fijian defense chief had agreed to the SFAB proposal, and our engineer team would work with Fijian Royal Engineers stationed out of Suva. I excitedly shared this good news with Capt. Spencer. The next step was to secure entry visas for the Brown Berets. This proved to be a longer process than anticipated and took four strikingly long weeks to navigate the bureaucratic gates. We also had to ask the RFMF for assistance to help the entry requirement paperwork get over a few hurdles. Luckily, they were a proactive sponsor and pushed the paperwork across the proverbial goal line. In the meantime, E-AT 5511 determined its flight route and contracting options to move its equipment. To reduce cost, they decided to pallet load their engineering equipment and parse it down to the simple essentials. Their precise calculations ended up saving us tens of thousands of dollars.

Finally, the day came, and the Brown Berets of E-AT 5511 took off, landing in Fiji in early April 2021. We were excited because their arrival meant our "start-up" battalion had deployed seventeen of our eighteen teams into a foreign country for our inaugural mission. That's a 94 percent success rate with a completely new organization. I was personally elated by the success.

The Fiji team was required to adhere to a two-week quarantine just like many of our other SFAB teams. The Brown Berets were pleased to learn that their quarantine hotel was located on the beach. And, as part of their quarantine procedures, they were allocated an hour each day for exercise and mental freedom outside of their rooms, which was usually taken on the picturesque beach. This small privilege was in our view a reward for the past sacrifices these soldiers had endured. The pictures Capt. Spencer sent of their time on the beach showed they were in a paradise-like environment with beautiful beaches.

Once their quarantine time was complete, the engineer team moved to the capital of Suva in anticipation of meeting with the Fijian Infantry Regiment (their army branch of their military forces) engineers. This was optimistic on our part since COVID was ramping up and Fiji began partial and complete lockdown status depending on locations. This ranged from a no-movement order in the capital, where the Brown Berets couldn't leave their hotel, to limited freedom, where they had the opportunity to shop in nearby stores. Unfortunately, the Fijian engineer unit members were more hesitant to meet with *anyone* in person, including personnel from the US Embassy attaché office. The result of the Fijian hesitancy meant the engineer Brown Berets remained in a standby mode for a little over four weeks waiting to meet with any representative from the Fijian Infantry Regiment.

COVID had consumed Fijian government and military resources. As such, the Fijian government focused on the escalating COVID crisis instead of the planned military-to-military engagement with the SFAB. Our Fijian engineer partners were assisting with the control and management of the national emergency. Our team wanted to help them, so they developed proposals to work with the Fijian military and aid them during this black swan crisis. Their proposals included assisting with command and control, logistics management, constructing temporary hospitals (the team had worked on the large one in Seattle in 2020), and several other humanitarian tasks. We thought we could work toward an amiable solution to benefit both parties.

Regrettably, the Fijian culture typically dictated face-to-face meetings prior to agreeing to work together or committing to a work plan and agreed-to activities. Unfortunately, due to the COVID conditions, it wasn't possible to meet in person to move forward with the relationship. Capt. Spencer and his team endeavored to text and make phone calls to their counterparts, but many went unanswered or were acknowledged with only a cursory response. Capt. Spencer considered several excuses to come over to the Fijian compound, including inspecting his equipment that had arrived and been secured on their compound. But that didn't work either. Once, our team was able to participate in a video conference between our attaché office and the Fijian Infantry Regiment command, but the meeting didn't manifest into any face-to-face interactions. All attempts to engage the Fijians in any in-person conversations or even a secure video conference fell on deaf ears. The lack of any engagement was frustrating. Our team could, nearly literally, see the Fijian engineer headquarters from their room hotel in Suva. They also drove past it on numerous occasions as they hoped to work with our partner force inside.

The Fijians had gone cold. They were not taking any chances in partnering with any outsiders. I made numerous calls and spoke to the new defense attaché Naval commander and the Army attaché and discussed options and opportunities to complete this training we had planned. I was told that we were not the only ones the Fijians were keeping at arm's length—the Australians, New Zealanders, and the Chinese were also unable to interact.

The Brown Berets had proven themselves to be quite resourceful. With these COVID delays they managed to work on better training for themselves. The team was diverse in talent, and this helped them to construct training that could benefit one and all. For example, the team consisted of a construction engineer, an electrician, and elite combat engineers known as sappers. The two junior members were scheduled to attend the Engineer's Sapper School in the late summer or early fall, so they focused classes and training that would best prepare them for the rigors of this premier Army school.

I talked with Capt. Spencer more frequently and left my virtual door open so we could chat more than the scheduled once per week that I arranged with each of my team leaders. The biggest thing I tried to convey to Capt. Spencer was maintaining a positive attitude and seeking opportunities. As the commander, I was also able to see themes and threads with our teams spread out across the entire Indo-Pacific. In this case, I had Capt. Spencer talk with Capt. Thimble and Capt. Clark in Thailand about the challenges they were facing working with or meeting with our partner forces. The teams in Thailand were working through many of the same frustrations and difficulties. All three of the teams needed to understand that they weren't the only ones facing issues with being the first SFAB team deployed as part of the entire 5th SFAB in the COVID environment.

By the end of May, things were still not moving forward for the Brown Berets in Fiji. I felt we really needed to make some hard decisions about this venture. I had considered giving the Fijians an ultimatum in hopes of forcing them to make a favorable decision on our behalf. After speaking with the defense attaché we concluded that decision day on whether or not to pull the plug on our Fijian venture would be May 28, which would allow us enough time to coordinate the team's equipment movement and purchase flight tickets that would get them through New Zealand and back to Seattle.

Decision day came a few days early due to more Fijian government mandated COVID restrictions. It was an unfortunate decision, but the Brown Berets had been sitting in the hotel waiting on something from the Fijians for over a month. I informed Col. Andy Watson of our recommended decision and ensured he had the necessary information to send to USARPAC and anyone else impacted by the situation. Technically, USARPAC decided to pull the team from Fiji, but we had the most reliable data and just needed them to endorse the decision and inform appropriate commanders and staffs.

Looking back, we probably should have made the decision earlier, but we were determined to "assume the yes" and maintain a positive attitude in every situation. We had seen COVID cases increase in other countries like Mongolia and the Philippines, and yet training continued in some form or fashion. But the Fijian government's many COVID policy additions and revisions were something we had not considered nor previously experienced. I was left feeling a bit defeated and deflated because the engineer team had been often requested but had yet to actually work with a partner force and build a trusting relationship for the future. In the end, both the chain of command and Team 5511 were comfortable with this failure and unfortunate situation.

Our Last Frontier— the Land of the Rising Sun: Tenacity

Given all we had accomplished getting Brown Berets to deploy to multiple countries in the winter and spring of 2021 we still had one company advisor team that did not have an assigned mission. Major Morgan Maier and his Brown Berets were eager for a mission as they watched others depart for their overseas missions. Selfishly Cmd. Sgt. Maj. Overway and I wanted to get them deployed as part of our command responsibility. We wanted to fulfill our recruiting pitch to these volunteers that they would gain experiences working alongside foreign army counterparts during their SFAB assignment. By the spring of 2021, we had not met that goal for one team.

On a large, big picture scale we wanted to deploy all our SFAB teams to demonstrate to the US Army and FORSCOM that they were getting a good return on investment in terms of filling the SFAB enterprise with talented and trained personnel and new equipment. To maintain SFAB enterprise personnel strengths FORSCOM wanted to know how many of the teams were getting used by the Army service component commands, USARPAC in our case. They didn't want this new car they had built just sitting in the garage with high maintenance costs. Preservation of the unit itself was part of the reason we wanted as many teams as possible to work with a partner force. As deployments and obligations in Iraq and Afghanistan decreased, the other regionally aligned SFABs struggled to figure out how to penetrate the bureaucratic processes related to the Army and geographic commands in South America, Africa, Europe, and even the Middle East.

For Maj. Morgan Maier and 1st Sgt. Duane Bochmann's CAT 5130, from our C Company, they could not yet demonstrate the return on investment to FORSCOM. The opportunities for their team we had anticipated in Thailand and Indonesia had not borne fruit. We needed to find another way to get our teams into our partner countries. What options did we have that we had not fully explored? After a monumental brainstorming session, Maj. Maier and I believed that reconnecting with Japan was our best alternative. The previous fall of 2020, a small 5th SFAB element led by Col. Andy Watson had participated in an exercise in Japan. It was short but Col. Watson had met a variety of people from US Army Japan (USARJ) that might be able to assist with partnering the Brown Berets of CAT 5130 with the Japanese Defense Force. Only the dogged tenacity displayed by Maj. Maier and CAT 5130 made this mission happen at all.

To inquire about potential opportunities there, I emailed and called the US Army Japan (USARJ)chief of staff and G3 operations officer. Their response was a tentative maybe, which we which we took as a "yes" opportunity and proceeded to develop courses of action. From Washington State, Col. Watson started a dialogue with USARJ senior leaders and Maj. Maier began working on details with USARJ staff officers located at Camp Zama, Japan.

This process moved along at a snail's pace. First, we needed to convince the USARJ staff and commander the SFAB concept for training was a good idea then, in turn, have them convince their Japanese counterparts a partnership was in their best interest. The group identified an exercise called ORIENT SHIELD that held some potential. The US Army and Japanese Ground Self-Defense Forces Middle Army (JGSDF) conduct the exercise annually and it was to be held from mid-June to mid-July of 2021. This bilateral field training exercise enlarged interoperability between the two parties by whetting and testing multidomain and cross-domain theories.[63] The 1st Battalion, 28th Infantry Regiment from the 3rd Infantry Division located at Fort Stewart was slated to participate in ORIENT SHEILD. We thought the exercise was a way we could initiate training with the JGSDF. After a series of back-and-forth phone calls and emails over the course of several weeks, Col. Watson and Maj. Maier received an official response. The JGSDF agreed to include Maj. Maier's Brown Berets as part of the exercise, and they could come early to conduct pre-interoperability training with the Japanese designated unit to allow a smoother integration of both units. We had managed to score another win. With CAT 5130 heading to Japan, every SFAB team from the 1st Battalion task force would travel to a foreign country.

Maj. Maier and his team worked with the 15th Japanese Infantry Rapid Deployment Regiment (RDR). Their capacity was one of advising and liaising between the Japanese and the US infantry battalion.

Maj. Maier planned on his CAT team arriving two weeks before the infantry battalion and working with the Japanese regiment at their military installation in Zentsuji. The SFAB had found this to be a beneficial way to plan for training exercises. This way they could train with our partner forces and be totally prepared to integrate when the larger US units arrived. Following their period of quarantine, they were able to accomplish all that they had previously set forth.

For two weeks in Zentsuji the Brown Berets and 15th RDR worked together to prepare for the exercise. The Brown Berets also learned about the unit. Maj. Maier and his team trained with the regiment on how to utilize their Type 96 Armored Personnel Carrier, which is similar to the US's Infantry Stryker, and their Type 16 Maneuver Combat Vehicle, similar to the US's Mobile Gun System Stryker. The JGSDF had designed the 15th RDR to respond within seventy-two hours to instances when Japan's territorial integrity was threated. Still, the 15th RDR was working on how it would specifically do that when notified. Rapid deployment requires a high level of training readiness, well-established standard operating procedures, and preplanned and rehearsed logistics to move the unit and supplies. These are certainly not easy tasks.

During the two weeks Brown Berets worked with the Japanese on basic infantry tactics and medical training, they found that the Japanese soldiers were very proficient on technical tasks and excelled as soldiers. The Brown Berets found the Japanese regiment was trying to update their doctrine and operating concepts on how to employ their unit against an enemy. As the team members realized this, they started to understand that the Japanese needed to work on performing joint operations with their air force and navy, developing their NCO corps, and operating in a contested or denied communications environment. Most of all, the Japanese were interested in leader development. Young Japanese officers were interested in the US Army's approach to leadership and how US officers interact and build relationships with their senior NCOs.

The Brown Berets lived with the 15th RDR soldiers at Zentsuji, which was another benefit of arriving a few weeks before the official exercise. They stayed in the same barracks, walked the same sidewalks, and ate in their dining facility. For some Brown Berets, adjusting to the local cuisine was challenging. Sometimes unfamiliar food didn't sit well. Others jumped right in and tried everything. When some Brown Berets started skipping certain meals and attempted to forage food on their own, the Japanese cooks took notice. To mend this, Maj. Maier had the cooks prepare some simple bowls of rice for those that had more sensitive palates or stomachs. This compromise patched things up and was a lesson for the Brown Berets. Sometimes one must stick it out and embrace elements of the culture they may not like as long as it doesn't violate any of our Army values or ethics. In this Japanese dining facility case, Brown Berets had to expand their dietary preferences from hamburgers and chicken.

After the initial two weeks of training in Zentsuji the 15th RDR and the Brown Berets of CAT 5130 relocated to the Aibano Training Area northwest of Kyoto for Exercise ORIENT SHIELD. Relocation is not complicated, but it was a new experience for many on the team who had not been to a foreign country. The team figured how best to integrate the US and Japanese tactical operations command posts. They helped to negotiate the optimal way to conduct simultaneous platoon live fires, which is an inherently dangerous training task. The stress level is always higher when live bullets and mortar shells are flying. Maj. Maier's experience in the Republic of Korea as the deputy division operations officer in the 2nd Infantry Division had helped prepare him for this particular mission. Understanding how different armies can work together helped him identify many of the details to make it successful.

The Brown Berets served as the primary liaison element between the Japanese 15th RDR and the US 1-29 IN during the exercise. That meant they helped clear up the details between the two parties. By serving this purpose, the Japanese and US units focused on preparing for the tactical portions of the exercise rather than just coordinating and interpreting orders. Between the SFAB's tactical voice bridge and other communications systems, the Brown Berets enabled the 1-29 IN and 15th RDR commanders to talk directly to each other during the large-scale battalion-level situational training exercise.

I was especially proud of Maj. Maier and 1st Sgt. Bochmann for keeping their team motivated and continuing to pursue a partnership mission. Most importantly, having the Brown Berets of CAT 5130 arrive two weeks before the start of the exercise allowed them to best prepare and inform both parties about how they operated. The SFAB had become quite good at determining how to integrate with our Japanese allies and prove Brown Berets could provide value to the 15th RDR and a conventional US Army unit. While coming at the end of the 1st Battalion employment window, the Japanese mission verified our officers and NCOs would doggedly pursue partnership opportunities and work to achieve national objectives.

Mongolia: The Far Reaches of America

Cmd. Sgt. Maj. Overway and I decided to accompany the Mongolian mission for two reasons. First because Lt. Col. Phil Luu had convinced the Mongolians that our battalion headquarters, a large element, could set up in Mongolia. Second, Mongolia seemed like a high-reward location for the SFAB in terms of building a relationship—especially considering Mongolia's neighbors. As a colonel, I would be the most senior ranking US Army officer in the country for a considerable amount of time, which gave us some clout, or as those of us who had spent time in the Middle East called it, *wasta*. Unofficially I also thought it would be cool—how many other people get to travel to outer Mongolia for work?

While Maj. Dan Ludwig and 1st Sgt. Travis Keen's teams, composed of their CAT 5110, MAT 5112, FA-AT 5421, LAT 5611, and the battalion headquarters Advanced Operational Node conducted their Mongolian quarantine at the end of February 2021, the rest of the battalion headquarters staff, led by Maj. Scott Orr, worked on getting the second C-17 flight into Mongolia. The second C-17 flight required extra attention because we needed to transport US-specific ammunition for some of CAT 5110 and MAT 5112's training with the Mongolian Army. We had to overcome some significant challenges in our collaboration with US Strategic Command, which controls worldwide movement of aircraft like the C-17 we used, the crew assigned to fly our particular mission, and the diplomatic clearances needed to pass through China's airspace. Ensuring this flight could deliver all the personnel and cargo took tremendous effort and coordination between 5th SFAB and Lt. Col. Luu's defense attaché team in Mongolia. Even with such concerted efforts, we were met with a delay in Japan. Our C-17, Brown Berets, equipment, and crew (which ended up getting swapped) remained in diplomatic limbo at Yakota Air Base, Japan. While there, we continued our battalion mission command functions and worked to get SFAB teams deployed, but we hated being stuck waiting for others to negotiate our flight plan. A small group of us did tempt fate at a local US Air Force Morale Welfare and Recreation on-base restaurant where we endeavored to complete the Route 16 Burger Beast Challenge. Here we attempted to eat a one-and-a-half-pound hamburger topped with twelve slices of bacon and all the trimmings, and of course with a hefty side of French fries. It's served on a twenty-four-inch platter.

Unlike John Candy's character from *The Great Outdoors* who finished "the Ol' 96er" steak, all of us failed miserably. However, after our gastronomical misadventure with the Burger Beast, our C-17 landed at Ghengis Khan Airport in the middle of the night in early March 2021. Landing the huge aircraft and offloading the ammunition and cargo was impressive, given the bureaucratic and diplomatic obstacles we encountered.

Because the team members had been vaccinated, the quarantine had been modified down to a mere seven days instead of the fourteen Maj. Ludwig and 1st Sgt. Keen had previously encountered. During my and Cmd. Sgt. Maj. Overway's time in quarantine, Maj. Dan Ludwig and his Brown Berets finalized training plans with the Mongolian Land Forces Command (LFC). They were excited to work with the United States Army and planned to bring officers and NCOs from around the country to participate in the training events. Initially, the training events were going to occur close to the national capital, Ulaanbaatar, commonly called "UB" by the younger Mongolian generation. Instead, they moved it further away from the capitol near a town called Zuunmod, south of UB, for reasons unknown to us. The LFC headquarters was located in Zuunmod and so was the 16th Mechanized Brigade, which hosted a sizable portion of the training conducted by the Mongolia SFAB Teams. CAT 5110, Capt. Chris Kosmyna's Field Artillery Advisor Team (FA-AT) 5421, and Capt. Simon Johnston's Logistic's Advisor Team (LAT) 5611 conducted medical, training management, military decision-making processes, mortar training and live fires, and logistics planning classes at this location. All training focused on preparing Mongolian officers and soldiers for their peacekeeping operations abroad.

Capt. Dan Lee's MAT 5112 and a few Brown Berets from CAT 5110 took a short detour south into Dalanzadgad in the Gobi Desert to conduct various training over a six-week period that they would replicate later in the western city of Khovd. On the road to Dalanzadgad is where we encountered the Bactrian camels on the road blocking our movement south. Capt. Dan Lee's slate for his time with new partners included medical training, short-range marksmanship shooting, small-unit tactics, and survival skills—all basic skills the Mongolians wanted to be proficient in when conducting their peacekeeping missions. The Mongolians devoured all the training Capt. Lee's Brown Berets provided them. Whether it was the smiles on their faces as they shot their rifles alongside Brown Berets like Staff Sergeants Rafael Soto and Ryan Dean or the pride they showed when displaying their medical training certificates, we knew we were making an impact with our Mongolian counterparts.

Capt. Lee's team eventually traveled to probably the most remote location of any SFAB team during our Indo-Pacific deployment when they arrived in Khovd, located at the very western edges of Mongolia where China, Russia, and Mongolia come together. When I say it's in the middle of nowhere, it means that it barely has roads to connect it to anywhere else and a functional, but not frequently used, runway. As we approached the remote town, we felt the vastness of the Mongolian steppe and how it seemed to stretch on forever. It was here that MAT 5112's Brown Berets had milestones in their training and experiences with the Mongolian culture.

Training of course was paramount in the eyes of the Mongolians and SFAB team members. The Brown Beret's short-range marksmanship training with the Mongolian Land Forces Command was arguably the most fun for both parties. Shooting for military members is always a positive bonding experience. Participants worked on basic weapons safety and proficiency with their pistols and rifles. They shot a lot of ammunition for such a small group. One day in Khovd, the Brown Berets were having lunch with their Mongolian counterparts. They bantered back and forth about who shot better, who was physically the strongest, and even discussed personal life events like the birth of a child or weddings. As they talked, one of the Brown Berets joked that it would be really cool if the Mongolian students conducted a night fire, something no one had considered before due to the inherent risks associated with night firing. All of a sudden everyone stopped eating and looked at each other and almost harmoniously said, "Yeah, why don't we?" Why not adjust the training to enhance the overall experience? The Brown Berets had safely conducted the shooting with other LFC soldiers, NCOs, and officers in Dalanzadgad in the Gobi Desert just a few weeks before. From that moment on, the Brown Berets jumped into action to make the idea a reality.

The NCOs thought through the equipment requirements, the adjustments necessary in the training methodology, and most importantly their risk assessment. Then they approach Maj. Ludwig (remotely, because he was several hundred kilometers south of UB at that time) and briefed him about their plan. After careful consideration, he recommended a few modifications then briefed me as the battalion commander. It made sense to Cmd. Sgt. Maj. Overway and me, so they proceeded.

Capt. Dan Lee's Brown Berets were excited when the day finally came. They familiarized the Mongolians with their night vision equipment, including goggles and night lasers mounted on their rifles They broke into small groups and rehearsed in the daylight how the shooting would go. Capt. Lee and the Brown Berets could see the excitement in their eyes as night drew near. The Mongolians could see how effective the night vision goggles and lasers could be during nighttime operations. Some had used them before with Germans and Russians but not to the extent the SFAB was willing to take them, shooting on their own at multiple targets. They started shooting at close range with targets at twenty-five to fifty meters and progressed to one hundred meters. Excitement radiated throughout the whole group of Brown

Berets and Mongolians. Shooting at night was a skill level the Mongolians had not experienced before. They rotated through the shooting stations repeatedly until they expanded all the available ammunition. Everyone was exhausted by the end of the night but knew it was an extraordinary experience.

Khovd was also an opportunity to experience some even more authentic and rural Mongolian culture—they went out of their way to be exceptional hosts. In Khovd, the Brown Berets were taken to a family that tended free range livestock, something common in Mongolia but certainly a tough life. Unsurprisingly, the family invited the Brown Berets into their *ger* (often referred to as a *yurt* outside of Mongolia) to share in a traditional meal. Milk tea, candies, biscuits, and cookies were the appetizers. Eventually the host brought out several large trays of cooked sheep innards that included intestines, the stomach, and several other unidentified items. Through an interpreter, Capt. Lee learned these particular items were only offered for esteemed guest on special occasions. And, as the senior member of the group, Capt. Lee had to be the first to take part of the delicacies. As Capt. Lee's eyes took in the platters and their contents, he broke out into a cold sweat and gulped. The spread did not exactly look like American home cooking. However, as a good American representative, he grabbed something that he later recalled looked like an intestine and took a bite. The words *chew, chew, chew, and don't swallow too fast* came to his mind as he smiled and took the first bite. It took everything in him to not run straight to the door of the ger and relieve himself of the delicacies. Thankfully, the traditional Mongolian barbecue meal that followed was served quickly afterward, and by now the Brown Berets were accustomed to it. The cultural meal in Khovd was certainly something the Brown Berets of MAT 5112 would never forget.

Meanwhile, Major Colin O'Toole's Engineer Company Advisor Team (ECAT) 5510 worked with one of the Mongolian engineer regiments teaching basic combat engineering, like sapper skills, demolitions with an unexploded ordinance focus, and counter-improvised explosive device planning. The culminating event for this training was a series of controlled explosions that demonstrated the skills the Mongolians had learned by controlling detonations with their assigned equipment. During this event Brown Berets and Mongolian engineers had the opportunity to create a bunch of explosions simulating those of unexploded ordnance or improvised explosive devices. Seeing explosions was the fun part. Throughout the day Brown Berets from ECAT 5510 and our EOD tech Sfc. Steve McNeil, along with their Mongolian counterparts, ran detonation lines to the simulated locations and carefully placed plastic explosives. Calculating the appropriate mix of explosives and shaping the charge was critical to the event. Watching the mountainside erupt into a series of detonations was thrilling. However, the final Mongolian-led event for the day was probably the most breathtaking.

To prepare Mongolian soldiers, NCOs, and officers for what it was like to be shelled by mortars and artillery, they had the Mongolian engineers prepare a series of explosions that sequentially crept closer and closer to dug-in foxhole positions. We had the opportunity to experience this. Once the Mongolian engineers arranged the charges, we all jumped into our shallow foxholes. Then they initiated the explosions. I'd experienced a rocket attack before in Afghanistan and Iraq, but I was shocked at how close the Mongolians laid the charges to our positions—it was safe, but still a little nerve-racking. The loud explosions and the visible black smoke plumes they created certainly felt as if an enemy artillery barrage was closing in on us. Dust, noise, and the smell of explosives filled the air. Once they were finished, the Mongolian safety officer gave us the all-clear signal. Brown Berets and Mongolians then crawled out of their foxholes with big grins on their faces and started patting each other on the back. It was a surreal experience for everyone, certainly one that many of us will not forget.

The Land Forces Command was completely committed to the SFAB training. So much so that they assigned permanent liaison officers to the battalion headquarters and Maj. Dan Ludwig's CAT. They even sent their command sergeant major, the most senior enlisted soldier in the Mongolian Army, to travel with Capt. Dan Lee's training group for the entire four months. Their commitment and dedication ensured all the training planned actually occurred. Despite COVID impacting the country, combined training with the Mongolian Armed Forces continued uninterrupted in many cases. The Land Forces Command liaisons and their command sergeant major assisted the Brown Berets with gaining exceptions from the Mongolian government and smoothing the bureaucratic processes to ensure that training and traveling could proceed.

In one such case, the Brown Beret engineer team prepared Mongolian soldiers for their real-world missions. The previous year some Mongolian soldiers had tragically drowned when rescue operations were hindered by the flooding season (the Mongolian government frequently has the armed forces assist with disasters). The leaders of the Mongolian Armed Forces were criticized publicly by politicians for the unfortunate accident and for not having a program to prevent such losses. Maj. Colin O'Toole and 1st Sgt. Rob Clark's engineer team, at the request of Mongolian Armed Forces leadership, developed a unique training plan that taught basic water survival and water rescue techniques. The Brown Berets had to conduct thorough research and preparation in Mongolia before they conducted the training. The training location was in a beautiful but remote area located in northern Mongolia along the Selenge River. Even in June the river was frigid. The Brown Berets trained the Mongolian officers and NCOs on important safety measures they could implement during any emergency rescue and recovery water operations in the future.

They had hoped to add a comprehensive heavy seas and rapid moving water safety swimmer program to that training, but the water was running too fast, and the temperatures were too cool for that. When I met with Maj. Gen. Ganzorig later, he was well aware of the training and profusely thanked us. We hoped it would help them prevent any future drowning losses.

The training and cultural experiences created a bond between the SFAB Brown Berets and Mongolian officers and NCOs. Both groups stayed out in frigid conditions shooting their rifles and pistols or manipulating their mortars and artillery pieces together. Culturally, the Brown Berets learned during off-duty excursions that a Mongolian barbecue was really a bunch of root vegetables, goat meat or mutton, and other unknown ingredients cooked in a pressure cooker on top of an open fire pit. Not exactly the same thing found in the United States. Throughout the experiences, the Brown Berets learned how the Mongolian Army operates. For example, Capt. Simon Johnstone's LAT 5612 came to understand and appreciate how Mongolian Armed Forces logisticians managed bases, supported training, and maintained supply systems. Some supplies and equipment the Mongolian logisticians procured locally from nearby vendors while others were sent from Ulaanbaatar.

One particular advantage we noticed with SFAB teams in Mongolia was having competent female Brown Berets present for training. Female Mongolian NCOs and officers felt much more comfortable with our female Brown Berets and interfaced with them much more frequently. Since we had female logisticians, medics, and mechanics, we had some diverse skill sets to connect with our counterparts. I particularly remember observing one our LAT 5611's logistics planning classes at Zuunmod. Once it was time for a break, the Mongolian female officers and NCOs tended to flock to S.Sgt. Kristina Hinojosa and talk with her. I believe having her and S.Sgt. Gennesis Raya around made them feel much more comfortable with the rest of our Brown Berets.

Learning, of course, was a two-way street. The 1/5 SFAB and the Mongolian Armed Forces taught and learned from one another. Many from the SFAB had no prior knowledge of the Mongolian's wide swath of expertise as part of the UN's peacekeeping missions across the globe. They had been working in the Democratic Republic of Congo, South Sudan, Western Sahara, and many other places. They had certainly been around. Many of the SFAB soldiers hadn't touched those areas and were humbled to learn from their counterparts. The seasoned Mongolian officers and NCOs freely discussed their missions and their assigned deployments to foreign countries. One particular officer described how they patrolled in muddy waters of the Democratic Republic of Congo and the challenges they faced logistically. We found the Mongolians were proud of their worldwide contributions. There were also points of overlap between our groups, sharing some bonds and similar experiences from places like Afghanistan or Iraq. Individuals would name places and people to see if they had been there at the same time or knew the same people. These unexpected connections brought them closer as friends and teammates.

The friendships and mutual training opportunities between the Brown Berets and Mongolian Armed Forces was only possible due to the absolute support the American Embassy gave the SFAB while we were in Mongolia. Lt. Col. Phil Luu and Ambassador Michael Klecheski, the US ambassador to Mongolia, were instrumental in making these training exercises occur. Lt. Col. Luu did a lot of work administratively and helped forge relationships in-country for us. Frequently Lt. Col. Luu spoke on our behalf to Mongolian senior officers about the opportunities with our Brown Berets. He even opened his home to us to let us know how much he appreciated our presence and assignments in Mongolia. He even cooked up some authentic American barbecue that made everyone feel like they were home. We all enjoyed his hospitality immensely.

The Battalion Headquarters

Gen. Miller, the Joint Special Operations Command (JSOC) commander while I served there several years ago, once said that a commander is only as good as his staff. He elaborated, saying that a commander could be brilliant, have a terrific vision, and know where to take the organization, but all that didn't matter unless the commander had a staff that could help put it into action. I felt the same way with the 1/5 Battalion staff. I was fortunate to have a battalion filled with significantly talented people.

While Maj. Dan Ludwig and his teams were training with the Mongolian Armed Forces daily, the battalion headquarters staff managed the command-and-control requirements of our multiple teams spread across the vast Indo-Pacific. Although my headquarters team was able to interact with our Brown Berets and their Mongolian Army counterparts at times, our primary function was still supporting the missions of the other teams simultaneously deployed in ten countries. The staff received reports, packaged information for USARPAC, coordinated logistics, and helped with country-entry requirements as Brown Berets deployed, redeployed, and trained with their partners. Every member of the headquarters was busy and had an important role to play to achieve mission success. If fact, everyone had two or more roles to play in the battalion headquarters. The SFAB operated much like a start-up in the business world. When a business is just starting out, the founder and their teams wear many hats because there is so much to accomplish and little funding to hire more people. This is commonly termed *working lean*. Most consider that a smart move since it saves money and prevents what is called *shrinks*, which is hiring more people to begin with and dropping them as things move ahead. All people juggle roles and responsibilities until things are up and running smoothly. Our SFAB did the same while we were in Mongolia; our staff officers and NCOs woke up early and worked late into the evening to coordinate activities, people, and programs across the entire region and back to the West Coast, including Hawaii, which was no short order. We were blessed to have some pretty amazingly capable people.

Foremost, we had to work in some capacity with our Mongolian host. At the national level, interactions did not necessitate daily meetings like they did for Maj. Ludwig and his teams, but they did require some mechanism to develop relationships. To achieve this, we created a small liaison cell that included, Captain Sebastian Bonilla, our battalion S1 (human resources officer) and, Captain Mark Goodwin, our battalion S6 (communications officer), who collaborated with Major Mobi, the Mongolian Land Forces Command and Mongolian Armed Forces primary liaison officer. This coordination cell mainly managed personnel movements, logistic requirements, and meetings between both parties. The battalion headquarters planning with respect to Mongolia focused primarily on long-term geopolitical initiatives or military-to-military training programs.

I always enjoyed the opportunity to discuss US Army and Mongolian Armed Forces relationships with their senior leaders. Maj. Gen. Ganzorig, the chief of the Mongolian General Staff, and his staff members engaged us in several meetings where we discussed the upcoming training and what other opportunities there might be between us. One interesting dynamic we had not previously considered when planning our Mongolian mission there was that we were there during an election year. Maj. Gen. Ganzorig had no interest in stepping into the middle of internal politics for that election year, but also was cautious to strike a balance between their national interests and those of their partners in China and Russia too. I did not envy his predicament but trusted his instincts and respected him a lot. Timing, perception, and our public affairs posture was very important to him.

It's not always easy to understand the nuances of what we can or should accomplish for our mission given our limited funding and resources. We wanted to do our very best for our Mongolian counterparts. Maj. Scott Orr, Maj. AJ Vogel, Capt. Jeff Lockwood, and a few others had witnessed what dumping money or equipment could do with Iraqi and Afghan forces when they did not have the sustainment and maintenance systems to support it. We were also trying to help the Mongolian Armed Forces develop options that would strengthen the defense of their country, further enable their forces for peacekeeping missions, and improve economic independence from their neighbor, China. Our discussions were challenging and complicated but also productive.

To develop good situational awareness, Cmd. Sgt. Maj. Overway and I had the opportunity to occasionally visit our Brown Berets and other potential sites to better determine the feasibility and return on investment of possible US long-term investments with regard to these missions in various locations. When we did so, we snatched a variety of staff members from our headquarters to get them out of our hotel and the city environment of UB. It was a nice change of pace for them, and they had the opportunity to see something different. Many times we had some rough drives to Dalanzadgad, Khovd (a full two-day drive from UB), and Khyalganat since many of the roads outside UB were not the best. The local commanders were exceptional hosts in each location and balanced our visit between work and some recreational exploration of the local area. In Khovd, Cmd. Sgt. Maj. Overway and I had the opportunity to enjoy the authentic Mongolian dinners and chat with Mongolian officers in the middle of the vast steppe. When the sun set the bright stars filled the entire night sky like nothing we had ever seen before. The temperature also dropped. We learned there that camel and horse dung can burn quite well when it's dried out and can keep you warm.

During these forays, the working relationships we made and reinforced in Mongolia were pretty fantastic and totally enjoyable. It was not, however, all wine and roses. The staff was focused on many issues or problems that might crop up during the SFAB's debut into the Indo-Pacific. Anticipating complications and obstacles were monumental tasks because there were eighteen subordinate teams spread out across eleven countries at various times. They required supervision and communication to keep everything humming along smoothly.

Creating reports was a big portion of what we did. These reports were critical for USARPAC and our brigade headquarters because they informed everyone who was an influential leader understand what we were learning from our partners and what we were learning about ourselves. Businesses during start-up and at every other phase also do their version of this and that entails collating the various information that can showcase meeting or missing targets or milestones that can provide business owners and managers insights that are important for performance strengths and weaknesses, as well as any opportunities for growth. This information should help them to reach their goals.

In our case, SFAB teams provided both daily and weekly reports. These reports provided the clarification and highlights for missions and training and included any required messages for FORSCOM as part of developing SFAB training methodology back home. Most important was the information we provided to USARPAC so they could best understand the operating environment across the Indo-Pacific. The weekly reports generated were overviews of what we had accomplished since the prior week. Some were created with storyboards and pictures that linked our tactical actions to our strategic objectives. Capt. Josh MacKenzie and Sfc. Joe Ooley were responsible for the delivery of these reports, and both had devised a premium information management system to efficiently synthesize the details.

Businesses oftentimes use what is called a *future report*, which includes what occurs at every level of operation and labels it from stable to efficient, to predictive, to future-ready.[64] This type of report helps to keep the operation working at peak efficiency while providing keen insights that can increase their capabilities and readiness for the future.

The SFAB had a similar report that looked into our future operations. This report went beyond our daily and weekly activities and tried to foretell any issues or problems that might crop up weeks in advance. They also helped the various teams to visualize their future of work so they could aptly request the resources that might be required to fulfill that task or obligation, especially for 2nd Battalion or 3rd Squadron, who would replace us after our inaugural Indo-Pacific mission. Capt. Josh Henry and Sfc. Eric Zacherson spearheaded this report for the SFAB. Capt. Henry was great with providing critical thought to the report and Sfc. Zacherson was a knowledge management guru at compiling all the essential data for analysis.

Sfc. Zacherson and Sfc. McNeil, our EOD expert who had worked a lot with our engineer team in Mongolia, were also responsible for our Defense Travel System program in the battalion. This program allows individual soldiers to travel to duty stations on behalf of the missions, in our case, helping our respective teams to travel from Washington State to their particular country. Personnel travel and equipment transportation constituted most of the cost to send Brown Berets across the Indo-Pacific. Sergeants First Class Zacherson and McNeil oversaw this entire program for the battalion and spent many late nights on phone calls with team representatives to make sure it ran smoothly. Neither had any extensive prior experience to draw upon and as such this was on-the-job training for them. They learned and excelled. They kept the entire organization in line with military travel regulations and likely prevented us from getting into any trouble.

We also had to ensure our missions were aligned with headquarters directives and direction. We had exactly three people who completely understood the operational environment and were capable of distilling those exhaustive and extensive strategic documents produced by USARPAC and INDOPACOM for our unit. Two were capable NCOs, Sfc. Bryant Murphy and Sgt. Nick Mickle, who were led by Capt. Jeff Lockwood. This small group comprised our entire intelligence section, which also doubled as our policy and planning staff. The collective information they produced from their various networks and understanding across eleven different countries was certainly two-to-three-star-general-officer worthy! No other conventional formation was able to replicate the quality and quantity of information that these three produced. There was a circulating rumor in the battalion that some of the products they produced actually did make their way up to senior US military leadership, but we were not able to verify that.

In addition to our operations and intelligence sections, the other part of the staff, personnel, logistics, and communications, was led by the battalion executive officer, or chief of staff, Maj. AJ Vogel. Oftentimes these sections do not get enough credit for the hard work they do. For instance, Capt. Pete Smith, Sfc. Omar Moore, and S.Sgt. Brenton Kirk were responsible for helping every team transport their equipment in and around countries, arranging life support contracts, and ensuring appropriate funding for other expenses. It's essentially all the activities that matter when people get into the country. New arrivals to a foreign country first focus on the basics. They want to know where they are eating, sleeping, and . . . where the latrines are. Fulfilling just the basic life support needs requires people to navigate a plethora of bureaucratic requirements. US rules for contracting were usually very different from the host nation's. Typically, this meant Capt. Smith and his team needed to coordinate with ten different embassies who were helping Brown Berets meet requirement. Normally, the US Army has contracting commands with people who are responsible for ensuring all this happens for the extensive exercises in the Indo-Pacific. We didn't have that expertise, so Capt. Smith and his team had to do a lot of learning. This team was constantly working with the lead logisticians on the SFAB teams to either help them understand their partner forces logistics challenges or ensure the Brown Berets had the correct life support requirements in place. They were always busy.

Our Human Resources (HR) section, known as the S1, was split between Mongolia and JBLM. S.Sgt. John Murray remained in Washington State to track the movement of various Brown Berets between the Indo-Pacific and the multiple places in the United States. People were always in transit. Accounting for them, wherever they were, took a concerted effort. We always wanted 100 percent accountability for all our Brown Berets. Meanwhile, Capt. Sebastian Bonilla went with the battalion headquarters to Mongolia. Between the two of them, they took care of all the administrative paperwork necessary for a unit to be deployed and many of the routine requirements typical for Army units. Capt. Bonilla also had the additional multitasking duties of working our public relations network and managing the command calendar. He was swamped, and if he had any hair, Capt. Bonilla would have pulled it all out. We were eternally thankful for our HR (S1) section.

The small communications section, S6, was also constantly troubleshooting with communications sergeants on one of their thirteen different communications systems while at the same time keeping everything running for the battalion headquarters itself.

Capt. Mark Goodwin, S.Sgt. Jinshik Kim, Sgt. Leslie Demalla, and Sgt. Angel Mercado were crazy busy. Not only did they keep the routine networks up and running, but they also established communications windows where teams set up their tactical systems to ensure they were still working. They were the entire formation's tech support and we relied on them constantly. Ensuring all of our communications equipment was working sometimes included a drive out to a Mongolian army base on the outskirts of UB. Here they would troubleshoot our equipment, set up the radios and satellite dishes, and wait for the teams to call in. Keeping the communications equipment functional was important because it kept the teams ready at all times and verified our contingency platforms were operable in an emergency or crisis situation.

Our battalion medics had a slightly different mission than many of our other staff sections. The Army designed the battalion medical section to treat casualties during a conflict as patients were evacuated from the battlefield and moved to higher medical care levels. Due to COVID, the battalion physician's assistant, Maj. Roland Salazar, and senior medic, Sfc. Dave Nagle couldn't go to the various teams and assist with medical evaluations or review medical evacuation procedures. Instead, they had to determine how to do it remotely. Both Maj. Salazar and Sfc. Nagle learned best practices to perform telemedicine and assist with medical planning. Sometimes, junior medics had to learn a foreign country's medical system, understand which hospitals could service their Brown Berets, and how an injured soldier could be evacuated back to a US medical facility. It is complicated to know how eleven different foreign medical systems work and learn what it takes to move a patient back to the United States from the point of injury. The well-established systems from the Global War on Terror to move patients from Iraq and Afghanistan to the United States didn't exist for us in the Indo-Pacific. The medics also had to make sure all parties knew how to accommodate medical costs through the military's medical insurance system, Tricare.

The junior medics on the battalion medical team got valuable experiences to augment the medical training Maj. Ludwig and 1st Sgt. Keen's teams provided to the Mongolian Armed Forces. Since medical training was so popular, they were asked to train almost constantly with their counterparts. Sgt. Duran was essential when we conducted the first casualty evacuation rehearsal using a Mongolian Air Force MI-17 to validate our medical plan for Mongolia.[65] Having a quality medical evacuation plan in place was important if we wished to deliver higher risk training for the Brown Berets and our foreign counterparts because it defined the transportation of injured soldiers or civilians from the point of injury to a medical or trauma facility where they could receive urgent medical care. The difference between a casualty evacuation (CASEVAC) and medical evacuation (MEDEVAC) is that a CASEVAC uses a nonstandard or nondedicated medical vehicle to move the patient.

The SFAB battalion had no assigned chaplain, but there was one at the brigade level. Maj. Dom Grotti was our chaplain, and he served the entire brigade. Chaplain Grotti was able to provide remote weekly services during our entire deployment into the Indo-Pacific. He was part of the 1st battalion in every way. Every Sunday morning, which was Saturday night in Washington State, he delivered a complete virtual service from his remote chapel, usually his quarters on JBLM, due to the date and time difference. All we had to do was dial in. The service was so creative and innovative that Chaplin Grotti could reach out to every person in our task force to minister to them. Anyone who has ever deployed understands the importance of having a chaplain available even if they weren't physically there. Nobody from our team was aware of any other Army chaplain holding services like Chaplain Dom Grotti. We were exceedingly grateful to him for his ministry to us.

The battalion staff was amazing! They managed to provide

support to eighteen teams spread out across eleven countries at any given time, which was nothing short of remarkable. Part of their excellence was their ability to develop new operating procedure standards that did not exist in the conventional Army or the SFAB enterprise. Sometimes this required the Brown Berets to experiment a bit with regard to reporting, coordination of differing agencies, and working with the higher-level staff.

CHAPTER 8

Exit Phase, Transitions

Back to Washington

Leaving countries was as important as coming into them for the SFAB teams. Flights, both for departing and incoming teams, equipment shipments or hand overs, etc. had to be coordinated between team leaders and the various battalion staff members, embassy country teams and or attaché offices so that all parties knew what was happening next. It was our hope to have this transition flow seamlessly, and in most instances it did. Doing so meant we needed to debrief the country teams and attachés on what the departing team had accomplished, what the incoming SFAB team was slated to do, and how all of that supported the embassy's overall Integrated Country Plan while meeting USARPAC and INDOPACOM objectives. Now our "green light" had transitioned from yellow to red. It was time for us to stop, head home, and regroup.

Cmd. Sgt. Maj. Overway and I knew from prior experience that having SFAB team members sitting around waiting for flights for days with nothing relevant to do could mean trouble, especially when in foreign countries. We did not want this to occur with our soldiers, NCOs, and officers. These Brown Berets had traveled to a lot of places, had some rather ambiguous missions, and were given a lot of freedom. We were fortunate that we had relatively few disciplinary incidents and nothing that would get the SFAB into any real trouble. Our goal was to keep it that way.

Ideally, we wanted face-to-face handoffs between the Brown Berets of 1st Battalion and 2nd Battalion. However, given the

COVID environment, that type of handoff was not always possible or even feasible in every case. Our foreign counterparts had specific entry requirements and COVID restrictions, including quarantines, that stymied personal introductions and other protocols that would have normally occurred. We worked around that as best as we could by conducting secure video conferences with our 2nd Battalion replacements and adding them to important email correspondence. Sometimes we were able to debrief our replacements in person when we returned to Washington State. The multifaceted approaches were less than perfect, but it worked out okay.

To keep the 5th SFAB headquarters informed, we conducted a full briefing with timings and decision points so that everyone in the chain of command up to USARPAC knew when we were leaving particular countries. Many senior USARPAC leaders had come to rely on our Brown Berets for ground-truth information on a particular country and we needed to make sure they knew when that knowledge might temporarily be unavailable for a specific time period. Since this was the first time SFAB teams had been deployed into the Indo-Pacific, we thought it important to overcommunicate what we were doing, so we sent more detailed information than normally would be required in any military operation. I also had to request permission to "jump," or move, my headquarters from Mongolia back to JBLM, Washington State.

In Army doctrine, the lower headquarters must ask permission from the higher headquarters to break down any communications links. For instance, during our JRTC rotation in November of 2020, we frequently moved the battalion tactical operations center, which had to be communicated to the brigade tactical operations center, the next level up, so they understood how to get ahold of us and that we were operating in a degraded capacity. We had to specifically let them know what communication platforms were and were not available—an important detail, as situations could change rapidly, and they might need to contact us. As an example, we pulled down the satellite link that, in turn, disrupted the brigade's ability to call us on our phone lines. Therefore, we had to communicate via our high-frequency radios.

When moving back from Mongolia to Washington, Col. Andy Watson needed to know that the bulk of my staff and I would no longer be on the western side of the international date line. This included Col. Watson telling USARPAC where all the SFAB units were across the Indo-Pacific. We had built a good reputation and the USARPAC enterprise had tapped our Brown Berets for some in-country tasks like they did in Indonesia and the Philippines. In case something came up, we wanted to make sure USARPAC knew which countries we were still in and which we were not.

Some SFAB teams had returned to Washington before the bulk of the battalion. They were instrumental in helping incoming Brown Berets returning from their deployments. Sometimes they had to pick up SFAB teams or equipment at airport in Seattle. The units who had served in the Maldives, India, South Korea, and Fiji all returned to Washington first and assisted with these tasks.

Internal to the battalion, we also established tasks to assist with bringing the people and equipment back to the United States. These consisted of closing out financial paperwork, accounting for equipment, and assisting Brown Berets as they reintegrated with their families. During the Global War on Terror, these types of tasks were planned and managed by the installation or a higher headquarters and were a very prescriptive series of events. Noncombat missions like ours extending over a long period of time had not previously happened for conventional units in the Indo-Pacific. Therefore, we had to manage these things ourselves and make sure our Brown Berets and their families were supported.

Luckily, we had anticipated this early on in the process and decided to keep some tasks centralized and others decentralized. Much of this was addressed by the battalion's field grade officers, Majors Orr, Vogel, Ludwig, Wallgren, and Maier, with significant input from the senior NCOs such as Command Sergeant Major Overway and First Sergeants Lane, Keen, Workman, and Bochmann. Brig. Gen. Taylor and I had discussed the timeline back in April and the SFAB had adhered to that perfectly. All teams were back by the June 30 deadline, with the exception of those who were flying back from Mongolia with our containers and Maj. Maier's 5130 team in Japan. A safe redeployment was just as important as a successful mission in a foreign country.

Final Farewell

Unfortunately, Cmd. Sgt. Maj. Overway and I would not be able to shake hands with all the Brown Berets from our battalion task force when they returned from their missions. He and I changed out of our positions the day prior, June 29. It was a simple ceremony in the Evergreen Theater on JBLM due to the unusually hot temperatures in Washington at the time. Some of our teams were literally flying back during the ceremony, with others enjoying a day off from flying back to Washington either over the weekend or the day before. Col. Watson officiated the ceremony as the acting commanding officer of the 5th SFAB. Col. Jon Chung, who was in attendance, took command of the 5th SFAB the following day, June 30. Col. Chung previously commanded 2nd Brigade (Stryker), 2nd Infantry Division. It was a bittersweet goodbye as I handed the unit colors off to Lt. Col. Marcus Hunter. Marcus and I knew that we would not get a lot of face-to-face time before the ceremony, given he had to complete school at the Army War College in early June and then drive with his family to Washington State. In anticipation of this scenario, we had conducted several video conferences and meetings over the previous few months while the battalion was deployed. Majors Vogel and Orr developed a plan to brief Marcus on the manning, training, and experiences of each of the staff sections, the companies, and SFAB teams. That way, Marcus understood the staff's personalities, capabilities, and backgrounds and each SFAB team he inherited. Additionally, each of the companies, led by Majors Ludwig, Wallgren, and Maier, conducted briefs for him so he could have a more detailed understanding of each organization and have a chance to ask questions.

The 1st Battalion change of command came at an opportune time for the unit. The start-up mentality that existed in the organization had been needed to get the SFAB concept in the Indo-Pacific going. It was now time for someone to solidify procedures, expansion, and growth. The unit needed to transition from a start-up to an established formation, something many organizations struggle with. In the business world some entities select to spin off rather than continue. If they continue, then they need to define the various roles of the organization and how they will interact with one another, i.e. who will manage what projects, etc. At this juncture there is also usually a crystallization of policies and procedures that support the function of the organization, in this case the missions of the SFAB.

That summer the Army selected Cmd. Sgt. Maj. Overway to take the command sergeant major position for 1st Brigade, 82nd Airborne Division—certainly, a prestigious reflection of his professionalism and leadership. Soon after his arrival at Fort Bragg, his unit conducted a last-minute deployment to Afghanistan to oversee the security of the final withdrawal of all Americans from the country. He was the last of five American service members to get on the final C-17 that left Afghanistan.

Amy and I drove across the country with our kids Zachary, Abigail, Isabelle, and Andrew. We headed to the Naval War College in Rhode Island. Along the way we stopped at some National Parks and visited the city of Chicago. We enjoyed this special family time together where we could see how beautiful the United States is and appreciate all that this country has to offer her people and visitors alike. The granite- and glacier-topped Rocky Mountains lined with evergreens, rolling plains of lush grassland in the Midwest, and old mountains of the Appalachians contrasted significantly with the vast rolling Mongolian steppe.

Many of the leaders had elected to stay with the SFAB. Their commitment provided some much-needed continuity to the organization and allowed them to capitalize on the experiences we had shared over the past couple of years. This entrepreneurial spirit lived on with those Brown Berets that stayed and even those that left and returned again. It was heartwarming to know they were in good hands.

CHAPTER 9

The Entrepreneurial Bureaucracy

STARTING SOMETHING—anything—from scratch is hard work. In the case of 1st Battalion, 5th SFAB, it took an entrepreneurial mindset, beginning with individual Brown Berets on teams, flowing to the captains and sergeants first class, team leaders and assistant team leaders, transferring through the captains and noncommissioned officers serving on the battalion staff, and taking hold with the majors and senior noncommissioned officers found throughout the organization to make it work. At every level these individuals displayed the characteristics and qualities associated with a start-up, in this case an Army start-up.

Like many start-up companies, the journey was a roller coaster of emotions but well worth the ride. Throughout the build-up, training, and inaugural deployment into the Indo-Pacific, the Brown Berets displayed the characteristics of entrepreneurs.[66,67] Throughout the organization, Brown Berets were intellectually curious. They discussed ways to get their team and equipment into a country then developed partner training plans for a foreign military they had never worked with before. The battalion and brigade conducted structured experimentation when developing the training exercises at JBLM and the Yakima Training Center to certify that SFAB teams were ready to deploy to a foreign country. At a macro level, Capt. Leshaun Smith and Maneuver Advisor Team 5132 experimented with different ideas in Indonesia as they moved around to different Indonesian National Military units.

The Brown Berets proved they were flexible and nimble when they pivoted flawlessly when asked to partner at multiple locations in Thailand and Indonesia. Nothing like this had ever been done before. Leaders like Majors Ludwig and Orr showed firm decisiveness when recommending launching C-17 aircraft on two occasions, an expensive endeavor, from Washington State to Mongolia as we waited for China's approval to fly over their airspace, which came at the last minute on both occasions. Cmd. Sgt. Maj. Overway and I watched Capt. Mat Brown and Sfc. Jeromee Javar build MAT 5113 into a solid outfit as they independently deployed themselves to Hawaii, joined their company for our Thailand mission, turned around and headed to JRTC at Fort Polk, Louisiana, then figured out how to make themselves a valuable partner with the Indian Army.

Maj. Colin O'Toole and 1st Sgt. Robert Clark exhibited calculated risk-taking when planning water confidence training in the cold waters of the Selenge River in Mongolia. The Brown Berets of ECAT 5510 made multiple site surveys to the training location there and implemented numerous safety precautions to conduct the Mongolian Land Forces Command's requested training. Capt. Chuck Spencer and Sfc. Stephen Botelho were able to forge ahead with their Fiji mission despite multiple obstacles with a positive attitude, only to ultimately fail to link up with their Republic of Fiji Military Forces engineer counterparts. In the end, we were all comfortable with bringing the Brown Berets of Engineer Advisor Team 5511 home from Fiji. Maj. Morgan Maier and 1st Sgt. Duane Bochmann displayed persistence repeatedly as they and their company leaders searched for missions for all their Brown Berets in Malaysia, Thailand, Indonesia, Brunei, and Japan. Maj. Maier and 1st Sgt. Bochmann never gave up, and at long last had their Company Advisor Team 5130 Brown Berets in Japan.

The battalion staff continued to innovate as we figured out how to conduct mission command of SFAB teams spread out over vast distances, borrowing existing techniques and processes from other units or assignments and then improving or adapting them to fit our unique model—they were simple things, but still innovative.

Finally, every Brown Beret leader in the organization considered the long-term impact, relationships, and legacy their actions would have with their foreign partner force, US Army Pacific (USARPAC), and the US Army. People like Capt. Sheynfeld and Sfc. Nate Peno, Capt. Alex Lara, and Sfc. Terrance Parrish were instrumental in laying the foundation in the Philippines for long-term partnerships and opportunities for future 5th SFAB and US Army activities with the Philippine Army.

The transition from a start-up to an established unit was only possible through learning and capturing the lessons to pass them to future 5th SFAB Brown Berets. The 1st Battalion and the 5th SFAB as a whole learned a significant amount about the Indo-Pacific and the potential roles of SFAB teams in the region. The most important contribution we made to the SFAC enterprise was demonstrating how SFAB teams could go into a region using different funding and authorities outside of declared armed conflict, such as Iraq and Afghanistan. While other SFABs had sent teams to Africa and South America, the 5th SFAB determined how to do it at scale across a wide range of geopolitical interests. Another significant contribution was providing an example of how to educate, inform, and sell SFAB capabilities to the Army service component command, which in our case was USARPAC. Many in the US Army were—and likely still are—unsure of what the SFAB is and how it can contribute to meeting geographic combatant command and country team requirements. In our own way, Brown Berets worked to achieve national security objectives by building relationships with our allies and partners in the Indo-Pacific. In every case, we were creating trust between two armies and two nations to forge bonds that could be relied upon during a crisis. We were also lucky that we had good relationships with those in Hawaii at USARPAC. The solid and trust-centric relationships between senior officers like Maj. Gen. Jon Braga, Brig. Gen. Curt Taylor, and Col. Jay Bartholomees helped set the framework to allow Brown Berets to work hand in hand with their foreign counterparts. Majors and captains from the 1st Battalion then followed up with the details and plans necessary to move the bureaucracy in the right direction.

I also learned a few things along the way that I'm sure apply to any entrepreneur. First, the organization moves at the speed of trust. Trust has to be earned both up and down the chain of command and laterally with sister units and supporting organizations. Doing so means having the right people in the right jobs and giving them some latitude to perform—in other words, if you hire the right people, the mission will take care of itself. I have no idea all the small details and concerns young NCOs and officers solved without input from me or Cmd. Sgt. Maj. Overway. That was only possible because we found the right people to be part of the battalion and allowed them to make decisions and act.

Second, predictability drives excellence. The further out we told our officers and NCOs what specific mission we were assigning them, the better it turned out. I often remember going to the ranges to build our baseline combat skills and watching the NCOs run Brown Berets through the training. I was once watching a range that was exceptionally well run and wondered how long the NCO had been preparing for it. When I asked him, his response was six weeks. His performance and the quality of training showed. On another occasion I watched a safely run, yet disorganized range. I inquired as to how long the NCO in charge had known about running the exercise and was told a scant two days. The takeaway there was that time knowing about the job helps increase productivity and efficiency.

Third, the old adage about leading by example matters at every echelon, and your subordinates are watching you whether you know it or not. We didn't realize it at the time, but when Cmd.

Sgt. Maj. Overway and I pitched in to do all the manual labor to put up our tactical operations center tent and communications equipment in Yakima, it helped establish a work ethic culture in the battalion that helped get our Brown Berets into eleven different countries six months later. Additionally, I was the first volunteer in the battalion to attend the Army's Survival, Evasion, Resistance, and Escape (SERE) school. Later I found out by talking with other Brown Berets that I had set the example that even the senior commander can go through challenging and demanding training. Soon thereafter, others attended the Army's SERE school.

Finally, Cmd. Sgt. Maj. Overway and I had to have consistent and persistent messaging in the organization, whether it was about training, standards and discipline, or a positive attitude. Having frequent one-on-one touchpoints with our team leaders and assistant team leaders while we were separated and deployed helped keep our personal connection with them and reenforce key messages we needed to emphasize.

Recruiting, building, training, and deploying the 1st Battalion, 5th SFAB into the Indo-Pacific in less than two years was a phenomenal accomplishment that simply would not have been possible had it not been for the talent and entrepreneurial spirit of the officers and NCOs. They are some of the best the US Army has to offer. I know that the future Brown Berets of the 5th SFAB will create some memorable experiences as I did on the dusty road in the Gobi Desert, where I met my first two-hump camel. I mean Bactrian!

INTO THE INDO-PACIFIC | 323

Mitchell Napier from MAT 5111 demonstrates proper transition shooting on barriers in the Maldives with the Maldives National Defence Force. Photo Courtesy of Matt Orders.

Brandon Gallup from MAT 5113 gives a tracking class to members of the Indian and US Armies at the Mahajan Field Firing Ranges in Rajasthan, India. Photo courtesy of US Army.

Tylor Williams from MAT 5113 trains with members of the Indian 11th battalion, Jammu and Kashmir Rifles and the US 1-2 SBCT at the Mahajan Field Firing Ranges in Rajasthan, India. Photo courtesy of US Army.

Warren Mohan, CAT 5110, demonstrates how to launch a small unmanned aerial surveillance platform while training with the Mongolian Army near Ulaanbaatar, Mongolia. Photo Courtesy of Dan Ludwig.

Members of CAT 5110 Train Mongolian NCOs and Officers on Short Range Marksmanship rifles and pistols in April 2021 near Ulaanbaatar, Mongolia. Photo Courtesy of Dan Ludwig.

Ryan Dean from MAT 5111 demonstrates proper rifle posture to Mongolian NCOs and Officers during a training event in Mongolia. Photo courtesy of 5th SFAB.

CJ Overway and the author pose with their Mongolian liaison officer, Major Mobi, in Khovd, Mongolia. Photo courtesy of the author.

During a recreation day in Mongolia, members of 1/5 SFAB make an attempt to ride Mongolian horses across the steppe in frigid temperatures. Photo courtesy of the author

INTO THE INDO-PACIFIC | 327

During a recreational day in Mongolia, in the middle of a snowstorm, the author along with other members of 1/5 SFAB make an attempt to do some camel riding. Photo courtesy of the author

The author meets with Major General Amgalanbaatar, the commander of Mongolian Land Forces Command. Photo courtesy of the author.

328 | GREEN LIGHT GO!

Members of MAT 5123 pose for a photo with their Filipino counterparts of the Philippine Army following a field training exercise. Photo courtesy of Tyler Matherson.

Andre Arienza and members of MAT 5123 conduct urban operations training with soldiers from the Philippine Army's 1st Brigade Combat Team at Fort Magsaysay, the Philippines. Photo courtesy of Tyler Matherson.

Medical NCO Eui Yoo from LAT 5612 teaches a medical treatment and evacuation class to soldiers from the Philippine Army. Photo courtesy of 5th SFAB.

Infantry NCO Jun Choh walks with Indonesian soldiers and officers following a training event in Indonesia. Photo courtesy of LeShaun Smith.

Infantry NCOs Jun Choh and Joseph Gesumaria practice close quarter combat skills with their counterparts in the Indonesian Army. Photo courtesy of LeShaun Smith.

Infantry NCO Jun Choh instructs an Indonesian soldier on dismounted individual infantry tactics. Photo courtesy of LeShaun Smith.

Michael VanMale from MAT 5133 gives a Thai NCO a unit patch following their platoon level situational training exercise. Photo courtesy of Emanuel Moore.

GLOSSARY OF TERMS

4187: Army Personnel/Human Resources general purpose form

1-2 SBCT : 1st Brigade, 2nd Division Stryker Brigade Combat Team

1-23 IN : 1st Battalion, 23rd Infantry

1st Sgt. : First Sergeant

AFRICOM: Africa Command

ASLA: Advise, Support, Liaise, Assess

BCT: Brigade Combat Team

BfSB: Battlefield Surveillance Brigade

Brig. Gen.: Brigadier General

Blue Force: Friendly Forces

C-17: Air Force Multipurpose Cargo Aircraft

CASEVAC: Casualty Evacuation

CAT: Company Advisor Team

CBRN: Chemical/Biological/Radioactive/Nuclear

CENTCOM: Central Command

COBRA GOLD: Bilateral Exercise in Thailand

Col.: Colonel

CONOP: Concept of the Operation

CONUS: Continental United States

Capt: Captain

Cmd. Sgt. Maj: Command Sergeant Major

CTC: Combat Training Center

DAT: Defense Attache

DIRLAUTH: Direct Liaison Authority

DOD: Department of Defense

DOS: Department of State

E-AT: Engineer Advisor Team

EOD: Expert Ordnance Disposal

ETT: Embedded Training Team

EUCOM: European Command

FA-AT: Field Artillery Advisor Team

FAO: Foreign Area Officer

FORSCOM: US Army Forces Command

FSC: Forward Support Company

GCC: Geographic Combat Command

Gen.: General

Green Force: Allied or Friendly Forces

HMMWV: High Mobility Multipurpose Wheeled Vehicle

HQPA: Headquarters Philippine Army

ICS: Integrated Country Strategy

INDOPACOM: Indo-Pacific Command

JBLM: Joint Base Lewis-McChord, Washington State

JGSDF: Japanese Ground Self-Defense Force

JRTC: Joint Readiness Training Center, Fort Polk (Johnson), Louisiana

JSOC: Joint Special Operations Command

JUSMAGPHIL: Joint United States Military Assistance Group - Philippines

JUSMAGTHAI: Joint US Military Advisory Group-Thailand

LAT: Logistics Advisor Team
LFC: Land Forces Command

LNO: Liaison Officer

Lt. Col.: Lieutenant Colonel

Lt. Gen.: Lieutenant General

LTP: Leader Training Program

MAF: Mongolian Armed Forces

Maj.: Major

MAT: Maneuver Advisor Team

MCP: Mission Command Post

MDMP: Military Decision-Making Process

MDTF: Multi-Domain Task Force

Maj. Gen.: Major General

MILES: Multiple Integrated Laser Engagement System

MINDEF: Minister of Defense

MiTT: Military Transition Team

MNDF: Maldives National Defence Force

MOS: Military Occupational Skill

MRE: Meals Ready to Eat

M.Sgt.: Master Sergeant

MWR: Morale, Welfare, Recreation

NCO: Noncommissioned Officer

NCOER: Noncommissioned Officer Evaluation Report

NETCOM: Network Command

NPA: Nasopharyngeal Airway

NTC: National Training Center

O/C-T: Observer/Controller - Trainer

OCONUS: Outside the Continental United States

ODC: Office of Defense Cooperation

OIC: Officer in Charge

OPFOR: Opposing Force

PCC: PreCommand Course

PDSS: PreDeployment Site Survey

PEQ-15: Advanced Target Pointer/ Illuminator/ Aiming Light

Pfc.: Private First Class

POLAD: Foreign Policy Advisor Program

PRC: Peoples Republic of China

PVS-14: Night Vision Goggles

RDR: Rapid Deployment Regiment

Red Force: Enemy Forces

RFMF: Republic of Fiji Military Forces

ROK: Republic of Korea

ROK-A: Republic of Korea Army

ROM: Restriction of Movement

RSOI: Reception, Staging, Onward Movement, and Integration

RTA: Royal Thai Army

RUBA:Rotational Unit Bivouac Area

S1: Personnel/Human Resources Section

S3: Operations Officer

S4: Logistics section

SBCT: Stryker Brigade Combat Team

SCO: Security Cooperation Office/Officer

SCOUT: Scalable Class of Unified Terminal

SERE: Survival, Evade, Resistance, Escape

SF: Special Forces

SFA: Security Force Assistance

SFAAT: Security Force Advisory and Assistance Team

SFAB: Security Force Assistance Brigade

SFAC: Security Force Assistance Command

Sfc.: Sergeant First Class

SFRG: Soldier Family Readiness Group

Sgt. Maj.: Sergeant Major

Sgt.: Sergeant

SIPR: Secret Internet Protocol Router

SOUTHCOM: Southern Command

SRCT: Stryker Regimental Combat Team

S.Sgt.: Staff Sergeant

TCCC: Tactical Combat Casualty Care

TCMCC: Tactical Combat Medical Care Course

TOC: Tactical Operations Center

Torbia: Fictional nation-state used for Army training

TOW: Tube-launched, optically tracked, wire-guided, heavy anti-tank missile weapon

TVB: Tactical Voice Bridge
UB: Ulaanbaatar, Mongolia

UH-60: US Army Utility Helicopter

USARJ: US Army Japan

USARPAC: United States Army Pacific

VFA: Visiting Forces Agreement

VTC: Video Telephone Conference

XO: Executive Officer

YTC: Yakima Training Center, Washington State

IMPORTANT FIGURES

Afarian, Christian: Communications NCO for 1/5 SFAB

Aherns, Tammy: Counter-Intelligence NCO for 5th SFAB

Angstadt, Tom: Commander of A Company, 1/5 SFAB

Antal, Jarret San: Medical NCO for CAT 5120

Aragon, Heydi Vaness : Mechanic NCO for MAT 5131

Arguello, Richard C: Communications NCO for MAT 5123

Arienza, Andre Francis: Infantry NCO for MAT 5123

Atchison, Chance Alexander: Infantry NCO for MAT 5112

Avila, Chris: Assistant Team Leader for MAT 5111

Bales, Travis: Infantry NCO for MAT 5132

Bales, Travis Grant: Fires Advisor for MAT 5132

Bartholomees, Jay: Operations Officer of USARPAC

Bavender, Joshua Todd: Communications NCO for MAT 5120

Berteaux, Joshua Joaquin: Medical NCO for MAT 5111

Bidwell, Michael: Assistant Team Leader of MAT 5132

Black, Jonathan Karl: Infantry Mortar NCO for CAT 5130

Blackmon, Rhett: Commander of 5/5 SFAB

Blas, Jordan: Medical NCO for CAT 5110

Bochman, Duane : 1st Sgt. of C Co., 1/5 SFAB; CAT 5130

Bonilla, Sebastian: Battalion S1 OIC, human resources, for 1/5 SFAB

Boone, Gunner William: Medical NCO for MAT 5113

Bordwell, Jared: Commander, 1-2 SBCT

Botelho, Stephen: Assistant Team Leader for E-AT 5511

Braga, Jon: Deputy Commanding General of USARPAC

Brambila, Jose Luis: Infantry NCO for MAT 5133

Brambilla, Javier: Medical NCO for HHC, 1/5 SFAB

Brogan, Ronald Patrick, Jr.: Infantry NCO for MAT 5131

Brown, Mathew: Team Leader for MAT 5113

Brown, Brad: Team Leader of FA-AT 5420

Brown, Barrett Nelson: Medical NCO for MAT 5133

Brown, Michael Andrew: Medical NCO for CAT 5130

Brzak, Scott: Senior Cmd. Sgt. Maj for USARPAC

Buckalew, Richard Allen: Engineer NCO for MAT 5112

Butler, Blair: Intelligence NCO for MAT 5132

Calderon, Patrick Ryan: Intelligence NCO for MAT 5121

Carter, Travis Lamar: Logistics NCO for CAT 5112

Cebulski, Ryan Andrew: Engineer NCO for MAT 5111

Ceniceros, Rodriguez Eduardo: Military Police NCO for MAT 5122

Chafin, Damien: Infantry NCO for MAT 5121

Cherry, Troy Alexander: Infantry NCO for MAT 5123

Choh, Jun: Infantry NCO for MAT 5132

Chung, Jon: Second Commander of 5th SFAB

Clark, Brenton: Team Leader for MAT 5133

Clark, Robert: First Sergeant of A Company, 5/5 SFAB; ECAT 5510

Clark, Jordan George: Intelligence NCO for MAT 5130

Conlon, Ashley: Medical NCO for ECAT 5510

Cooper, James Edward, III: Logistics NCO for CAT 5122

Cox, Travis: DAT and SCO for the Maldives

Craft, Joshua Caleb: Mechanic NCO for MAT 5111

Craven, Robert: CSM for 5th SFAB

Cynkar, Michael Spencer: Engineer NCO for MAT 5122

Davis, Mario: I Corps Chief of Staff

Dean, Ryan: Infantry NCO part of MAT 5111

Deberg, Justin: Fires Advisor for CAT 5110

Delort, Jessica Renee: Medical NCO for 1/5 SFAB

Demalla, Leslie: Satellite Systems Operator for 1/5 SFAB

Devall, Jordan Andrew: Military Police NCO for MAT 5133

Dimaria, Pietro: Intelligence NCO for MAT 5110

Dimilia, James: Assistant OIC for ECAT 5510

Dixon, Joseph Earl: Logistics NCO for CAT 5113

Dougherty, Daniel: Assistant Team Leader of MAT 5131

Doyle, Darnell: Senior Operations NCO for 1/5 SFAB

Duran, Richard: Medic for 1/5 SFAB

Dydasco, Joseph Derrick : Chemical, Nuclear, Biological NCO for 1/5 SFAB

Echevarria, Jesus Mathew: Infantry NCO for MAT 5122

Eckhardt, Joshua Louis: Infantry NCO for MAT 5113

Ellis, Blaine Mitchell: Logistics NCO for CAT 5120

Elward, Wesley: Construction Engineer NCO for E-AT 5511

Enebrad, Jesse Lee: Fires Advisor for MAT 5111

Fay, Shane Patrick: Infantry NCO for MAT 5120

Felix, Andrew Hurtado: Engineer NCO for MAT 5120

Ferguson, Tim: Commander of 3/5 SFAB

Figueredo, Yuslandy Ed: Infantry Mortar NCO for CAT 5120

Fisher, Brian Joseph: Fires Advisor for MAT 5120

Flores, Franky Juan: Medical NCO for MAT 5121

Fong, Bradford Jonathan: Infantry NCO for MAT 5111

Fox, Shawn Christopher: Communications NCO for MAT 5111

Francis, Ian: US Army Attaché and ODC Chief for Indonesia

Franco, Edgar: Engineer NCO for MAT 5130

Freeman, Dustin: Team Leader of MAT 5121

Gallop, Brandon: Military Police NCO for MAT 5113

Ganzorig, Dovchinsurengiin: Chief of Staff of the Mongolian Armed Forces

Garcia, Danny: Assistant Operations Officer of B Company, 1/5 SFAB

Gesumaria, Joseph Anthony, II: Mechanic NCO for MAT 5132

Goodwin, Mark: Battalion S6, communications, for 1/5 SFAB

Gore, Anthony: Commander of 2/5 SFAB

Grace, Jaron K: Mechanic NCO for MAT 5113

Gross, Matt: Deputy US Army Attaché and ODC Chief for Indonesia

Grotti, Dominic: Chaplain for 5th SFAB

Guminski, Andrew: Fire Control NCO for FA-AT 5421

Gutierrez, George: Infantry NCO for MAT 5122

Gutierrezbustos, Omar: Mechanic NCO for MAT 5122

Hai, Hang: Logistics NCO for CAT 5121

Hall, Brian Christopher: Mechanic NCO for MAT 5110

Handley, Eric Charles: Intelligence NCO for MAT 5133

Heintz, Amber: Intelligence NCO for MAT 5120

Heinz, James Anthony: Infantry NCO for MAT 5131

Henry, Josh: Operations Planner for 1/5 SFAB

Herman, Travis: Assistant Team Leader of MAT 5121

Hilton, Robert : Assistant Team Leader for LAT 5611

Hinojosa, Kristina: Medical NCO for LAT 5611

Hoffman, Charles Joseph, III: Fires Advisor for MAT 5133

Homan, Derek Derek: Engineer NCO for E-AT 551

Hopson, Antonio: Supply NCO for LAT 5612

Howard, Cameron Robert: Infantry NCO for MAT 5130

Hunter, Marcus: Second Commander of 1/5 SFAB

Hunter, Pieter Hendrik: Engineer NCO for MAT 5123

Irwin, Michael: Counter-Intelligence Technician for MI-AT 5540

Jackson, Scott: Commanding General of SFAC

Javar, Jeromee: Assistant Team Leader for MAT 5113

Johnston, Simon: Team Leader for LAT 5611

Keen, Travis: First Sergeant of A Company, 1/5 SFAB

Kennedy, Jamaal: Assistant Team Leader for MAT 5122

Kennedy, James Alexander: Intelligence NCO for MAT 5112

Keyonnie, Orlando: Mechanic NCO for CAT 5120

Kim, Jinshik: Communications NCO for 1/5 SFAB

Kim, Ryan Hwan: Fires Advisor for MAT 5112

Kirk, Brenton: Assistant Logistics NCO for 1/5 SFAB

Klecheski, Michael: US Ambassador to Mongolia

Konrade, Alec James: Communications NCO for MAT 5113

Kosmyna, Chris: Team Leader for FA-AT 5421

Lacamera, Paul: Commander of USARPAC

Lane, Richard: 1st Sgt. of HHC, 1/5 SFAB

Lara, Alex: Team Leader of LAT 5612

Lee, Dan: Team Leader of MAT 5112

Lentz, Greg: Team Leader for MAT 5122

Link, Robert: Assistant OIC for FA-AT 5420s

Livingston, Hunter Ethan: Military Police NCO for MAT 5123

Locke, Andrew Michael: Medical NCO for MAT 5112

Lockwood, Jeff: Intelligence officer for 1/5 SFAB

Louis, Tavarus Kamden: Engineer NCO for MAT 5121

Lovins, Thomas Jacob: Infantry NCO for MAT 5133

Ludwig, Dan: Company Commander of A Company, 1/5 SFAB; CAT 5110

Lugo, Eric: Supply NCO for LAT 5611

Luu, Phil: Defense Attaché for Embassy Mongolia

Lyons, Sean: Commander, 1st Battalion, 23rd Infantry (Stryker)

Mackenzie, Josh: Operations Planner for 1/5 SFAB

Maier, Morgan: Commander of C Co., 1/5 SFAB; CAT 5130

Major, David Matthew: Mechanic NCO for MAT 5123

Marlar, Davis Buckner: Assistant OIC for CAT 5210

Matherson, Tyler: Medical NCO for MAT 5123

Mayo, Neal: Commander, 2nd Brigade, 25th Infantry Division

McConville, James: Chief of Staff of the Army 2019-2023

McCord, Thomas Brandon: Assistant Team Leader for FA-AT 5421

McDaniel, Daniel: Australian Deputy Commander for USARPAC

McDowell, Daquois: Logistics NCO for CAT 5133

McKinley, Robert Douglas, Jr.: Infantry Mortar NCO for CAT 5110

McNeil, Steve: Senior EOD Tech for 1/5 SFAB

McNeil, Zachary Quinn: Intelligence NCO for MAT 5123

Meier, Dylan David: Communications NCO for MAT 5130

Melchione, Joseph Alangeroni: Military Police NCO for MAT 5112

Mendola, Zachary: Medical NCO for MAT 5132

Mendoza, Juan Antonio: Engineer NCO for MAT 5132

Mercado, Angel: Network Support NCO for 1/5 SFAB

Mickle, Nickolaus: Intelligence sergeant for 1/5 battalion headquarters

Miller, Pierre A: Senior Fires NCO for FA-AT 5420

Milley, Mark: Chief of Staff of the Army 2015–2019. Chairman of the Joint Chiefs of Staff 2019–2023

Mobi: Mongolian Land Forces Command LNO to 1/5 SFAB

Mohan, Warren Spencer: Engineer NCO for MAT 5110

Moore, Omar: Senior Supply Non-Commissioned Officer for 1/5 SFAB

Moore, Emmanuel: Assistant Team Leader of MAT 5133

Murphy, Bryant: Senior Intelligence NCO for 1/5 SFAB

Murphy, Tucker Franklin: Fires Advisor for MAT 5122

Murray, John: Battalion S1 NCO, human resources, for 1/5 SFAB

Musser, Woodruff Leroy: Assistant Team Leader for MAT 5112

Nagle, David: Senior Medical NCO for 1/5 SFAB

Napier, Mitchell: Infantry NCO part of MAT 5111

Nededog, Cody Joel: Mechanic NCO for MAT 5130

Oliver, Christopher Edward: Mechanic NCO for MAT 5133

Ooley, Joseph: Operations NCO for 1/5 SFAB

Orders, Matt: Team Leader MAT 5111

Orr, Scott: Operations officer of 1/5 SFAB

O'Toole, Colin: Company Commander of A Company, 5/5 SFAB; ECAT 5510

Overway, CJ: Command Sergeant Major of 1/5 SFAB

Paris, William Charles Jackson: Intelligence NCO for MAT 5131

Parker, Marcus: Fires Advisor for MAT 5113

Parrish, Terrance: Assistant Team Leader of LAT 5612

Patrick, James Dean, Jr.: Engineer NCO for MAT 5113

Pena: Royal Thai Army Division Commander

Peno, Nate: Assistant Team Leader for MAT 5123

Perkasa, Andika: Indonesian Army Chief of Staff

Petty, Chad Ray: Communications NCO for MAT 5122

Politano, Steven: Infantry NCO for MAT 5132

Powell, Aaron Lee: Infantry NCO for MAT 5122

Ramos, Fernando David: Infantry NCO for MAT 5131

Ramsey, Stephen Fredrick: Logistics NCO for CAT 5132

Raya, Gennesis: Logistics NCO for CAT 5110

Richards, Monique: Logistics NCO for MAT 5123

Rodriguezalvarez, Carlos Jos: Communications NCO for MAT 5121

Royster, Joseph M: Assistant OIC for CAT 5110

Salazar, Roland: Battalion Physician's Assistant for 1/5 SFAB

Salazar, Jadin Isiah: Fires Advisor for MAT 5121

Shaw, Kijuan Dwayne: Communications NCO for MAT 5133

Sheynfeld, Oleg: Team Leader for MAT 5123

Sikon, Lee: Commander, HHC 1/5 SFAB and LNO in Singapore

Simmonds , Lucas L.: Maintenance NCO for LAT 5612

Smith, Pete: Senior logistics officer for 1/5 SFAB

Smith, Leshaun: Team Leader for MAT 5132

Smith, Garrett Devon: Infantry NCO for MAT 5121

Sobocinski, Kurtis Edmund: Infantry NCO for MAT 5111

Soto, Rafael: Infantry NCO for CAT 5110

Sparks, Allex Christopher: Infantry NCO for MAT 5121

Spencer, Chuck: Team Leader for E-AT 5511

Stackhouse, Parker Levi: Fires Advisor for MAT 5123

Stackhouse, Zachary N: Assistant OIC for CAT 5130

Starnes , Kenneth: Medical NCO for FA-AT 5420

Taylor, Curt: Commander of 5th SFAB

Taylor, Ahkiem Anderson: Logistics NCO for CAT 5130

Tenorio, Rafael: Fires NCO for FA-AT 5421

Thimble, Matt: Team Leader for MAT 5131

Trahan, Andrew: 5th SFAB Adjutant, aka "Tray"

Tucker, Toby Michael: Communications NCO for MAT 5112

Turnbull, Wayne: Defense Attaché for Embassy Thailand

Underwood, Evan Thomas: Intelligence NCO for MAT 5111

Vaaia, Tau: Intelligence NCO for MAT 5113

VanMale, Michael Grant: Engineer NCO for MAT 5133

Vilca, John David: Logistics NCO for CAT 5111

Vogel, Aj: Executive Officer 1/5 SFAB

Wagner, Russ: Senior O/C-T for 1/5 SFAB at JRTC

Wallgren, Chris: Commander of B Company, 1/5 SFAB; CAT 5120

Walsh, Liam: Operations Officer 5th SFAB

Washington, William Berry, III: Medical NCO for MAT 5131

Watson, Andy: Deputy Commander of 5th SFAB

Welch, Michael: Military Police NCO for MAT 5132

Wettlaufer, William Frederic: Mechanic NCO for MAT 5121

Williams, Tylor: Infantry NCO for MAT 5113

Williams, Brandon N.: Maintenance NCO for LAT 5611

Wilson, Jonny Thomas: Medical NCO for 5122

Wohlgemuth, Marty: first commander 4/5th SFAB

Workman, Chad Halston: 1st Sgt. for B Company, CAT 5120

Yalung, Gabriel: Communications NCO for MAT 5132

Yoo, Eui: Medical NCO for LAT 5612

Zacherson, Eric: Senior Fires NCO for 1/5 SFAB

1/5 SFAB TIMELINE

Brown Berets Timeline

April 2018—phone call between the author and Colonel Brian Ducote

June 16, 2019—5th SFAB established

July 2019—Author arrival to JBLM, Washington State and meets CSM CJ Overway

August 2019—First 1/5 SFAB Hail (official welcome to the unit). Received the battalion sign outside battalion headquarters.

August 2019—1/5 SFAB sponsors the Royal Thai Army Stryker Driver training at JBLM, Washington.

September 2019—Author, Anthony Gore, and Tim Ferguson attend the Combat Advisor Training Course at Fort Benning, GA.

October 2019—Weapons arrive for 1/5 SFAB

November 2019—Recruiting trip to Fort Hood, Texas

December 2019—Headquarters US Army announces 5th SFAB to align with the Indo-Pacific rather than Afghanistan or Iraq.

January–February 2020—Author, Anthony Gore, Tim Ferguson attends the Survival, Evade, Resistance, Escape (SERE) school at Fort Rucker, Alabama (recently renamed Fort Novosel).

February 2020—Author and 1st Sgt. Chad Workman travel to Fort Carson, Colorado.

March 2020—Capt. Matt Orders attends planning conference in Fiji

May 18, 2020—5th SFAB Officially Activated

July 2020—MAT 5113 travels to Hawaii to train with the Royal Thai Army at 25th Infantry Division's training exercise.

August 2020—1/5 SFAB mission to Thailand

September–November 2020—primary time window 1/5 SFAB leaders contacted US Indo-Pacific embassies and associated US military embassy staff members and attachés.

September 2020—5th SFAB's brigade training exercise in Yakima, Washington State.

October 2020—Leader Training Program at JRTC.

November 2020—JRTC Rotation to Fort Polk, Louisiana.

December 2020—the US Army announced that advisor teams from the 5th SFAB would deploy to the Indo-Pacific region during the winter of 2020–2021.

January 2021—Deployment and utilization time window for 1/5 SFAB begins.

Deployment Timeline

FEBRUARY 2021

February 2021—LAT 5612 deploys and trains in South Korea

February 2021—MAT 5113 begins training with Indian Army in India

February 2021—Capt. Sikon deploys to Singapore

February 2021—CAT 5110, MAT 5111, FA-AT 5421, ECAT 5510, LAT 5611 deploy to Mongolia.

February 2021—MAT 5111 deploys to the Maldives

MARCH 2021

March 2021: MAT 5123 and LAT 5612 arrive in the Philippines

March 2021: MAT 5122 arrives in the Republic of Korea.

March 2021: Training in Mongolia is interrupted by COVID restrictions.

March 2021: MAT 5132 arrives in Indonesia

March 16, 2021: Author, Cmd. Sgt. Maj. Overway, and Maj. Scott Orr meet with Mongolian CHOD, Maj. Gen. Ganzorig

March 2021: MAT 5111 completes training in the Maldives at the end of the month and conduct closing ceremonies with USARPAC Maj Gen (AUS) McDaniels and CSM Brzak.

APRIL 2021

April 2021: MAT 5122 trains with ROK-A Commandos

April 2021: MAT 5111 departs the Maldives.

April 2021: MAT 5132 travels throughout Indonesia training with and partnering with Indonesian National Military units.

April 2021: MAT 5123 and LAT 5612 begin training with Philippine Army units.

April 2021: E-AT 5511 arrives in Fiji.

Mid-April 2021: Author, Cmd. Sgt. Maj. Overway, and Maj. Scott Orr travel through a winter snowstorm to Khovd via Bayankhongor, Mongolia. End of April 2021: Author, Cmd. Sgt. Maj. Overway, and ECAT 5511 travel to Selenge River training site.

End of April 2021: MAT 5131 arrives in Thailand

May 2021: MAT 5122's training with ROK-A commandos ends and returns to JBLM, WA.

May 24, 2021: Author attends Mongolian Armed Forces Day with Ambassador Klecheski and was presented Mongolian Presidential Medal from Mongolian President Khaltmaagiin Battulga

End of May 2021: CAT 5130 arrives in Japan.

End of May 2021: Decision to have E-AT 5511 depart Fiji and return to JBLM, Washington State.

End of May 2021: MAT 5131 moves to Chon Buri and MAT 5133 moves to Chachoensao in Thailand to begin training with the RTA.

JUNE 2021

June 2021: SFAB Teams in Mongolia conduct Air CASEVAC training with Mongolian LFC units.

June 7, 2021: Ambassador Klecheski oversees closing ceremonies for Mongolian training.

June 2021: CAT 5130 begins training with Japanese 15th Rapid Deployment Regiment.

Beginning of June 2021: E-AT 5511 departs Fiji.

June 2021: 1/5 SFAB teams depart Mongolia.

June 2021: MATs 5131 and 5133 depart Thailand

June 2021: MAT 5123 and LAT 5612 depart the Philippines.

June 2021: MAT 5132 departs Indonesia

ENDNOTES

1. General Flynn mentions ten countries in an interview with Defense News. I include Singapore as well since we had Brown Berets there as part of our mission. "The Pacific has one such team [1/5 SFAB], which has deployed to ten different countries, including Mongolia, South Korea, Japan, Philippines and Indonesia, Gen. Charles Flynn, US Army Pacific Command commander, told Defense News in a Sept. 30 interview." Judson, Jen. "Post-Afghanistan, the US Army Wants to Carve Out its Role in the Pacific." DefenseNews, Oct 11, 2021. https://www.defensenews.com/digital-show-dailies/ausa/2021/10/11/post-afghanistan-the-us-army-wants-to-carve-out-its-role-in-the-pacific/.
2. Lopez, C. Todd. *Milley: Army on Cusp of Profound, Fundamental Change.* The Pentagon: Army. mil, 2016.
3. Montcalm, Rick. *Three Imperatives for the New SFABs.* Arlington, Va: Association of the United States Army, 2018.
4. Franklin Institute. "Edison's Lightbulb." Accessed Feb 22, 2022. https://www.fi.edu/history-resources/edisons-lightbulb.
5. Carlson, Eugene. "American Entrepreneurs: Thomas Alva Edison's 'Invention Factory'." *Wall Street Journal,* Feb 7, 1989.
6. See recent Administrations' National Security Strategies, especially the last three under Presidents Trump, Obama, and Bush. https://history.defense.gov/Historical-Sources/National-Security-Strategy/
7. Karbler, Dan. "Boots on our Ground, Please!: The Army in the Pacific." Washington, DC: War on the Rocks, 2014.
8. Balestrieri, Steve. "Army Chooses Security Forces Over Green Berets for Counter-Drug Deployment to Colombia." SOFREP Media Group, Jun 1, 2020. https://sofrep.com/news/army-chooses-sfab-not-special-forces-for-counter-drug-deployment-to-colombia/; Myers, Meghann. "Army Chief: SFABs Will do a Completely Different Job than Special Forces." Accessed Nov 8, 2021. https://www.armytimes.com/news/your-army/2017/10/31/army-chief-sfabs-will-do-a-completely-different-job-than-special-forces/.
9. For more information on the differences between SFAB Maneuver Advisor Teams (MATs) and Special Forces Operational Detachment Alphas (ODAs), see Chris Thielenhaus' article in Infantry Magazine. Thielenhaus, Christopher R. "Special Forces Vs SFAB: It's Not a Competition." *Infantry Magazine* no. Summer 2021 (Jun 22, 2021): 18-23. https://www.benning.army.mil/infantry/magazine/issues/2021/Summer/pdf/7_Thielenhaus_txt.pdf.
10. WTVC. "2nd Brigade Selected for Iraq Deployment." Accessed Nov 27, 2021. https://newschannel9.com/news/local/2nd-brigade-selected-for-iraq-deployment.
11. Myers, Meghann. "Army Chief: SFABs Will Do a Completely Different Job than Special Forces." Accessed Nov 8, 2021. https://www.armytimes.com/news/your-army/2017/10/31/army-chief-sfabs-will-do-a-completely-different-job-than-special-forces/.
12. During the surge in the Iraq and Afghanistan wars between 2007 and 2013, the United States Army expanded in size. One of the expansions included building new BCTs in many of its operational divisions. The creation of the SFAB differs from these new BCTs in that these new BCTs had the same mission, organization and purposes as other similar brigades. They were built to alleviate the strain of unit rotations to and from Iraq and Afghanistan. Eventually the Army inactivated many of these brigades in 2013. Feickert, Andrew. *US Army's Modular Redesign: Issues for Congress* (RL32476). Washington, D.C.: Congressional Research Service, 2007; Lopez, C. T. "Brigade Combat Teams Cut at 10 Posts Will Help Other BCTs Grow." Accessed March 14, 2022 Grow." https://www.army.mil/article/106373/brigade_combat_teams_cut_at_10_posts_will_help_other_bcts_grow.
13. Moore, Harold G. and Joseph L. Galloway. *We were Soldiers Once . . . and Young: Ia Drang - the Battle that Changed the War in Vietnam.* New York City: The Random House Publishing Group, 1992.
14. Richardson, Michael, and George W. Casey. "Keep 'Em Moving": The Role of Assessment in US Cavalry Operations Against the Plains Indians." *In Assessing War: The Challenge of Measuring Success and Failure,* edited by Leo J. Blanken, Hy Rothstein, and Jason J. Lepore, 96–110. Georgetown University Press, 2015.

15. McConville, James. "Army Transformation." https://vimeo.com/358166082, Sep 10-12, 2019, Sep 12, 2019.
16. The US Army Pacific (USARPAC) is the Army Service Component Command (ASCC) that supports the Indo-Pacific Combatant Command (INDOPACOM) and synchronizes Army activities in the Indo-Pacific on behalf of the INDOPACOM commander. Therefore, 5th SFAB coordinated all its activities with the USARPAC Headquarters. For more information, see McInnis, Kathleen J. *Defense Primer: Commanding US Military Operations*. Washington, D.C.: Congressional Research Service, 2020. https://crsreports.congress.gov/product/pdf/IF/IF10542/8
17. Thielenhaus, Christopher R. "Special Forces Vs SFAB: It's Not a Competition." Infantry Magazine, Summer, 2021, 19.
18. SFAC Recruiting and Retention. What is a Company Advising Team (CAT)?. Facebook Photo: SFAC Recruiting and Retention, 2018.
19. Myers, Meghann. "Army Chief: SFABs Will do a Completely Different Job than Special Forces." Accessed Nov 8, 2021. https://www.armytimes.com/news/your-army/2017/10/31/army-chief-sfabs-will-do-a-completely-different-job-than-special-forces/.
20. For more information on the contrast between Special Forces and SFABs, see Maj. Christopher Thielenhaus' article "Special Forces vs SFAB: It's Not a Competition" in *Infantry Magazine*, Summer 2021. https://www.benning.army.mil/infantry/magazine/issues/2021/Summer/pdf/7_Thielenhaus.pdf
21. Department of the Army. *Army Training Publication* (ATP) 3-96.1: Security Force Assistance Brigade. Washington, D.C.: Department of the Army, 2020, pg 1-2.
22. Kimmons, Sean. *Army to Build Three Multi-Domain Task Forces using Lessons from Pilot*. Washington, D.C.: United States Army, 2019.
23. US Army. "Army Establishes Army Cyber Command." Accessed Feb 25, 2022. https://www.army.mil/article/46012/army_establishes_army_cyber_command.
24. Grazier, Dan. Preventing Train and Defeat in Future Conflicts. Washington, D.C.: Project on Government Oversight (POGO), 2020.
25. Office of the Assistant Inspector General for Special Plans & Operations. Report on the Assessment of US and Coalition Plans to Train, Equip, and Field the Afghan National Security Forces. The Pentagon: Department of Defense, 2009.
26. Special Inspector General for Afghanistan Reconstruction. Reconstructing the Afghan National Defense and Security Forces: Lessons from the US Experience in Afghanistan. The Pentagon: Department of Defense, 2017, p. 179.
27. Wojcicki, Susan. *Johns Hopkins University 2014 Commencement Speaker: Susan Wojcicki*, YouTube CEO. John Hopkins University: YouTube, 2014.
28. Feickert, Andrew. *Army Security Force Assistance Brigades* (SFABs). Washington, D.C.: Congressional Research Service, 2021.
29. The Joint Readiness Training Center located at Fort Polk, Louisiana, is one of three combat training centers (CTCs) that the Army used to test and validate its combat formations. Its focus is improving unit readiness by providing life-like, taxing, joint and combined arms training and operations across a cornucopia of current and future conflict sequences with emphasis on contingency force missions. Each training scenario is specific to the participating organizations mission-essential task list. These exercises are intended to be as close to the actual operations that the organization is scheduled to conduct.
30. The Army formalized this process and created the Center for Army Lessons Learned (CALL) to capture best practices and share them with the rest of the force. CALL is located at Fort Leavenworth, Kansas and sends out regular updates to leaders throughout the Army. Reading these publications before conducting training or going to combat training centers helps units best prepare for forthcoming challenges. https://www.army.mil/call
31. Pedron, Anna. "One Platoon's Bravery Becomes an Army Legacy." Accessed Dec 21, 2021. https://www.army.mil/article/149762/one_platoons_bravery_becomes_an_army_legacy.
32. FORSCOM is four-star command responsible for providing trained and ready forces to the combatant commanders. FORSCOM certifies brigade combat teams for deployment primarily by testing them at JRTC, NTC, and JMRC.
33. Torreon, Barbara and Sofia Plagakis. Instances of use of United States Armed Forces Abroad, 1798-2022 (R42738). Washington, D.C.: Congressional Research Service, 2022.

34. According to Army Regulation 350-50, Combat Training Center Program, "CTCs provide a crucible experience for units and leaders training in a complex and highly realistic decisive action training environment (DATE) designed to replicate combat by stressing every warfighting function with operations against tough, freethinking, realistic, hybrid threats under the most difficult conditions possible." In layman's terms, it's where the Army's combat units go to practice against an adversary on their home turf. There are primarily three CTCs. The National Training Center (NTC) in California is primarily used to trained mechanized and motorized formations. The Joint Readiness Training Center (JRTC) in Louisiana trains primarily light and airborne units. The Joint Multinational Readiness Center (JMRC) located in Germany trains a variety of US Army formations, including NATO allies. US Department of the Army. Army Regulation 350–50 Combat Training Center Program. Washington, D.C.: United States Army, 2018, p. 1.
35. Christensen, Clayton M., Michael E. Raynor, and Rory McDonald. "What is Disruptive Innovation?" *Harvard Business Review* no. December 2015 (Dec, 2015). https://hbr.org/2015/12/what-is-disruptive-innovation.
36. Ibid.
37. In Army slang, mermite is often used as a verb—one mermites the food to the field.
38. Fort Bliss, MWR. "Soldier Family Readiness Groups (SFRG)." Accessed Dec 24, 2021. https://bliss.armymwr.com/programs/family-readiness-groups-frg.
39. US Army Training and Doctrine Command, TRADOC, has a complete overview of the Pacific Decisive Action Training Environment. US Army Training and Doctrine Command (TRADOC). "Decisive Action Training Environment (DATE)-Pacific." Accessed May 22, 2022. https://odin.tradoc.army.mil/DATE/Pacific/South_Torbia/Pacific.
40. For more reading on the By, With, and Through approach see Gen. Garrett's *The By-With-Through Approach an Army Component Perspective* article. Garrett, Michael X., William H. Dunbar, Bryan C. Hilferty, and Robert R. Rodock. "The by-with-through Approach an Army Component Perspective." Joint Forces Quarterly 2, no. 89 (2018): 48-55. https://ndupress.ndu.edu/Portals/68/Documents/jfq/jfq-89/jfq-89_48-55_Garrett-et-al.pdf.
41. *Chain of Command*. Web. Directed by Boggins, Scott. National Geographic, 2018.
42. See also Michael Gordon's brief article in the Wall Street Journal that discusses the By, With, Through efforts during the counter-ISIS fight. Gordon, Michael R. "How the War Against ISIS was Won." *The Wall Street Journal*, Jun 3, 2022, online. https://www.wsj.com/articles/how-the-war-against-isis-was-won-11654271174.
43. Maj. Morgan Maier had only arrived in August 2020 to take command and then deployed very quickly to Yakima for the brigade training event the following month. 1st Sgt. Duane Bochmann arrived in October 2020, just before heading to JRTC in November 2020. 1st Sgt. Ron Hansen, the first 1st Sgt. of C Company, had left earlier the in the summer of 2020 to attend the Sergeant Major's Academy at Fort Bliss, Texas, so there was a four-month gap where C Company was without an assigned first sergeant.
44. "Keris Strike consists of several subject matter expert exchanges designed to develop the capacity to quickly respond to the crisis with greater interoperability and increased mission effectiveness." Kriess, Jason. "Exercise Keris Strike Begins in Malaysia." United States Army. https://www.army.mil/article/218360/exercise_keris_strike_begins_in_malaysia.
45. "Bersama Warrior is a joint and bilateral exercise sponsored by US Indo-Pacific Command and hosted by the Malaysian Armed Forces . . . The aim of this exercise is to enhance interoperability and build capacity to plan and conduct joint and multinational operations at the operational level; it provides a great opportunity for all participants to exchange ideas and experiences as the multinational force." Teeter, Alyson. "6th Annual Bersama Warrior Exercise Underway in Malaysia." Washington Air National Guard. https://www.army.mil/article/233722/6th_annual_bersama_warrior_exercise_underway_in_malaysia.
46. According to the Department of State, the Integrated Country Strategy is "the four-year strategy that articulates the US priorities in a given country is developed that is referred to as the Integrated Country Strategy (ICS). This ICS is led by the Chief of Mission to develop a common set of Mission Goals and Objectives through a coordinated and collaborative planning effort among Department of State and other US Government agencies with programming in the country. Higher-level planning documents and strategies, such as the National Security Strategy, the State-USAID Joint Strategic Plan (JSP), and Department regional (JRS) and functional bureau strategies (FBS) inform the ICS. Once completed the ICS frames and

informs the annual Mission Resource Request and Mission-level performance management requirements." Department of State. *Integrated Country Strategies*. Washington, D.C.: Department of State, 2022.
47. Sometimes military officers posted at US Embassies fulfill multiple roles, such as serving in both a Joint US Military Advisory Group, the attaché office, or the security cooperation office. The duties and authorities are derived from various US statutory and fiscal law.
48. "Status of forces agreements (SOFAs) and status of mission agreements (SOMAs) are bilateral or multilateral treaties that define the legal status of military forces and civilian personnel deployed abroad with the consent of the host State. They typically deal with such issues as the entry and departure of foreign personnel, the carrying of arms, taxation, the settlement of claims, and the exercise of criminal jurisdiction over members of the visiting force or mission." Sari, Aurel. "The Conclusion of International Agreements by the European Union in the Context of the Esdp." *The International and Comparative Law Quarterly* 57, no. 1 (2008): 53-86.
49. South, Todd. "SFAB Soldiers are Heading Out in Smaller Teams to More Places." *Army Times*, Oct 13, 2021. https://www.armytimes.com/news/2021/10/13/sfab-soldiers-are-heading-out-in-smaller-teams-to-more-places/.
50. Biden, Joseph Jr. *Interim National Security Strategic Guidance*. Washington, D.C.: The White House, 2021, pg. 10.
51. Mongolian "officials have adopted a policy of actively seeking strong partnerships beyond Russia and China, an effort they call the Third Neighbor Policy. The most important Third Neighbors have been Japan, the US, and Korea, followed by Germany and India. The government also uses different categories to refer to the strength or importance of these relationships." Narangoa, Li. "Mongolia in 2011." Asian Survey 52, no.1 (2012): 81.
52. The headquarters, the command team, and the headquarters company (i.e. the rest of the battalion staff in the case of the SFAB) was commanded by an experienced Army captain. The company itself was small, so Capt. Lee Sikon had some capacity to do additional tasks on behalf of the entire battalion.
53. US Embassy Singapore. "Navy Region Center Singapore." Accessed Jun 27, 2022. https://sg.usembassy.gov/navy-region-center-singapore/.
54. The VFA, signed in 1998, supports the Mutual Defense Treaty, which was agreed upon in 1951 and outlines what support will be allocated in the case of a foreign attack. Under the VFA both countries agreed to have bilateral training and military exercises and procedures for how to resolve any issues that may come about due to the presence of these US forces. Schaus, John. *What is the Philippines-United States Visiting Forces Agreement, and Why does it Matter?*. Washington, D.C.: Center for Strategic & International Studies, 2020.
55. General Andika Perkasa later became the Indonesian military commander in charge of all Indonesian Armed Forces.
56. In Indonesian, the army's official name is the Tentara Nasional Indonesia, hence Indonesian National Military or Indonesian National Military.
57. "POLADs advise US military combatant and component commanders, as well as leadership in the Office of the Secretary of Defense, the Joint Staff, and throughout the DOD enterprise. These experienced diplomats ensure that US military operations, planning, and exercises benefit from their expertise, which enhances overall cooperation between the DOS, DOD, and other interagency partners." These State Department senior officials help military commanders understand operations and activities from the State Department's perspective. US Department of State. "About Us—Office of State-Defense Integration." Accessed Dec 30, 2021. https://www.state.gov/bureau-of-political-military-affairs-office-of-state-defense-integration-pm-sdi/.
58. United States Army Pacific (USARPAC): America's Theater Army for the Indo-Pacific. Fort Shafter, Hawaii: United States Army Pacific (USARPAC), 2021, pg. 17.
59. Capt. Brenton Clark had to depart Thailand early because his wife's pregnancy due date was near, and we didn't want him to miss the birth of his second child.
60. US Embassy Bangkok. "Cobra Gold 21 Showcases Strength of our Security and Health Partnerships." Accessed May 12, 2022. https://th.usembassy.gov/cobra-gold-21-showcases-strength-of-our-security-and-health-partnerships/.
61. Some of the training highlighted in Exercise COBRA GOLD include military training, civic action, humanitarian assistance, disaster relief and medical trauma response Garrison, Spencer. "US, Royal Thai Armed Forces Complete 40th Exercise Cobra Gold." Accessed May 12, 2022.

https://www.army.mil/article/249675/us_royal_thai_armed_forces_complete_40th_exercise_cobra_gold.
62. Sagvold, Mark. "US Army Teams with Fijian Military for Exercise Cartwheel 2019." Accessed Dec 30, 2021. https://www.army.mil/article/225083/us_army_teams_with_fijian_military_for_exercise_cartwheel_2019.
63. Unknown. "Orient Shield 2019, a Soldiers View." Accessed Dec 30, 2021. https://www.army.mil/article/227520/orient_shield_2019_a_soldiers_view.
64. Sharma, Manish and Kaushal Mody. "Fast-Track to Future-Ready Performance." Accessed Dec 30, 2021. https://www.accenture.com/us-en/insights/operations/future-ready-operations.
65. The official definition is a "Casualty evacuation is the movement of casualties aboard nonmedical vehicles or aircraft without en route medical care." US Department of the Army. CASUALTY EVACUATION Army Training Publication (ATP) 4-02.13. Washington, D.C.: United States Army, 2021.
66. The Harvard Business School succinctly discusses ten characteristics of successful entrepreneurs that many of the 1st Battalion's members displayed in some form or another. Miller, Kelsey. "10 Characteristics of Successful Entrepreneurs." Accessed Nov 8, 2021. https://online.hbs.edu/blog/post/characteristics-of-successful-entrepreneurs.
67. The US Chamber of Commerce defines a variety of entrepreneur characteristics as well. Walsack, Joyce. "Entrepreneurs Reveal the 6 Personality Traits that make them Successful." Washington, D.C.: US Chamber of Commerce, 2020. https://www.uschamber.com/co/grow/thrive/p

ACKNOWLEDGMENTS

First I'd like to thank my wife, Amy and our kids, Zac, Abi, Izzy, and Andrew for allowing me the time to write down the historic experiences of 1st Battalion, 5th Security Force Assistance Brigade even after enduring the long days, frequent trips during our build-up and training, and finally the time away working with our Indo-Pacific Region partners and allies. Amy is the best thing that ever happened to me and is truly my better half.

Second, I want to thank God for the wisdom and guidance He has brought to me through my family and career. I am grateful for the insights He has given to me, and the decisions He has helped me with to get to where I am today. Through my military journey, God has grown my trust and developed my confidence. Thank you God!

Third, I'd like to recognize and thank all the men and women who volunteered to don the brown beret, take a risk with their Army careers, and make our inaugural deployment into the Indo-Pacific Region possible. Without their dedication, ingenuity, and hard work, none of this would have been possible. I'd be remiss if I failed to especially thank CJ Overway, my SFAB partner for over two years, for his support, counsel, and inspiration. I'd also like to thank our first field grade officers, Tom Angstadt and Scott Orr, who took my ideas and concepts and turned them into tangible results including 5th SFAB's first training mission in Thailand and our eventual deployment to eleven Indo-Pacific countries. I especially want to thank my boss in 5th SFAB, (brigadier general) Curt Taylor, who was a trusting and inspiring boss that worked tirelessly to help make the successes of 1st Battalion, 5th SFAB a reality.

Fourth, I'd like to thank those who believed in me, this work, and encouraged me along the way to make *Green Light, Go* possible. My dad, Don Rowland, who suffered through the first draft of this book and gave me tons of feedback. My first editor, Michelle Malsbury, who started the polishing work to make the manuscript a viable product then continued to coach and encourage me along the way as I navigated the publishing process. I'd also like to thank Kevin Eubanks during our time together at the Naval War College in Rhode Island and his "pro bono" work instructing me on how to develop my writing skills and seeing *Green Light, Go* as a viable manuscript.

Fifth, my launch team who provided feedback, kept me focused, and helped me navigate the publishing and marketing aspects of creating a book. Scott Orr, Andrew "Tray" Trahan, Will Marm, Chris Curry, and Shahin Uddin were, and are, invaluable partners. Thank you for your time, ideas, and wise counsel.

Finally, I want to thank John Koehler, editor Becky Hilliker, and graphic designer Christine Kettner for investing the time and resources from Koehler Books to take the manuscript from a document to an actual, tangible book.

Printed in the USA
CPSIA information can be obtained
at www.ICGtesting.com
CBHW031824171123
1936CB00005B/5

9 798888 241530